D0578615

AWESOME
ALMANAC™

THE GREAT SEAL OF THE STATE OF MINN
L'ETOILE DU NORD
1858

MINNESOTA

**Created by
Jean F. Blashfield**

**Compiled and Written by
Jean F. Blashfield**

B&B Publishing, Inc.

B & B Publishing, Inc.
P. O. Box 393
Fontana, Wisconsin 53125

Editor – **Nancy Jacobson**
Photo Researcher – **Margie Benson**
Computer Design and Production Manager – **Dave Conant**
Computer Specialist and Indexer – **Marilyn Magowan**
Cover Design – **Gary Hurst**

Publisher's Cataloging in Publication

Blashfield, Jean F.
　　Awesome almanac—Minnesota / Jean F. Blashfield.
　　p. cm.
　　Includes index.
　　Preassigned LCCN: 92-074710
　　ISBN 1-880190-07-9

1. Minnesota—Miscellanea. 2. Minnesota—History. 3. Almanacs,
American—Minnesota. I. Title.

F604.B53 1993

　　　　　　　　　　　　　　977.6'003
　　　　　　　　　　　　　　QBI93-577

Printed in the United States of America

93 94 95 96 97　　　　5 4 3 2 1

AWESOME ALMANAC is a trademark of B&B Publishing, Inc.

ATTENTION SCHOOLS AND BUSINESSES:
　　*This book is available at quantity discounts with bulk purchases for educational, busi-
　　ness, or sales promotional use. For information, please write to B&B Publishing, Inc.,
　　P.O. Box 393, Fontana, WI 53125*

DISTRIBUTOR TO THE BOOK TRADE:
　　Publishers Distribution Service, 6893 Sullivan Road, Grawn, MI 49637

TABLE OF CONTENTS

St. Croix River

THE NORTH STAR STATE

Welcome to Minnesota, land of 10,000 lakes, or is it 15,721, or maybe even 22,000? Let's just say there's lots of water—beautiful "Sky-Blue Waters"—making up the lakes and the rivers that have played such a vital role in Minnesota's history, as well as in its present enchantment for visitors from all over the world.

But Minnesota isn't just a place to visit. It is consistently rated one of the best places to live in the whole country. Its business enterprises are known the world over. It has cared about education since the days of the earliest settlers. And in recent years it has been the focus of all eyes for major sporting events. Come on up and get acquainted—the water's fine!

MINNESOTA'S NUMBERS

The land

Area – 84,402 square miles – 12th largest state
Water area – 4,854 square miles
Longest distance from north to south – 411 miles
Widest distance from east to west – 357 miles
Average width – 240 miles
Northernmost point in the contiguous 48 states – Northwest Angle
Highest point – Eagle Mountain in Cook County, 2,301 feet
Lowest point – The shore of Lake Superior, 602 feet
Geographic center – Crow Wing, southwest of Brainerd

Northwest Angle

Northwest Angle is a jut of land that extends into Lake of the Woods. It is the northernmost point of land (except Alaska, which seems to be an exception to everything) in the entire United States, as well, of course, as the northernmost point of Minnesota. Actually, it isn't even attached to the rest of Minnesota. It is across the lake and connected to the province of Manitoba (see p. 14).

THE GOVERNMENT

Admitted to the Union

May 11, 1858 – 32nd state admitted

The executive branch

Minnesota's original constitution (which is still in force), instead of providing a strong single governor, called for six equally powerful positions: the governor, lieutenant governor, secretary of state, auditor, treasurer, and attorney general. Over the years, however, the governor has been given increasing powers, resulting in a single head of state. The main change was instituted by Governor Harold E. Stassen, who created a Department of Administration, functioning under the governor. The people in the six positions are elected for four-year terms.

In office (until January 1995)
Governor – Arne Carlson, Republican
Lieutenant Governor – Joanell Dyrstad, Republican
Secretary of State – Joan Anderson Growe, Democrat
State Auditor – Mark Dayton, Democrat
Attorney General – Hubert H. Humphrey III, Democrat
State Treasurer – Michael McGrath, Democrat

The legislative branch

The legislative branch consists of an upper chamber, the senate, with 67 members who serve for four-year terms, and a lower chamber, the house of representatives, with 134 members, who serve two-year terms. Minnesota has two U.S. senators and eight congressmen, making 10 electoral votes.

The judicial branch

The judicial, or court, system includes three levels. At the top is the Minnesota Supreme Court, with a chief justice and eight associate justices. They are elected by the citizens to serve for six-year terms. The court of appeals has twelve members, elected to serve for six-year terms. At the bottom level are various county and municipal courts, the judges of which serve for six-year terms.

THE PEOPLE

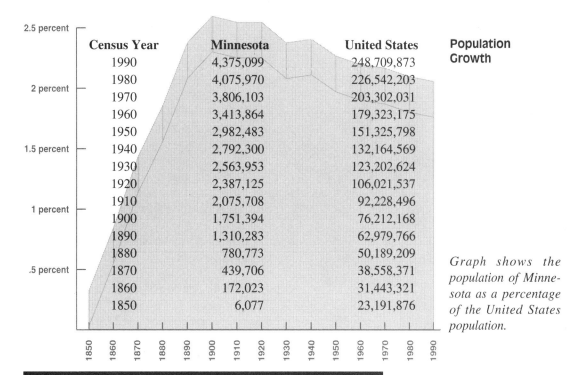

Census Year	Minnesota	United States
1990	4,375,099	248,709,873
1980	4,075,970	226,542,203
1970	3,806,103	203,302,031
1960	3,413,864	179,323,175
1950	2,982,483	151,325,798
1940	2,792,300	132,164,569
1930	2,563,953	123,202,624
1920	2,387,125	106,021,537
1910	2,075,708	92,228,496
1900	1,751,394	76,212,168
1890	1,310,283	62,979,766
1880	780,773	50,189,209
1870	439,706	38,558,371
1860	172,023	31,443,321
1850	6,077	23,191,876

Population Growth

Graph shows the population of Minnesota as a percentage of the United States population.

1990 Population
4,375,099

Gender
Male - 2,145,183
Female - 2,229,916

Age
Under 18 - 26.7%
65 and over - 12.5%
Median age - 32.5 years

• *Only Hawaiians have a longer average life span than Minnesotans*

Race
White - 4,130,395 (94.4%)

African-American
94,944 (2.2%)

Asian or Pacific Islander
77,886 (1.8%)

Hispanic - 53,884 (1.2%)

American Indian, Eskimo, or Aleutian - 49,909 (1.1%)

Other - 21,965 (0.5%)

NAMES AND NICKNAMES

"Minnesota" is from the Indian words *Minne sota*, meaning "sky-tinted water." To anyone who has been there, it more clearly translates as "Land of Sky-Blue Waters." The first time the possibility of state-hood came up in Congress, the state's name was spelled "Minasota."

Meaning of the state name

Nicknames   The closest thing to an official nickname is "North Star State," based on the fact that the state seal bears the words *L'Etoile du Nord*, meaning "Star of the North."

"The Gopher State"   When Minnesota became a state in 1858 there were no railroads. An ambitious St. Paul politician saw railroads as a necessity if Minnesota were to keep up with the rest of the nation and grow. The question was: Where was the money to come from? In April 1858, Minnesotans voted to let the state borrow $5 million and lend it to four companies to build railroads. These companies took the money but didn't finish any railroads. The citizens felt they had been cheated and their feelings were expressed in this cartoon, which appeared in newspapers all over the state. Just as gophers destroy farmers' crops, the businessmen had destroyed the state's dreams for railroads and had "eaten" public money.

The name "gophers" for Minnesotans quickly entered the songs of the period, including one with a line referred to neighboring Wisconsin: "We're good as any badgers, or any in the land."

Bread and Butter State   When Minnesota Day was held at the Pan-American Exposition in Buffalo, New York, on June 18, 1901, visitors first saw the state's superior exhibits of wheat, flour, and dairy products. The state quickly earned the nickname "Bread and Butter State."

SYMBOLS, SEALS & FLAGS

State tree: Norway Pine, adopted in 1953

The Norway pine (also called red pine) doesn't grow in Norway, but it does grow in Maine near a town called Norway. Since many of Minnesota's early loggers came from Maine, it is thought that the tree was named after this Maine town. Itasca State Park is home to the state's tallest Norway pine—300 years old and 120 feet high.

State bird: Loon, adopted in 1961

Designated as state bird in 1961, the common loon, or great northern diver, is the earth's oldest living bird species, dating back 60 million years. Although loons are excellent fliers, divers, and underwater swimmers, they are best known for their wild, sad cry. Over 12,000 loons come to Minnesota lakes in the summer months and head south in the fall.

State fish: Walleye, adopted in 1965

The walleye was chosen by an almost unanimous vote—128-1. The one dissenting vote was probably from a crappie fisherman, according to a walleye fan.

State Flower: Pink-and-white lady's slippers

Some pink-and-white lady's slippers are four feet high, making them one of the largest wildflowers in the country. The flower is very rare and is most often found in the swamps, bogs, or woods of eastern and northern Minnesota. It grows very slowly due to the fact that a special fungus must be present for the roots to get nourishment from the soil.

Some more state symbols

State muffin - blueberry
State mushroom - morel
State gemstone - Lake Superior agate
State grain - wild rice

State animal - white-tailed deer

State Song

"Hail! Minnesota" was written in 1904 and 1905 by two University of Minnesota students, Truman E. Rickard and Arthur E. Upson, as the University of Minnesota song. It became the official state song in 1945. Only one phrase had to be changed—instead of "Hail to thee our college dear" it became "Hail to thee, our state so dear!"

Hail! Minnesota

Minnesota hail to thee!
Hail to thee, our state so dear!
Thy light shall ever be
A beacon bright and clear.
Thy sons and daughters true
Will proclaim thee near and far.
They shall guard thy fame and ádore thy name;
Thou shalt be their northern star.

The seal of approval

Minnesota has had four seals, three for the state and one for the territory. The first design for the territorial seal showed an Indian family giving a peace pipe to white settlers, but many delegates thought there would never be peace in Minnesota until all the Indians were moved out. Since they couldn't agree on a design, they decided to let Governor Ramsey and Henry Sibley, delegate to Congress, decide. They chose a picture drawn by the commanding officer at Fort Snelling, Seth Eastman. He had sketched a white settler plowing near the Falls of St. Anthony with an Indian in the background galloping into the sunset (or, as some people claimed, being pursued by the farmer). *Quo sursum velo videre* ("I want to see what lies beyond") was chosen to show the pioneer spirit of Minnesotans. However, after the seal was cast, errors were discovered. Two of the Latin words were misspelled and the picture was backward. The Indian was actually galloping east toward Wisconsin and not into the setting sun of the West. The mistakes were corrected when Minnesota became a state in 1858. The Latin words were replaced with a French phrase, *L'Etoile du Nord*, meaning "Star of the North."

1849-1858

1858-1971

This seal was used for over 100 years until the 1960s when people began to question its implications to Native Americans. In 1968 the Minnesota Human Rights Commission asked the state government to develop a seal that all Minnesotans could be proud of. So the second state seal changed the Indian to another settler. In 1983, Minnesota decided to design the present state seal (see the cover). It added Norway pines and put the Native American back in—galloping *toward* a farmer—to represent the state's great Indian heritage.

1971-1983

The state flag

In 1891, Minnesota decided to sponsor an exhibit at the 1893 Columbian Exposition in Chicago but had no flag to display. A Women's Auxiliary Board was formed, and they picked a six-person state flag committee, which held a statewide contest to pick a design. Amelia Hyde Center of Minneapolis won the contest on February 28, 1893. She was given $15 for her winning design. The flag was officially adopted by the legislature on April 15, 1893.

The flag adopted was made in two layers, white on the front and light blue on the back. It was both too heavy to fly well and too expensive for most people to buy. Also it had a mistake—the white lady's-slippers shown on it don't grow in Minnesota, pink-and-white lady's-slippers do. So a new version of the flag was adopted on March 18, 1957.

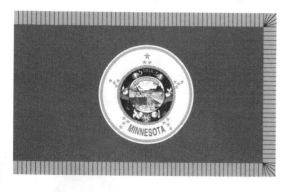

THE SHAPE OF THE STATE

▞ Before it became a state, part or all of Minnesota Territory was successively under the flags of France, England, Spain, the colony of Virginia, the Northwest Territory, and the territories of Louisiana, Indiana, Illinois, Michigan, Missouri, Iowa, and Wisconsin.

Land of twelve flags

What, when, and where — a topsy-turvy history

Up to 1803 - Western Minnesota was part of the territory controlled by France, until President Thomas Jefferson bought the whole area as the Louisiana Purchase.

1804 - The Louisiana Purchase was split in half. The northern half, including western Minnesota, was attached to Indiana Territory.

1812 - Missouri Territory was created, with plans for making it into six states. The western part of Minnesota was attached to it.

1821 - Western Minnesota left Missouri Territory when Missouri became a state. It was left unorganized for the next 13 years.

1834 - Eastern and western Minnesota were placed in Michigan Territory— together for the first time!

1836 - Wisconsin Territory was established, including all of Minnesota.

1838 - Iowa Territory, including western Minnesota, was formed. Many Iowans hoped that when the territory became a state, they would keep all of western Minnesota. But . . .

1846 - Western Minnesota was left with no government after Iowa was admitted as a state.

Up to 1784 - Eastern Minnesota was part of the land claimed by Virginia. After the American Revolution it remained unorganized for three years.

1787 - Eastern Minnesota was included in the Northwest Territory.

1800 - Indiana Territory was established with eastern Minnesota included.

1809 - Illinois Territory was created when Indiana became a state. Minnesota east of the Mississippi River was attached to it.

1818 - Michigan Territory, including eastern Minnesota, was established when Illinois bacame a state.

1838 - When Iowa Territory was formed with western Minnesota, eastern Minnesota remained part of Wisconsin Territory.

1846 - Eastern Minnesota separated from Wisconsin when Wisconsin started the drive to become a state. Eastern Minnesota was left without a government.

1848 - The movement to get Congress to establish a separate Minnesota Territory began.

1849, March 3 - The Territory of Minnesota established by Congress.

MINNESOTA COUNTY ALMANAC

87 counties

Largest by population - Hennepin, the 30th largest in the U.S. and the largest in Minnesota, with 1,032,431 people

Smallest by population - Cook, with 3,868 people

Largest by area - St. Louis County, with 6,612 square miles

Smallest by area - Ramsey, with 154 square miles

First county established - 9 counties were established by the territorial legislature on October 27, 1849. Only Benton, Dakota, Itasca, Ramsey, Wabasha, and Washington remain

Last county established - Lake of the Woods, in 1922

MINNESOTA COUNTIES

COUNTY	1990 POP.	COUNTY SEAT	SQ. MI.	CREATED	NAMED FOR
Aitkin	12,425	Aitkin	1,834	5/23/1857	Fur trader William Aitkin
Anoka	243,641	Anoka	430	5/23/1857	Sioux word: on both sides
Becker	27,881	Detroit Lakes	1,312	3/18/1858	Not-quite congressman George Loomis Becker
Beltrami	34,384	Bemidji	2,507	2/28/1866	Italian explorer Giacomo Beltrami
Benton	30,185	Foley	408	10/27/1849	Missouri senator Thomas Hart Benton
Big Stone	6,285	Ortonville	497	2/21/1862	Big Stone Lake
Blue Earth	54,044	Mankato	497	3/5/1853	Blue Earth River
Brown	26,984	New Ulm	610	2/20/1855	Pioneer Joseph Renshaw Brown
Carlton	29,259	Carlton	864	5/23/1857	Pioneer Reuben B. Carlton
Carver	47,915	Chaska	351	2/20/1855	Connecticut explorer Jonathan Carver
Cass	21,791	Walker	2,033	9/1/1851	Michigan Territory Governor Lewis Cass
Chippewa	13,228	Montevideo	584	2/21/1862	Chippewa River
Chisago	30,521	Center City	417	9/1/1851	Chippewa word: large and lovely
Clay	50,422	Moorhead	1,049	3/18/1858	Henry Clay
Clearwater	8,309	Bagley	999	12/20/1902	Clearwater Lake
Cook	3,868	Grand Marais	1,412	3/9/1874	Civil War hero Michael Cook
Cottonwood	12,694	Windom	640	5/23/1857	Cottonwood tree
Crow Wing	44,249	Brainerd	1,008	5/23/1857	Translation of Chippewa name
Dakota	275,227	Hastings	574	10/27/1849	Dakota Indians
Dodge	15,731	Mantorville	439	2/20/1855	Wisconsin Governor Henry Dodge and son

COUNTY	1990 POP.	COUNTY SEAT	SQ. MI.	CREATED	NAMED FOR
Douglas	28,674	Alexandria	643	3/8/1858	Senator Stephen A. Douglas
Faribault	16,937	Blue Earth	714	2/20/1855	Fur trader Jean Baptiste Faribault
Fillmore	20,777	Preston	862	3/3/1853	President Millard Fillmore
Freeborn	33,060	Albert Lea	705	2/20/1855	Legislator William Freeborn
Goodhue	40,690	Red Wing	763	3/5/1853	Newspaper editor James M. Goodhue
Grant	6,246	Elbow Lake	547	3/7/1868	Gen. Ulysses S. Grant
Hennepin	1,032,431	Minneapolis	541	3/6/1852	Father Louis Hennepin
Houston	18,497	Caledonia	564	2/23/1854	Texas leader Sam Houston
Hubbard	14,939	Park Rapids	936	2/26/1883	Governor Lucius F. Hubbard
Isanti	25,921	Cambridge	440	2/13/1857	Band of early Sioux
Itasca	40,863	Grand Rapids	2,661	10/27/1849	Lake Itasca, named by Schoolcraft
Jackson	11,677	Jackson	699	5/23/1857	Pioneer merchant Henry Jackson
Kanabec	12,802	Mora	527	3/13/1858	Chippewa word: snake
Kandiyohi	38,761	Willmar	784	3/20/1858	Sioux word: lakes
Kittson	5,767	Hallock	1,104	2/25/1879	Pioneer Norman W. Kittson
Koochiching	16,299	International Falls	3,108	12/19/1906	Cree word: rainy river
Lac qui Parle	8,924	Madison	772	3/6/1871	French word: the lake that talks
Lake	10,415	Two Harbors	2,053	3/1/1856	Lake Superior
Lake of the Woods	4,076	Baudette	1,296	11/28/1922	Lake of the Woods
Le Sueur	23,239	Le Center	446	3/5/1853	French explorer Pierre Charles Le Sueur
Lincoln	6,890	Ivanhoe	538	3/6/1873	President Abraham Lincoln
Lyon	24,789	Marshall	714	3/7/1868	Gen. Nathaniel Lyon
McLeod	32,030	Glencoe	489	3/1/1856	Fur trader Martin McLeod
Mahnomen	5,044	Mahnomen	559	12/27/1906	Chippewa word: wild rice
Marshall	10,993	Warren	1,760	2/25/1879	Governor William Rainey Marshall
Martin	22,914	Fairmont	706	5/23/1857	Landowner Henry Martin or territorial organizer Morgan Lewis Martin
Meeker	20,846	Litchfield	624	2/23/1856	State court justice Bradley B. Meeker
Mille Lacs	18,670	Milaca	578	5/23/1857	French word: thousand lakes
Morrison	29,604	Little Falls	1,124	2/25/1856	Fur-trading Morrison brothers
Mower	37,385	Austin	711	2/20/1855	Stillwater lumberman John E. Mower
Murray	9,660	Slayton	702	5/23/1857	St. Paul official William Pitt Murray
Nicollet	28,076	St. Peter	440	3/5/1853	French explorer Joseph N. Nicollet
Nobles	20,098	Worthington	714	5/23/1857	Prominent pioneer William. H. Nobles
Norman	7,975	Ada	877	2/17/1881	Norwegian immigrants or Red River Valley promoter Norman Kittson
Olmsted	106,470	Rochester	655	2/20/1855	St. Paul Mayor David Olmsted
Otter Tail	50,714	Fergus Falls	1,973	3/18/1858	Otter Tail Lake
Pennington	13,306	Thief River Falls	618	11/23/1910	Railway president Edmund Pennington
Pine	21,264	Pine City	1,421	3/1/1856	Pine River
Pipestone	10,491	Pipestone	466	5/23/1857	Indian pipestone quarry
Polk	32,498	Crookston	1,982	7/20/1858	President James Polk
Pope	10,745	Glenwood	668	2/21/1862	General John Pope
Ramsey	485,765	St. Paul	154	10/27/1849	Governor Alexander Ramsey
Red Lake	4,525	Red Lake Falls	433	12/24/1896	Red Lake River
Redwood	17,254	Redwood Falls	882	2/6/1862	Translation of Indian name
Renville	17,673	Olivia	984	2/20/1855	Fur trader Joseph Renville
Rice	49,183	Faribault	501	3/5/1853	Delegate Henry Mower Rice
Rock	9,806	Luverne	483	5/23/1857	Red quartzite outcropping
Roseau	15,026	Roseau	1,677	12/31/1894	Roseau Lake
St. Louis	198,213	Duluth	6,125	3/3/1855	St. Louis River
Scott	57,846	Shakopee	357	3/5/1853	General Winfield Scott
Sherburne	41,366	Elk River	435	2/25/1856	State court justice Moses Sherburne
Sibley	14,366	Gaylord	593	3/5/1853	Henry H. Sibley
Stearns	118,791	St. Cloud	1,338	2/20/1855	Legislator Charles T. Stearns
Steele	30,729	Owatonna	431	2/20/1855	Minneapolis pioneer Franklin Steele
Stevens	10,634	Morris	560	2/21/1862	Soldier/statesman Isaac I. Stevens
Swift	10,724	Benson	743	2/18/1870	Governor Henry A. Swift
Todd	23,363	Long Prairie	941	2/20/1855	Fort Ripley commander John Blair Todd
Traverse	4,463	Wheaton	575	2/21/1862	Lake Traverse
Wabasha	19,744	Wabasha	537	10/27/1849	Sioux chief Wabasha
Wadena	13,154	Wadena	538	6/11/1858	A trading post on Crow Wing River
Waseca	18,079	Waseca	422	2/27/1857	Indian word: richly providing (soil)
Washington	145,896	Stillwater	390	10/27/1849	President George Washington
Watonwan	11,682	St. James	435	2/25/1960	Watonwan River
Wilkin	7,516	Breckenridge	751	3/7/1868	Established earlier but renamed for Colonel Alexander Wilkin
Winona	47,828	Winona	630	2/23/1854	Sioux relative of chief Wabasha
Wright	68,710	Buffalo	672	2/20/1855	New York statesman Silas Wright
Yellow Medicine	11,684	Granite Falls	758	3/6/1871	From Sioux name for medicinal root

MINNESOTA'S BORDERS

Well, at least three of them

On the east, with Wisconsin — Mississippi River to Hastings, north along the St. Croix River, then straight north to the first rapids of the St. Louis River at the head of Lake Superior. It was determined by Wisconsin's Statehood Enabling Act of August 6, 1846, to the disgust of many Wisconsinites who wanted their state's border to follow the Mississippi River all the way up to its source and then to the border of Canada.

On the south, with Iowa — the 42°30' parallel, established in 1846 when Iowa was made a state.

On the west — along the 96°50' line of longitude, going through two lakes in South Dakota and meandering with the Red River of the North in North Dakota. This boundary was defined in the Minnesota statehood papers of 1858.

What about the north?

The northern border was a problem for almost 150 years.

The Treaty of Paris signed in 1783 established the U.S.-Canada border at the "northwest corner of Lake of the Woods" because the commissioners drawing up the treaty relied on an error-ridden map and called for the northern border to go from the "northwest corner to the Mississippi River." But the river didn't exist that far north! And no one knew quite where the "northwest corner" was. It's pretty difficult to identify the "northwest corner" of a lake with a shoreline that changes direction every few feet.

In 1818, another treaty defined the northern boundary as the 49th parallel, running through Rainy River and a collection of long, narrow lakes. The shape of it, especially at the jog of Lake of the Woods, where a totally disconnected section called the Northwest Angle is not even attached to the rest of the state, has been described as a "politico-geographical curiosity." But even that was open to interpretation, so both the U.S. and Canada began to make demands for more land. The Webster-Ashburton Treaty of 1842 placed the boundary at the Pigeon River, thus giving the rich iron mines of northern Minnesota to the United States. It also drew a specific border along the northern lakes of what is now the Boundary Waters Canoe Area Wilderness.

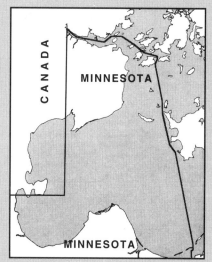

Another twitch of the treaty

Even that didn't finish things. In one place the compromise had to get more specific. A new treaty signed on February 24, 1925, exactly defined the northernmost point in Lake of the Woods as 49°23'04.49" north and 95°09'11.61" west. Under the treaty the United States gave up $2^1/_2$ acres of water to Canada.

There was no problem with Minnesota becoming a state—everything was ready, no one had any problems with it. By January 26, 1858, all was set, but then Congress decided to tie Minnesota's statehood in with Kansas's—and Kansas was caught up in the slavery question. Southerners wanted it to come in as a slave state. Northerners disagreed, and the residents of Kansas itself didn't seem to have any say in the matter. Finally, in May, the "English Compromise" was accepted that let Minnesota be admitted. The Kansans got a say in their own destiny, and things could get moving again. Minnesota's statehood was passed on May 11, 1858. The first governor was Henry H. Sibley, a Democrat who had come from Michigan.

Achieving statehood

THE CAPITAL

When Minnesota was made a territory, Congress specified St. Paul as the capital. However, Stillwater and Minneapolis (then called St. Anthony) both laid claim to the honor. In a compromise, St. Anthony got the university, Stillwater the penitentiary, and St. Paul the capital, although St. Peter made a good try at taking it away (see p. 71).

Which would you choose?

The first meeting of the legislature of the Minnesota Territory took place on September 3, 1849, in the dining room of a St. Paul hotel, the Central House. Presiding was the territory's first governor, Alexander Ramsey, who was appointed to the post by President Zachary Taylor. Among the legislature's first deeds was the creation of a system of free education.

A hotel for a capitol

The first real capitol building, built in 1853 near 10th and Cedar streets in St. Paul, was used during the end of Minnesota's days as a territory as well as during its first years of statehood, until 1881, when it burned down. After spending two years in the old Market House, the state's second capitol was built on the site of the first one. However, it became clear right away that they should have built it larger, and plans were made for another building.

The capitol building

Today's capitol was designed by Ohio-born St. Paul architect Cass Gilbert. It was begun with ground-breaking ceremonies on May 6, 1896. On July 27, 1898, the cornerstone was laid. The building was completed in late 1904. It is 433 feet long, east to west, with an average width of 120 feet. The central portion is 228 feet from north to south. Outer walls are 69 feet high, and the dome is 220 feet. It has the biggest unsupported marble dome in the world. In the central area stand six marble statues of idealized figures, created by Daniel Chester French. They represent the six virtues of "Wisdom, Courage, Bounty, Truth, Integrity, and Prudence."

MINNESOTANS IN STONE

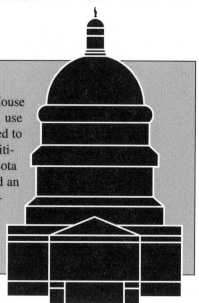

Henry Rice

When the United States Capitol was expanded and the House of Representatives got a new chamber, Congress decided to use the old House chamber as a Statuary Hall. Each state was asked to send statues of two of its most prominent citizens. The first citizen selected was Henry Mower Rice, who had come to Minnesota as a fur trader and stayed to grow with the territory. He played an influential role in the formation of the state. Elected a U.S. senator when statehood was achieved, he supported antislavery and pro-Union measures. Rice's statue, sculpted by Frederick Ernest Triebel, was sent to Washington in 1916.

Maria Sanford

Minnesota went another 42 years before sending a second statue to join Rice's. Then it was the statue of a woman, Maria L. Sanford. Among the first women in the United States to be made a full professor, she taught elocution and rhetoric from 1880 to 1909 at the University of Minnesota. Connecticut-born, she came within a hair's-breadth of becoming

a county superintendent of schools in Pennsylvania in 1869. She moved on to the new Quaker college, Swarthmore, where she was appointed professor of history. Her enthusiasm for the school dampened by an unhappy love affair with a married man, she was ready to move on when University of Minnesota president Folwell invited her to Minneapolis. Incredibly popular with her students but anathema to much of the faculty, she spent a good part of her later years having to fend off efforts to get her dismissed. But Maria Sanford got the last laugh when the state of Minnesota chose her in 1958 to go to Washington, D.C., as a prominent citizen. Her statue was sculpted by Evelyn Raymond.

NATURE AND ENVIRONMENT

It's doubtful that anyone knows for sure how many lakes Minnesota has. Of course, it's called the "land of 10,000 lakes," but estimates of the true total vary from 11,000 to 22,000. Officially, Minnesota has 15,291 lakes (and about 12,000 loons). It also has more shoreline than Florida, Hawaii, and California put together.

Oddly enough, it also has some ancient shoreline that adds to the interest of the state's landscape. In very ancient times, when glaciers kept the rivers of Minnesota from draining northward into Hudson Bay, a lake was formed that covered Minnesota, Dakota, and much of Canada. Called Lake Agassiz, it was about 700 by 200 miles in area and lasted several thousand years. When the glaciers retreated, the water drained away, leaving several major lakes, including Lake of the Woods, and some high-and-dry beaches in its wake. One such beach is visible in Old Mill State Park. Even those beaches are upstarts compared to the 3.6-billion-year-old rocks—among the oldest in the world—found in Brown and Renville counties.

Clearly, Minnesota's lakes, rivers, prairies, and even the ground beneath our feet and weather around us are awesome. Come and see!

- Rocks, Ridges & Caves
- What the Pioneers Found
- Feathers and Fur
- Endangered Species
- Rivers and Falling Water
- Lots of Lakes
- State and National Forests
- Protecting the Environment
- Stormy Weather

ROCKS, RIDGES & CAVES

Winona and the Mississippi Bluffs

No glaciers, please

When the last great glacier covered much of North America (up to about 12,000 years ago), it missed a spot in Minnesota. The area is filled with spectacular bluffs and the closest thing that Minnesota has to mountains. The region, called the driftless area, includes three counties—Houston, most of Fillmore, and southern Winona.

Mystery of the rocks

❋ England has its Stonehenge, Illinois has its Monk's Mound, and Minnesota has its mysterious Blue Mounds. At the south end of Blue Mounds State Park in Rock County, a line of rocks extends 1,250 feet from east to west. Nothing is known about who built the line of rocks, but it is clearly of human origin. Sunrise and sunset line up perfectly with the rocks on the first day of spring and the first day of autumn.

A farmer's lost pigs

❋ Oh where . . . Oh where had his little pigs gone? A farmer near Harmony kept losing his pigs. One day he heard squealing from a hole in the ground where he found his pigs and a beautiful cave of stalagmites and stalactites which is now the Midwest's largest cave—Niagara Cave. It now has five miles of underground trails, and the main feature is a waterfall dropping 60 feet, 200 feet below the earth's surface.

A wondrous cave

❋ Edward L. Wells was just a lowly accountant by day, but after hours he was a fiction writer. Interested in developing his town, St. Anthony, he and the Chute brothers made a plan to build a tunnel along the Mississippi to divert water for power generation that could be sold for industrial development. The excavation was begun but quickly came to a standstill and the project was abandoned.

Wells decided to promote the man-made "cave" and his town in a totally fictitious article. He described the wonders of the cave—it was 5,000 feet in depth and full of "innumerable natural curiosities, such as fish, snakes, bats, buffalo, horns, and bones of all descriptions." Others joined in on the hoax when inquiries arrived from out of state.

Colonel David Edwards, town merchant, wrote . . . "in the center was a huge stalagmite . . . called the tower of St. Anthony . . . circumference two hundred feet. . . . In a corner we found the skeleton head and body of a serpent of incredible size."

Wells penned the original article under the name of Nesmith and the whole hoax ultimately became known as the Nesmith Cave Hoax. It was a long time before the deception was exposed outside the state. Later, when the area became a vacation spot for Southerners, interest in the man-made cave was revived by a Mr. Pettingill. He built a resort at the entrance to the abandoned tunnel, sold snacks, and took vacationers up and down the tunnel—by then flooded with about 10 inches of water—on a flat-boat.

Rooting out a mystery

When it was found in 1937, Mystery Cave was simply a very peculiar spot next to a bluff where the waters of the Root River disappeared into a hole. An adventuresome farmer decided to trace the missing water and found his way into a cavern now known to be at least 12 miles long and filled with fascinating chambers, stalactites and stalagmites, and magnificent "waterfalls" of colorful flowstone. It is located in Forestville State Park.

In the pink

The major granite-producing area in Minnesota—second only to Barre, Vermont—is a small area in Sherburne and Stearns counties. In 1868, two partners opened a quarry in what is now part of the State Reformatory property and soon "Reformatory Pink" became a popular granite for use in cemetery monuments. Red and gray granites from Minnesota were used in such important buildings as the Louisiana State Capitol, the Chicago Tribune Tower, and the cathedral in St. Paul.

Stone for pipes of peace

The Indians fought for generations over the ownership of the pipestone quarries located near Lake Benton. They believed that the Great Spirit had created man here and the red stone was their ancestors' flesh hardened by the Great Flood. According to Omaha and Yankton legend, Wahegela, the Omaha wife of a Yankton Sioux, found the pipestone while trailing buffalo. The Omaha claimed the area because Wahegela was one of them; the Sioux claimed it because she lived and died with their people. The Indians finally declared the ground holy and neutral and shared the soft red stone to make their pipes. Indians came from hundreds of miles away to get the stone for their peace pipes. The stone, called catlinite, was named for artist George Catlin, who explored the quarry in 1836. In 1937, 115 acres that included the quarries were designated by Congress as Pipestone National Monument (pictured at right).

WHAT THE PIONEERS FOUND

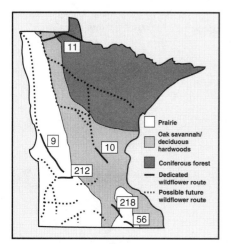

Prairie
Oak savannah/ deciduous hardwoods
Coniferous forest
Dedicated wildflower route
Possible future wildflower route

Three regions in Minnesota

Three main types of vegetation occur in Minnesota. To the far northeast is a large coniferous forest (dark area on map) which used to cover 38 million acres. The first commercial cutting of Minnesota white pine was at Franconia on the St. Croix River. One percent or less is all that remains today. There are only 3,000 acres of old white pines outside the Boundary Waters Canoe Area Wilderness. The BWCA may have about 20,000 acres of white pine forest, which includes aspen and birch. The total actual acreage of white pine left in the state would fit into a 2.25 mile square. One-fourth of that acreage is located in Itasca State Park.

The southwestern and western portion of the state (white area) is covered with prairie grass, and was once thought to be unfertile. Less than 1 percent of the more than 18 million acres of original prairie survives today.

The transition zone (shaded area), formerly known as "Big Woods," used to be a 100-mile-wide zone of hardwoods such as sugar maples, white elm, and basswood. The "Woods," which stretched from Mankato to approximately 110 miles north of Minneapolis-St. Paul, were cut down long ago and the land used for farming and grazing.

Minnesota wetland   ❋ About 3 percent of the land in Minnesota is wetland, where water stands in or on the ground during much of the year. For many decades, this wetland was harvested for its marsh hay, but farmers soon began to see that they would earn more by draining the land and planting regular crops. Machines such as the Buckeye Traction Ditcher could dig a ditch and fill it with drain tile at a rate of half a mile a day. About 50 percent of Minnesota's wetlands have been drained. Today, however, land managers realize that draining wetlands increases flooding and destroys wildlife.

Much of Minnesota's wetland is in a strange form called prairie potholes. These are often rounded depressions in the ground left as the glaciers receded, which then filled with water and plants. Unfortunately, it was easy for farmers to just fill in potholes and use them as part of their cropland. Today, many farmers plow around the contours of the remaining potholes in an attempt to preserve these natural areas.

Where the wildflower grows

"I had always thought I was standing knee-deep in weeds!" So said Le Roy Mayor Everett Kinter at the dedication of the state's first wildflower route, Highway 56 from Le Roy to Rose Creek. Minnesota has since designated parts of state highways 9, 11, and 56, and U.S. highways 10, 212, and 218 as wildflower routes. Along these hundreds of miles of highway are sections of the state's original plant life. Eventually there will be a Wildflower Route system throughout Minnesota. In the map above, bold lines mark dedicated wildflower routes and dotted lines mark possible future routes.

❄ The **Anoka Sand Plain** is a triangular area (858 square miles) north of the Elk River where the wind has eroded all the top soil and huge sand dunes—some as high as 20 feet—have been created.

The area of southern Minnesota now known as **Rice Lake State Park** was originally part of a region called the **Southern Oak Barrens**. It was a vast oak savanna, a type of growth making up as much as 7 percent of the entire state. It was prairie with occasional stands of burr oaks. Today Southern Oak Barrens is the rarest type of plant community in the state.

Goat Prairie in **O.L. Kipp State Park** near Winona has a very specialized type of plant that grows on a slope so steep that "only goats can graze it." It's a type of prairie grass that absorbs sun like a solar collector and can withstand the strong sun during daylight hours followed by freezing at night. Other plants, especially woody stemmed ones, cannot grow in such rapidly changing conditions.

Curious places

FEATHERS AND FUR

Birds of prey

St. Paul—big city, rushing people—right? Yes, but it is also the home of the Raptor Center, a rehabilitation center for birds of prey, where wounded hawks, eagles, falcons, and other large birds such as trumpeter swans are sent from at least 37 states. Associated with the University of Minnesota, the center was founded by Dr. Patrick Redig and Dr. Gary Duke. Between 1975 and 1989, they put 639 endangered bald eagles back into the air. Most of the birds had been injured by cars, collisions with powerlines, and shot pellets. The 3M Corp. donates medical supplies to the center, which has become very adept at dealing with lead poisoning in birds. Dr. Redig, along with Dr. Harrison Tordoff, also started and coordinates a program designed to reinstate the nesting of peregrine falcons in the Midwest. They supervise the release into the wild of birds bred in captivity.

Land of 12,000 loons

Often referred to as the land of 10,000 lakes, Minnesota also has almost 12,000 loons, according to a recent count—more than twice as many as any other state. The Department of Natural Resources uses volunteers to track the loon population every five years. The next count is scheduled for 1995.

Herons in a pig's eye

More than 8,000 great blue herons migrate to Minnesota every spring from the south to nest and rear their young. There are 13 heron colonies in the Twin Cities area alone with the largest on Pig's Eye Island, only five miles from St. Paul's city center. Created in 1986, the Pigs Eye Island Heron Rookery Scientific and Natural Area (whew!) is home to 2,400 great blue herons that nest high in the cottonwood trees. The St. Paul Port Authority was about to destroy the area in the early 1980s by dredging when a group of citizens organized the Pig's Eye Coalition and sued to stop the plans.

Oil brings death

✳ We tend to think of an oil spill as something that happens on the ocean, but rivers get them, too—in fact, even more frequently! In 1963, oil was accidentally spilled in the Mississippi just south of St. Paul before the major migration of ducks and other gamebirds began. It seeped into the wetlands along the riverbanks, poisoning the animals when they landed in their usual resting and feeding spots. More than 10,000 birds died.

Bearly welcome

✳ Civilization hadn't totally taken over in Duluth in 1929. On August 18, a black bear, estimated to weigh at least 350 pounds—and very hungry—wandered into the lounge of the Hotel Duluth. Panicked employees called the police, who came and shot it.

Oh deer!

In 1990, when there were 4,375,099 people in Minnesota, there were also 1 million deer. That year, three people were killed and 437 injured in vehicle-animal collisons, most of them involving deer. The Minnesota Department of Transportation estimates that almost 16,000 deer are hit each year. In the Twin Cities alone, 3,000 deer are hit each year.

Hot TIP

Wildife is important to Minnesotans and poaching of any kind isn't tolerated. When the state instituted the TIP (Turn In Poachers) program in 1981, little did they realize that 3,500 poachers would be convicted by 1991. Even kids get involved. One boy called TIP when another child killed a duck for no reason. A resort owner phoned in when some of his guests came back with more fish than the legal limit. A bigger "fish" was caught when tipsters alerted authorities to a commercial fisherman who had $65,000 worth of illegal fish. He was convicted on 12 federal counts and paid $3,000 in fines.

Giving them the bird

Rothsay is located near the traditional "booming grounds" of the greater prairie chicken, a.k.a. pinnate grouse. At mating time, the large males strut and dance on small knolls, hoping to attract females. It seems unlikely that the females won't pay attention—the males develop large, orange-colored sacs on their throats in which they make a resonant booming noise that can be heard a mile away. Rothsay celebrated the nation's bicentennial by constructing the "world's largest prairie chicken." It weighs $4^1/_2$ tons and can't fail to attract visitors, if not another $4^1/_2$-ton prairie chicken.

The grasshopper miracle

The first invasion of grasshoppers in Minnesota occurred in June of 1873. They seemed to enjoy what Minnesota had to offer—a smorgasbord of plant life. By 1877 the word must have gotten out because billions of the pesky grasshoppers were busy eating everything in their path and driving many farmers off their land. Weary farmers said the grasshoppers sounded like "hundreds of hogs turned into the fields" and sometimes "piled up in the fields and along the road to a depth of one or two feet." The menace was so real and so devastating that Governor Pillsbury asked citizens of the state to join in a day of prayer on April 26, 1877, to ask for divine intervention in ridding the state of the pests. It must have worked. During the next two days a late winter storm hit, freezing the pests in flight.

❋ Winona is headquarters for one of the country's most popular wildlife refuges, the Upper Mississippi River National Wildlife and Fish Refuge. Known as "Upper Miss," it is up to three miles wide and over 260 miles long, from Reads Land, Minnesota, to Rock Island, Illinois. It provides habitat for 100 kinds of fish, 35 types of amphibians and reptiles, 57 kinds of mammals, and over 265 species of birds The refuge accommodates about 3.5 million visitors each year.

Upper Miss

More refuges

Some other wildlife refuges include:
- Agassiz, near Thief River Falls – 61,500 acres on the Mississippi Flyway
- Big Stone, at Ortonville – 11,114 acres along the Minnesota River
- Mille Lacs – 0.6 acre
- Minnesota Valley, at Bloomington – 12,500 acres of wetland habitat
- Rice Lake, McGregor – 16,369 acres of wild rice and wild celery to feed arriving waterfowl
- Sherburne, Princeton – 29,606 acres of marsh and tamarack swamps
- Tamarack, near Detroit Lakes – 34,518 acres for waterfowl. Captive-bred trumpeter swans are released there.

ENDANGERED SPECIES

❋ Two of the most famous animals in America are on the federal Endangered Species List but are not labeled endangered in Minnesota—the bald eagle and the gray wolf.

But not in Minnesota

Minnesota and Wisconsin have the largest populations of nesting bald eagles in the continental United States. In 1989, there were 390 breeding pairs. Eagles mate for a lifetime and return to the same nests each year. Eggs are laid in March and incubated for about 35 days. By late June or July, the young are ready to fly. The first successful nesting of bald eagles in central Minnesota in over 30 years took place in 1983 at Sherburne National Wildlife Refuge. About 50 to 75 bald eagles winter in the Wabasha area of the Mississippi where the water remains unfrozen. They arrive in November and stay until March. During the day, they simply perch on the tall trees at the edge of the river.

The wolf pack of the Lower 48

❄ Although wolves still live throughout several of the northern states, albeit in very small numbers, Minnesota has more wolves than any other state except Alaska. Minnesota has been fortunate in that most of the northeastern part of the state is largely uninhabited and has not been widely farmed. The huge national forests and national parks in that part of the state have generally protected the wolf populations. In addition, Minnesota wolf country adjoins that of Ontario across the border—a border that wolves don't recognize—so the population is continually replenished.

Minnesota wolves number perhaps 1,700 and the population remains fairly stable, but only because the animal is protected. Even so, an estimated 20 percent of the wolves are killed illegally in some years. On June 26, 1993, the International Wolf Center opened at Ely. It includes a captive wolf pack, sponsors "Wolf Weekends" into the wilderness, and generally spreads the word that we need to protect the wolves that remain.

MINNESOTA'S ENDANGERED SPECIES

Minnesota has fewer endangered species than most states in the eastern half of the nation because it still has so much open land. Its Endangered Species List was established in 1984. Those with asterisks (*) after their names are on the federal Endangered Species List.

Mammals - none

Mollusks
Higgin's eye mussel*
Fat pocketbook mussel

Butterflies
Assiniboia skipper
Uncas skipper
Uhler's Arctic

Fish - none

Birds
Sprague's pipit
Baird's sparrow
Burrowing owl
Chestnut-collared longspur
Piping plover (Duluth harbor population)*
Peregrine falcon*

Amphibians and Reptiles
Five-lined skink

Plants
There are 45 species of plants regarded as endangered in Minnesota.

✳ Plants and animals that are brought into an area can cause severe problems for the native species. Minnesota, especially around the Twin Cities, is suffering from at least two such species. Eurasian watermilfoil, an imported plant, makes huge vegetation mats that crowd out native plants and clog boat propellers. Just a tiny fragment of the plant on a boat hull can begin the infestation of a whole lake. Currently, 40 Minnesota lakes suffer from the problem. A state law makes it illegal to "transport any watermilfoil over a public road."

Importing trouble

Zebra mussels have been found in Duluth-Superior Harbor and the Mississippi River. They are brought in on oceangoing ships and have multiplied rapidly, clogging municipal water intake lines, destroying beaches, and damaging lake ecosystems. In 1992, two species of fish called gobies were found in the Great Lakes, but they were welcome because they love to gobble up mussels. Only time will tell—and only time will tell whether the gobies themselves will become a problem.

RIVERS AND FALLING WATER

The Falls of St. Anthony

A waterfall on the Mississippi River, named the Falls of St. Anthony by Father Hennepin in 1680 (see p. 36) for St. Anthony of Padua. It's not spectacular as waterfalls go. The drop in the river is only about 16 feet high, and the waterfall stretches across the river perhaps 200 feet. But it became vitally important in the development of Minnesota. It created a barrier to exploration and transportation up the Mississippi, and provided power for the first sawmills and gristmills, which allowed Fort Snelling to develop. It served as the source of power for the first hydroelec-

Explorer Jonathan Carver created this image of the Falls of St. Anthony for his book of travels, published in 1778. Today, the falls are surrounded by Minneapolis.

tric station in the United States, opened in 1882, and for turning Minneapolis into the Flour Capital of the Nation. Today, the Falls of St. Anthony are barely noticeable in the rush of the Twin Cities. River traffic bypasses the falls through locks, and the famed Stone Arch Bridge blocks the view.

✳ A tunnel was being constructed under Hennepin Island in 1869 as part of the milling operations being developed. On October 4, the ground beneath the Falls of St. Anthony started to collapse into the tunnel. If it had been allowed to continue, the falls would have disappeared along with the power to run the mills. Everyone in the city who was able worked for weeks to shore up the falls. They had the work done by the time winter set in, at a cost of more than $1 million.

When the falls almost died

MINNEHAHA FALLS IN WINTER

Laughing water

Minnehaha Park in Minneapolis is made up of 142 acres of woodland bordered by the Mississippi River on the east. In the park are the famous Minnehaha Falls, made famous by Longfellow's poem, *The Song of Hiawatha*, published in 1855 (see p. 94). The falls are a 53-foot drop in the Minnehaha Creek to the Mississippi River, but the poet's description is much better:

Where the Falls of Minnehaha
Flash and gleam among the oak-trees,
Laugh and leap into the valley.

The name *Minnehaha* is from the Dakota words for "laughing water."

The source of it all

❄ Walk across the Mississippi River?! You gotta be kiddin'! No—you can do that, stepping on stones, soon after the "Father of Waters" emerges from Lake Itasca as a mere babe of waters. Itasca State Park is Minnesota's oldest state park and the second largest (the largest is St. Croix). It was established by an act of the state legislature on April 20, 1891. Lawyer, surveyor, and archeologist Jacob V. Brower led the three-year fight to preserve the area's red pines by confronting the logging industry's powerful lobby. Brower was named commissioner of Itasca State Park. The park is nationally significant, for it contains the source of the Mississippi River. During the early 1930s, the outlet of Lake Itasca (a.k.a. the first portion of the Mississippi River) was called "a swampy, muddy, and dirty sight" in a park report. It needed "improving" and so the first 2,000 feet of the Mississippi were rerouted and the swamps eliminated with 40,000 cubic yards of fill. Today the park contains more than 300 lakes and covers 32,000 acres.

Through the spit for spite

The city of Superior, Wisconsin, has a natural entrance into St. Louis Bay through the long, narrow spit of land in Lake Superior called Minnesota Point. Duluth, jealous, wanted one too. So they started building a canal through the spit that would allow boats to dock in the bay. Superior reacted by getting a legal injunction to make the Duluth residents stop. However, Duluth heard that the injunction was on its way, and the eager citizens dug night and day to get the work finished before the legal paper arrived. The famed Aerial Lift Bridge now spans the opening dug by the tricky citizens.

Minnesota Point

Duluth

Lake Superior

MINNESOTA

WISCONSIN

Superior

First "Wild and Scenic"

❄ In 1968, Congress passed the Wild and Scenic Rivers Act which recognizes the importance of rivers and seeks to keep them—or at least major segments of them—safe for future generations. The first river to be given the Wild and Scenic designation was Minnesota's St. Croix River and its tributary, the Namekagon (which means "place of the sturgeon"). Dakota people called the 200-mile river *Hogan-wahnkay-kin* or "the place where the fish lies." A Dakota legend told how a hunter was changed into a big fish after he drank water from the river.

LOTS OF LAKES

✳ Michigan geologist Henry Rowe Schoolcraft accompanied Governor Cass's expedition in 1820, which concluded that the lake they named Cass was the source of the Mississippi. (Minnesota was part of Michigan Territory at the time.) But the geologist was not really satisfied that they were right. He hired an Indian guide to take him up the river. On July 13, 1832, the Indians led him to *Omushkos*, meaning "Elk Lake," which he realized was the source of the Mississippi River.

The search for truth

Schoolcraft didn't much like *Omushkos* as the name for such an important lake, so he combined two Latin words, *veritas* meaning "truth" and *caput* meaning "head." When the first three letters of *veritas* and the last three letters of *caput* were dropped, Schoolcraft came up with *Itasca*. Certainly sounds better than "Veriput!"

The neighborly lighthouse

In western Lake Superior huge amounts of iron ore in the lake bed cause magnetic compasses to malfunction. Navigators needed something to help them find their way. Then, in 1905, between November 24 and 27, a huge storm caused at least 26 vessels to either sink or be stranded. The U.S. government acted immediately to purchase 763 acres of land on a bluff for the construction of Split Rock Lighthouse (at right). By 1910, the warning equipment was in place—two steam-compressed air foghorns that could be heard five miles away and a lantern. The station was officially opened on July 31, 1910. Through the years, the keepers have shone the powerful light on nearby houses so people could read at night. And one keeper sounded the foghorn in the fall to help lost deer hunters find their way home. When the first road to the lighthouse was completed, it became an overnight tourist attraction. By the late 1930s, over 100,000 people were visiting the lighthouse annually. The Split Rock Lighthouse was closed by the Coast Guard on January 1, 1969, and turned over to the state of Minnesota. Split Rock State Park was established in 1970 when 112.57 acres were added to the lighthouse holdings.

✳ More than a million years ago, Lake Agassiz was created when the glaciers melted. It was larger than all the Great Lakes combined. A glacial river, called the Warren, began draining Lake Agassiz more than 8,000 years ago. It carved the Minnesota River Valley, and the northern end drained into Hudson Bay as the ice-dam melted, leaving behind the Red River Valley. The remains of the giant lake can be seen in Minnesota's Lake of the Woods and Canadian Lakes Winnipeg, Winnipegosis, and Manitoba.

An ancient lake

Lakes and Facts

Officially, Minnesota has 15,291 lakes. It also has more boats per capita than any other state in the United States—at least one for every six residents. Lake country is centered in north-central Minnesota. Many tourists come to the state to experience the "canoe and loon syndrome"—being all alone on a lake when the sun goes down.

There are 11,842 lakes of at least 10 acres in Minnesota, and 5,483 of these are fishing lakes—for a grand total of 3.8 million acres of fishing lakes excluding Lake Superior. These numbers do not include the more than 10,000 wetlands that are smaller and shallower!

Some lakes have beautiful names such as Minnetonka, but others have weird names such as Jack the Horse, Full of Fish, Dirty Nose, Big Spunk, Pug-Hole, Split Hand, Big Mantrap, Shoe Pack, and Stingy. There are 118 Long Lakes and 201 Mud Lakes, but only one talking lake, Lac Qui Parle!

Lake of the Woods

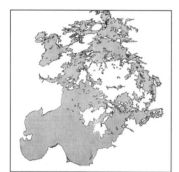

❄ The 20-year-old fur trader from Canada, named Jacques De Noyon, must have thought he was in an endless labyrinth when, in 1688, he became the first white person to see the famed Lake of the Woods, which makes up part of the border between Minnesota and Ontario, Canada. The spectacular 2,000-square-mile lake contains 14,000 islands, so that almost nowhere is it possible to feel completely surrounded by water. Only Big Traverse Bay in the southwest corner is wide open.

North of Big Traverse Bay is the small chunk of Minnesota called the Northwest Angle. It is completely separated from the rest of the state's land and was, until the acquisition of Alaska, the northernmost point of the United States. Most of the Angle is Red Lake Indian Reservation.

STATE AND NATIONAL FORESTS

First state forest was treeless

❄ In 1899, the John S. Pillsbury estate donated 1,000 acres that became the first state "forest." The forest was wishful thinking at that time, however, because the trees had all been cut down. The land had to be reseeded to become a forest again.

Women and mistakes make a forest

❄ The Minnesota Federation of Women's Clubs started protesting in the late 1890s about the amount of logging being done in Minnesota. The women used their personal influence in a major campaign that resulted in Congress establishing the Minnesota National Forest in 1908. Its name was later changed to Chippewa National Forest. It covers more than 2 million acres, taking up most of Cass, Itasca, and Beltrami counties, with headquarters at Cass Lake. The forest got a special bonus because of a mapping error made by the federal government in 1882. The error showed a 40-acre section of virgin forest as a part of Coddington Lake. The "Lost Forty" contains giant red and white pines now almost 350 years old and measuring between 22 and 48 inches in diameter. Because of the error, the loggers missed the trees completely!

Superior National Forest

President Theodore Roosevelt, on February 13, 1909, signed a proclamation setting aside 35,000 acres as Superior National Forest. Today it encompasses 3.7 million acres and, with Canada's adjacent Quetico Provincial Park, forms an area of unspoiled wilderness. More than 2,000 lakes with beautiful islands dot the landscape. In 1926, parts of the national forest were declared roadless. A major portion of the forest is now the Boundary Waters Canoe Area Wilderness. The once booming mining town of Ely is now the gateway to the area.

A million acres of canoe trails

A wilderness area of 1 million acres of rivers and lakes comprises the Boundary Waters Canoe Area Wilderness. Called BWCA (which can't be pronounced), it runs 150 miles with Canada's Quetico Provincial Park along the border from Lake Superior to International Falls. Vehicles are not allowed in the wilderness area and planes have to fly at a certain altitude. All trash must be carried out of the area and no bottles or cans are allowed in. It is the largest federal wilderness east of the Rocky Mountains, as well as the first one anywhere.

❄ Young Minnesotan Geoff Steiner survived the Vietnam War, at least in body, but his mind was a different matter. For years after his return home, he was sunk in despair, depression, and alcoholism. Then, knowing that he could not cope with other people, he moved into the woods, where he would impose his depression on no one else. But in that woods, the depression began to lift, because he discovered a joy and a purpose—the planting of trees. So far, he has single-handedly planted almost 40,000 trees in the Living Memorial Forest, in commemoration of the dead and missing from the Vietnam War. His ultimate goal is to build a healing center for veterans in his forest.

Smokey Bear at International Falls

The healing forest

One of the newest national parks

Voyageurs National Park, established in 1975, is best seen by water or on foot, mainly because there are so very few roads through the 217,892 acres, which contain 30 lakes. Named after the hardy French-Canadian fur trappers and canoemen who helped open up the region, the park's larger lakes—Rainy, Namakan, Sand Point, and Kabetogama—played an important role in creating the water highway used by both the voyageurs and Native Americans.

PROTECTING THE ENVIRONMENT

The hazardous garden

✳ The sewage-disposal plant on St. Paul's Pig's Eye island—now a Superfund site—opened on May 16, 1938. Through the years, so much hazardous waste was dumped there that it eventually became a Superfund site, one of hundreds across the country slated for high-priced cleanup by federal and state governments. But something special is happening at Pig's Eye.

In 1991, Pig's Eye Landfill became home to "Revival Field," an artistically designed garden of plants called "hyperaccumulators," which absorb certain hazardous materials from the soil. It is an experiment headed by New York artist Mel Chin to see if the plants will work to pull such elements as arsenic, cadmium, chromium, lead, and mercury—called heavy metals—from the soil. These are the main hazardous chemicals at the site, and they can cause human health problems.

A nuclear spill

✳ The water used to cool a nuclear reactor becomes radioactive in the process and cannot be returned to the water source; it must be stored. On November 19, 1971, the storage tank at the Northern States Power Company's reactor in Monticello spilled over. An estimated 50,000 gallons of radioactive water accidentally reached the Mississippi River, and some even got into St. Paul's water supply.

The toxic cloud

✳ At 2:30 A.M. on June 30, 1992, 14 cars of a Burlington Northern freight train were derailed while crossing the Nemadji River between Wisconsin and Minnesota. When a tank car ruptured that was carrying a benzene-based chemical, the air was filled with a toxic chemical cloud that forced the evacuation of 30,000 to 85,000 people in Duluth and northeastern Wisconsin. Residents were allowed to return to the area after rain caused the cloud to dissipate.

Salt and snow

✳ In 1988-89, Hennepin County spent over $2 million to battle snow and ice, and used over 18,000 tons of salt during 47 snow "emergencies." Snow- and ice-control functions use one-sixth of the world's yearly consumption of salt. Between 400 and 1,200 pounds are used on each mile of highway every year. And when the snow melts, it runs off into the ground, harming the soil and polluting the underground water supply.

SUPERFUND SITES

Two of Minnesota's Superfund sites have been cleaned up and deleted from the list:
  • Morris Arsenic Dump, Morris, deleted 3/7/86
  • Union Scrap Iron & Metal Co., Minneapolis, deleted 9/91
But there are still 41 sites where cleanup has not begun. One of them—FMC Corp. in Fridley— is on the short list of the 20 most hazardous waste sites in the U.S.

Adrian Municipal Well Field, Adrian

Agate Lake Scrapyard, Fairview Township

Arrowhead Refinery Co., Hermantown

Boise Cascade/Onan Corp/Medtronics Inc., Fridley

Burlington Northern, Brainerd/Baxter

Dakhue Sanitary Landfill, Cannon Falls

East Bethel Demolition Landfill, East Bethel Township

FMC Corp., Fridley

Freeway Sanitary Landfill, Burnsville

General Mills/Henkel Corp., Minneapolis

Joslyn Manufacturing & Supply Co., Brooklyn Center

Koch Refining Co./N-Ren Corp, Pine Bend

Koppers Coke, St. Paul

Kummer Sanitary Landfill, Bemidji

Kurt Manufacturing Co., Fridley

LaGrand Sanitary Landfill, LaGrand Township

Lehillier/Mankato Site, Lehillier/Mankato

Long Prairie Ground Water Contamination, Long Prairie

MacGillis & Gibbs Co./Bell Lumber & Pole Co., New Brighton

Naval Industrial Reserve Ordnance Plant, Fridley

New Brighton/Arden Hills, New Brighton

NL Industries/Taracorp/Golden Auto, St. Louis Park

Nutting Truck & Caster Co., Faribault

Oak Grove Sanitary Landfill, Oak Grove Township

Oakdale Dump, Oakdale

Olmsted County Sanitary Landfill, Oronoco

Perham Arsenic Site, Perham

Pig's Eye Landfill, St. Paul

Pine Bend Sanitary Landfill, Dakota County

Reilly Tar & Chemical Corp., St. Louis Park

Ritari Post & Pole, Sebeka

St. Augusta Sanitary Landfill/Engen Dump

St. Louis River Site, St. Louis County

St. Egis Paper Co., Cass Lake

South Andover Site, Andover

Twin Cities Air Force Reserve Base (Small Arms Range Landfill), Minneapolis

University of Minnesota Rosemount Research Center, Rosemount

Waite Park Wells, Waite Park

Washington County Landfill, Lake Elmo

Waste Disposal Engineering, Andover

Whittaker Corp., Minneapolis

Windom Dump, Windom

STORMY WEATHER

❄ • Record low temperature - On February 9, 1899, Leech Lake Dam reached minus 59° Fahrenheit. Pokegama Falls reached the same low on February 16, 1903.

The weather report

• Record high temperature - On July 29, 1927, Beardsley reached a high of 114° F. Nine years later, on July 6, 1936, Moorhead, not to be outdone, matched it.

• Although much of the state doesn't average more than 20 inches of snow per winter, Minneapolis got 24 inches in 24 hours on November 1, 1991.

❄ Watch the national weather reports on TV regularly and you'll find out why International Falls is called the "Nation's Icebox." Week after week during the winter it tends to have the coldest temperatures in the contiguous United States. And International Falls is proud of the fact! It even has a thermometer 22 feet high that stands where every visitor can see it and gasp. But as you can see from the facts given above, International Falls doesn't get the record low temperatures.

Wear your woolies!

The value of snow

A French proverb says "A proper snow is worth a pile of manure." That's because a snow blanket absorbs nitrates, calcium, potassium, and sulfate from the air and releases them into the ground. Minnesota farmers think of snow as a fertilizer worth about $20 an acre.

The Blizzard of '73 (18, that is)

❄ One of the worst blizzards in Minnesota history began on January 7, 1873, and lasted three full days. The temperature dropped almost 40 degrees in one minute and a hurricane-force wind came up that lasted almost 52 hours. After the storm there were reports from 12 counties that 800 people died from exposure or were frozen to death. That proved to be an exaggeration—only 70 were killed. A student in New Ulm had started for his home across the road and his frozen body was found eight miles away. Another lost man found a stable where he stayed two days, only to find when the storm subsided that he was just a few yards from his own house.

Now where did Mom put my favorite blanket after she washed it? The St. Patrick's Day Blizzard of 1966 literally piled snow as high as the clothesline poles.

Great Armistice Day Blizzard

To Minnesotans, November 11, 1940, was the day of the Great Armistice Day Storm "when all hell broke loose" and snowflakes "seemed as large as baseballs." The U.S. Weather Bureau had forecast "Cloudy with snow flurries, considerably colder Sunday; Monday continued cold. 24-hour high 42°F. at 4 P.M.; low 40°F. at 2 A.M." They were wrong. When the storm hit, the temperature dropped so fast that one hunter died standing in the river bottom, frozen where he held a willow branch, his feet anchored in the ice. Because so many hunters were out, 59 Minnesotans died. A total of 16.2 inches of snow fell in Minneapolis in 14 hours. Winona stunt pilot Max Conrad (nicknamed the "flying grandfather") was the hero of the day. Flying in 50-knot winds, he used his Piper Cub to search for dead or trapped hunters and dropped whiskey, matches, and 5-gallon pails of food. He flew each day until every hunter was accounted for.

The giant of storms

❄ In 1913, a storm that can only be called a hurricane settled in over the Great Lakes for four days, from November 7 to 11. It stretched from Lake Huron to the shores of Lake Superior at Duluth. In the melee, 17 steamships were lost, along with hundreds of sailors.

Great tornadoes

❄ On June 22, 1919, Fergus Falls was literally ripped in half by a violent tornado. It destroyed one half of the town, killing 59 people and destroying 228 houses, and left the other half untouched.

Some other major twisters:
• August 21, 1918 - A tornado wiped out Tyler's business district, killing 37 of its residents.
• July 21, 1883 - A tornado left a path of destruction through Mankato, Sleepy Eye, St. Peter, Kasota, Mantorville, Waseca, New Ulm, Owatonna, and Elgin (where every house was destroyed).
• April 14, 1886 - Sauk Rapids was leveled and 79 people were killed.

MINNESOTA MILESTONES

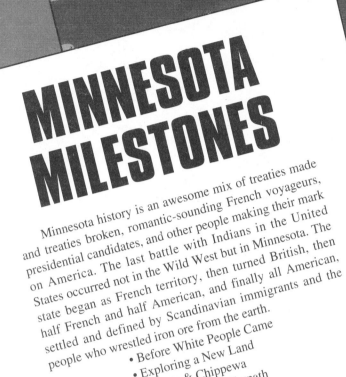

Minnesota history is an awesome mix of treaties made and treaties broken, romantic-sounding French voyageurs, presidential candidates, and other people making their mark on America. The last battle with Indians in the United States occurred not in the Wild West but in Minnesota. The state began as French territory, then turned British, then half French and half American, and finally all American, settled and defined by Scandinavian immigrants and the people who wrestled iron ore from the earth.

- Before White People Came
- Exploring a New Land
- Dakota & Chippewa
- Dakotas on the Warpath
- Indians in Later Years
- The Pioneers
- Slavery and the Civil War
- Gubernatorial Gossip
- Quest for the White House
- Minnesotans in Washington
- Minnesotans at War
- Public Men
- Public Women

BEFORE WHITE PEOPLE CAME

Digging up remains

⭐ The fossilized skeletal remains of a young woman, perhaps only 15 years old when she most likely drowned, were dug up in 1931 by a crew of road builders working at an ancient lake bed near Pelican Rapids. After much study, she was judged to be about 20,000 years old, and thus earlier than either Indians or Eskimos and perhaps the oldest known female in America. Though the skeleton was female, she came to be known to scientists as "Minnesota Man" and to the public as "Lady in the Lake" or "Miss Minnesota." An elk-antler knife and a conch shell were found with her.

Two years later, another ancient skeleton was found, this time in Browns Valley, by amateur archeologist William H. Jensen. The "Browns Valley Man" lived perhaps 8,000 to 10,000 years ago. He was buried with a knife made of brown chalcedony. The gravel in which he was found was probably laid down when ancient Lake Agassiz (see page 27) was draining away. Browns Valley Man represents the Unknown Indians referred to as Paleo Indians.

Another two years passed, and another ancient man was found, this time in Sauk Valley near West Union. The discovery of three such ancient skeletons in widely separated times and locations makes Minnesota rare among the states.

Jeffers petroglyphs

Unlike early rock paintings that abound the world over, Minnesota possesses rock pictures done by early residents that are carved into the rock instead of painted on it. Arising out of the prairie land near Jeffers is a dome of quartzite rock that has been exposed for thousands of years. And throughout those years, the human residents of the area carved nearly 2,000 objects into the rock. The carvings, or petroglyphs, show animals, human activities, and other, more abstract, figures. A smaller collection of petroglyphs can be seen on Picture Island at Nett Lake.

Grand Mound and more

More than 10,000 Indian burial mounds were located in Minnesota a hundred years ago. Most were rounded, but some were shaped to resemble birds, turtles, fish, and other animals (most of these have been plowed under). Many of the mounds have since been paved or bulldozed. The few remaining mounds have been excavated. Researchers have found human remains, tools, decorative beads, and utensils. Many of the skulls have holes cut into them, making scientists assume that the Mound Builders ate the brains of the recently dead for the power it could give them. The Mound Builders probably flourished between 2,000 and 1,000 years ago. The largest mound, at Laurel, near International Falls, is called Grand Mound. About 40 feet high and 325 feet around, it has not been systematically excavated, although several nearby smaller mounds have been opened.

EXPLORING A NEW LAND

The French should have listened

Probably the first steps of white men into Minnesota were taken by two Frenchmen who had to sneak away from their Montreal homes in 1659 because they did not have royal approval to make the journey. Pierre Radisson and his brother-in-law, Médard Chouart, Sieur des Groseilliers, paddled into Lake Superior and made their way along the southern shore. They built a house on Chequamegon Bay and then wintered—in the midst of famine—at an Ottawa Indian village in Wisconsin. They took furs back to their home in Montreal to show the potential and abundance of wealth in the forests around the Great Lakes. However, they were arrested for trading without a license, and all their furs were confiscated.

Angry at the French monarch, Radisson and Groseilliers went to England where they sold King Charles II on the idea of investigating the huge northern bay (Hudson Bay) the Indians had told them about. The plentiful furs they found there led to the founding in 1670 of the Hudson's Bay Company, which played a major role in the development of Canada and which still exists today.

The French map-maker

Joseph Nicolas Nicollet (not to be confused with Jean Nicolet who discovered Lake Michigan two centuries earlier) was a French astronomer and geographer, whose name is now busily used in Minnesota. He first showed up at Fort Snelling in 1836, intent on exploring Lake Itasca, but two years later, the U.S. government sent him through the North to map the region between the Mississippi and the Missouri. A talented artist, he created beautiful maps that provided the best cartography of Minnesota for many decades.

The great enforcer

⭐ Daniel Greysolon, Sieur Du Luth (also written Du Lhut, but we'll ignore that), was a French soldier who sought personal glory and adventure. In a meeting at the Dakota (Sioux) village of Mille Lacs, in 1679, he claimed all of the area for France by nailing the royal emblem to a tree. He spent the next 10 years in the area dealing with factions of Indians, trying to enforce French authority, though he would rather have been blazing his way across the continent. In 1680 he heard that a band of Sioux were holding three white men prisoner. Taking it as a personal affront that the Indians had challenged his king's authority, Du Luth went after the prisoners. Thus he found and released Hennepin, Auguelle, and Accault (see next page) and guided them back into Canada, after making sure that the Sioux understood who was boss. When a French fur-trading post called Fond du Lac, on Lake Superior, began to grow, it was renamed with Du Luth's name.

The kidnapped missionary

⭐ Franciscan missionary Louis Hennepin came into the Minnesota territory from Illinois in 1680 at the urging of Sieur de La Salle. He and his companions, Auguelle and Accault, were taken captive by a band of Sioux Indians in April 1680. While prisoners, they became the first white men to see Lake Pepin. Legend says that Hennepin named the wide area of the Mississippi "Lake of Tears" because some of their captors cried when they were not allowed to kill at least one of the prisoners. During a hunting expedition with the band, Hennepin and his companions became the first white men to see the falls they named after St. Anthony. They were freed in July by Sieur Du Luth. Father Hennepin, whose name now appears on many Minneapolis-area sites, returned to France and disappeared out of American history.

Minnesota's first travel writer

⭐ Jonathan Carver was a New Englander in search of the Northwest Passage to the Orient. The British sent him out from Fort Mackinac to meet with the Dakota Indians. While spending the winter of 1766-67 with them, Carver visited the Indian burial ground, now the site of St. Paul, and stayed briefly in a cavern now known as Carver's Cave. He published his travels in a book called *Travels through the Interior Parts of North-America* (see p. 25), which aroused interest in Minnesota. His heirs tried to claim a large tract of land that they said the Indians had granted him, but the U.S. government refused to let such a grant stand. His namesake cave was later destroyed by railroad construction.

Getting the British out

⭐ The British continued to control the upper Mississippi Valley for many years after the American Revolution. Lt. Zebulon M. Pike (later famous for Pike's Peak) headed an expedition to the Minnesota area in 1806. At Leech Lake they found the Union Jack flying over a post of the North West Company and proceeded to shoot it down, replacing it with the Stars and Stripes. Then they returned south. In all likelihood the British just hauled up another Union Jack and went on about their business.

Pike's Fort?

⭐ Zebulon Pike was on a quest for good locations for military forts when he set up camp on an island at the junction of the Minnesota and Mississippi rivers in 1805. For 60 gallons of whisky and $200 worth of trinkets, he acquired military sites at the mouths of the Minnesota and St. Croix rivers from the Dakota Indians. Sixteen years later Fort St. Anthony was built on the island Pike first explored. Its name was officially changed on January 7, 1825, to recognize the original commander, Josiah Snelling. Soon after the fort was opened, the soldiers harnessed the Falls of St. Anthony to power a sawmill and a grist mill. Zachary Taylor, who would later become president of the United States, was the commander of the fort in 1828-29. Today, Fort Snelling, now a museum, has as its neighbor the Minneapolis-St. Paul Airport.

⭐ At the very northeast tip of the state (the tip of the Arrowhead) stands the site of the busiest fur-trading post in North America in the late 1700s. At that time, the North West Company controlled the fur trade of the entire continent. The Grand Portage consisted of a nine-mile uphill path where even the earliest Indians had to carry their canoes around the falls on the lower Pigeon River. The first explorer to record having been there was Pierre de la Vérendrye, in 1731. When the British took over the region, they began to build up the area. Partners in the North West Company included Alexander MacKenzie, the first white man to cross the continent north of Mexico, and David Thompson, who discovered a route through the Rocky Mountains.

The grand town of Grand Portage

A fort was built at Grand Portage in 1778, and the only troops involved in the American Revolution stationed in Minnesota were dispatched to it. After the British lost the area, the North West Company moved its headquarters to Ontario, and John Jacob Astor's American Fur Company took over at Grand Portage. In 1792 it became a busy trading town boasting French fashions, police, shops, and, of course, drinking establishments. The stockade was surrounded by 16 log buildings, beyond which were camps of "pork-eaters" (the nickname given to canoe men of the Great Lakes) and "North Men" (the men who spent the winters in the lonely wilderness), Indian wigwams, and a canoe yard that could hold 150 canoes. Archeological studies of the Grand Portage area began in the 1930s, and it became a national historic site in 1951.

⭐ French-Canadian voyageurs were superb boatmen, and their job was to take trading goods (blankets, firearms, tobacco, metal traps) from headquarters out to the trading posts in distant places. There, they would leave the goods and collect the furs that Indians had brought in during the previous year and take them back to headquarters. Eventually the furs, especially beaver skins, reached Europe, where top hats made of beaver skin were all the rage.

The voyageurs

The voyageurs have been described as "unmoral and boastful," but their loyalty and faithfulness to their contractual obligations made the fur trade prosper. And when they came to the Minnesota town of Grand Portage for trading negotiations everyone turned out from miles around for the celebration that followed—dancing to violins and bagpipes and drinking gallons of rum. Afterward, the voyageurs disappeared into the wilderness for another year.

Muscular voyageurs

The voyageurs dealing at Grand Portage carried 90-pound packs of furs going out of Minnesota or goods going into the fur traders in the area. Each man taking the Grand Portage Trail between the Lake Superior shore and Port Charlotte on the Pigeon River was required to transport eight packs. Because it was a distance of 18 miles (half of it uphill) there and back to move one pack, the men frequently carried two at a time, or 180 pounds.

DAKOTA & CHIPPEWA

The Dakotas

⭐ Native Americans called Dakotas or Sioux occupied Minnesota after about 1000 A.D. They split up into several tribes, called council fires, which included four tribes known as Santee Dakota—Mdewakanton, Wahpekute, Wahpeton, Sisseton. Three others—Teton, Yankton, and Yanktonai—lived primarily on the prairies, farther west, in the Dakotas and all the way to the Grand Teton Mountains. When whites began to arrive in the seventeenth century, the Mdewakanton (the name means "people of the spirit lake") Dakota controlled Minnesota from their main village, Kathio, on Mille Lacs at the mouth of the Rum River. The name "Sioux" is actually a derisive one that developed from a Frenchified Chippewa name, Nadouessioux, meaning "snake."

The Chippewa or Ojibway

The Ojibway, or Chippewa (which was a white man's version of the name), Indians originally lived in Canada, north of Lake Huron. The Ojibway moved southward along Lake Superior, usurping the territory of the Dakota Indians, who had no firearms. That began the long-lasting animosity between the Dakota and the Ojibway. They established a "capital" on Wisconsin's Madeline Island named La Pointe. It was here that 10 tribes ceded northeastern Minnesota to the whites for $1 million and a reservation, Fond du Lac. They didn't know that this area would eventually yield billions of dollars in lumber and iron ore.

The Indian with the personal fort

⭐ Joseph Renville, son of a French fur trader and a Sioux woman born near St. Paul, served as a guide for Zebulon Pike and then became a captain in the British Army during the War of 1812. He returned to Minnesota to marry an Indian woman and established a large estate (sometimes called Fort Renville) at Lac qui Parle with herds of cattle and sheep and many acres of farmland. Because the Sioux and Ojibway were enemies, he also maintained a force of Sioux warriors to defend his land. Renville, who had spent part of his childhood in a Catholic school in Montreal, helped missionaries in the area and was involved in the translation of the French Bible into the Dakota, or Sioux, language.

A change of heart

⭐ When Kee-e-he-ie, a Sioux Indian who lived near the Falls of St. Anthony, couldn't pay his debt to Philander Prescott, one of the famed fur traders, he offered his daughter in payment. Mary Kee-e-he-ie was willing, and they were married the way all white men were to Indian squaws—they just started living happily together. But as more children and more responsibility came, Prescott became tired of it all, and he sold all his possessions and left for Texas and Louisiana. Failing in two to three years to find the opportunities he sought, Prescott started drinking heavily and probably would have died if he hadn't attended a religious camp meeting one day. There he underwent a change of heart and decided to rectify the wrong he'd done. He discovered that his wife had taken the children to live with the Sioux. When he found her, he insisted that the marriage be made legal. The couple lived among the Indians and became quite prominent in the territory and later in the state. Prescott was the first white man to make a record of a visit to the Pipestone Quarry (see p. 19). He was killed in the Dakota Uprising in 1862.

⭐ The Lac qui Parle Mission was begun in 1835 by Dr. Thomas S. Williamson (who was both a physician and a minister), at the invitation of Joseph Renville. Ten years later the mission chapel had the first bell in Minnesota.

Dakota ABCs

Stephen R. Riggs was a Presbyterian missionary to the Dakota Indians who spent a lifetime translating the Old Testament and other materials into the Dakota language. He developed the Dakota alphabet working with two men named Pond—Gideon and Samuel. In 1852, Riggs published a *Grammar and Dictionary of the Dakota Language*. He also created a series of verbal "sketches" of many of the prominent Indians he knew in the vicinity of Lac qui Parle. During the 1850s, he became influential in a movement to create an Indian nation within Minnesota, to be called the Hazlewood Republic.

an ox
TATANKA

barn
TATANKA TIPI

cart
CANPAHMIHMA

yoke
CAN NAPINPI

Leech Lake

Leech Lake is Minnesota's third largest lake, with 154 miles of shoreline. It was named by the Ojibway for a giant leech that they saw swimming across the lake. It is believed that, as the glaciers melted, as many as six different lakes occupied the present Leech Lake Basin with the Mississippi River running through. The remains of a forest were found on the lake's bottom in the 1800s by a lumberman who saw stumps, loosened by the ice, on the shore. The Ojibway took possession of the area in the 1700s. When they ceded all the North Shore and most of Upper Mississippi Valley in 1854 and 1855, they were given large areas of land that became White Earth and Leech Lake Indian Reservations.

⭐ In 1859, the Protestant Episcopal Church named New York-born Henry Benjamin Whipple as the bishop for Minnesota. He moved to Faribault, where he remained as bishop for the next 42 years. But his work covered the entire state, and he was especially interested in relations with the Indians. Discovering that the U.S. system of "caring" for Native Americans was in reality gradually killing them, he began to protest to the federal government and to work for change in the system. The Sioux and Chippewa gradually learned to trust him and called him "Straight Tongue." He lost a great deal of his influence with the whites after the Dakota Uprising because he's the one who convinced President Lincoln to go easy on the warriors. But the man who came to be called "Apostle to the Indians" later played a major role in persuading the government to provide more humane treatment of the Native Americans.

The bishop who cared

DAKOTAS ON THE WARPATH

The Dakota Uprising

★ While most of the nation stewed in the horrors of the Civil War, Minnesota had its own horror going in a war between the settlers and the Dakota Indians. This action of 1863 has been called the Sioux Uprising, Sioux War, Sioux Outbreak, and Dakota Conflict.

The federal government was intent on making farmers of the Dakotas, but they weren't ready to settle down, especially on the long, narrow strip of land south of the Minnesota River that had been left to them. They continued to hunt, often leaving their reservations and entering the white settlers' territory. By 1862, after a major crop failure, the Indians were hungry and dissatisfied. Because of the Civil War, the federal government was unable to pay the tribes their annuities (both food and money) on time.

On August 17, 1862, four young, hot-headed Santee Dakotas who had been hunting stopped at a farm in Acton in Meeker County. After being refused liquor, they shot four adults and a little girl. The Indian leader, Little Crow, was reluctant to follow up the attack, knowing that in the long run it was hopeless. He said, "Kill one, two, ten, and ten times ten will come to kill you." But he finally agreed to go to war.

The next morning, 1,500 braves under Little Crow's command attacked the Redwood Indian Agency. As many as 200 whites died on that first day of action. One of the first men killed was Thomas Galbraith, head

The rest of the United States received their vision of the Dakota Uprising from such inflammatory newspaper etchings as this one, published at the time.

of the agency, who had been heard to say some days before: "So far as I am concerned, if they are hungry, let them eat grass." He was found with his mouth stuffed full of grass.

The deadly action continued for a month. The Dakotas raided German settlements, killing entire families. Settlers in 23 counties—an area 200 miles long and 50 miles wide—fled to safety. Fort Ridgely was attacked twice. The town of New Ulm was almost completely burned. An estimated 486 white settlers died in the conflict. The main action ended on September 23, in the Battle of Wood Lake, when General Henry Hastings Sibley, the former governor, forced the Dakotas to surrender.

⭐ Although 303 Indians were sentenced to death after the Dakota Uprising, President Lincoln reviewed each case personally, granting a reprieve from hanging to all but 38 men at the urging of Bishop Whipple (see p. 39). On December 26, 1862, in Mankato, the warriors were led single file to the 24-foot gallows while singing an Indian war song. A man who had lost his whole family in the uprising, W.H. Dooley, cut the rope that hanged all men simultaneously before 4,000 cheering citizens. It was the largest mass execution in American history.

On March 3, 1863, Congress passed a law calling for the Indian Department and the military to remove the Dakota Indians as punishment for the uprising. The removal of Dakota Indians from Minnesota began on May 4, when 770 people, primarily women and children, were forced to board the steamboat *Davenport* anchored at Fort Snelling for the long journey to reservations in bleak Dakota Territory. Little Crow, the chief who had been reluctant, was killed later in Meeker County.

⭐ Snana was a Christian Indian woman married to Good Thunder. Eight days before the uprising started in 1862, her daughter died and she went into deep mourning. The arrival of another young woman brought her out of it. Mary Schwandt, an immigrant maid, was the only survivor of a Dakota attack on the family she worked for. She was taken to the Dakota village and became the property of a young Indian warrior, until Snana, still in mourning for her own daughter, offered to trade her best pony for the girl. Repeatedly during the following months, Snana protected Mary from marauding warriors, even to the extent of putting herself in danger. When the uprising was quelled, Mary was delivered back to her people, but Snana was left heartbroken.

⭐ Major Joseph R. Brown bragged that he could "smell Indians afar off." But in August of 1862, his sense of smell was way off. The major left Fort Ridgely with 150 men to patrol the Minnesota River Valley where the Sioux had been causing trouble. When they stopped for the night in Birch Coulee, Brown told the men they could sleep safely. But a Sioux scout saw the unsuspecting soldiers. The Indians surrounded the soldiers during the night and attacked at dawn, wounding 60 and killing 20 of Brown's patrol. The remaining soldiers hastily built dirt barricades and held the Indians off for 31 hours, a task not made simpler by the fact that the ammunition they'd been given at Fort Ridgely was the wrong size for their guns. Reinforcements arrived only because a soldier at Fort Ridgely thought he heard gunfire in the direction of Birch Coulee and a patrol was sent toward the sound.

⭐ Guri Endreson (Rosseland) and one daughter, who lived near Willmar, were left alive after marauding Dakotas killed her husband and a son, kidnapped two daughters, and shot another son. Taking no time for self-pity, Guri ignored the danger and went to a neighboring farm, where she nursed several wounded people and drove them in a wagon through the night for help. The state of Minnesota later erected a monument to the immigrant heroine, as well as other monuments to settlers who fought and died in the uprising.

Vengeance

The protective mother

**Brown's Last
Stand . . . almost**

The heroine of Willmar

INDIANS IN LATER YEARS

Leftover from the uprising

⭐ When news arrived in the Twin Cities that Little Six and Medicine Bottle—two really bad Dakotas—had been captured, there was cause for rejoicing. It was 1864 and the two Indian warriors had terrorized white settlers during and after the Dakota Uprising of 1862. Little Six, referred to as the "Prince of Devils," claimed responsibility for killing 17 women and roasting babies. Medicine Bottle's reputation was just as bad.

The two men were captured illegally in Canada while the British looked the other way. Major Edwin A.C. Hatch crossed the border to apprehend the braves and sent some men to trick them into going to Fort Garr. The soldiers drank water and stayed sober while the two Indians passed out from liquor laced with laudanum. They were strapped onto a dogsled and taken across the border where they waited for ten months at Fort Snelling to stand trial. When told he was going to die, Little Six said, "I am no squaw—I can die whenever the white man wishes." On November 11, 1865, the Indians marched to the gallows bravely and were hanged.

The unnecessary ride of Sam Brown

⭐ When Sam Brown began his 150-mile ride on April 19, 1866, he thought he was saving western Minnesota from an Indian uprising after receiving reports that danger was imminent. After covering 60 miles in five hours, and warning settlers along the way, he made his report at a scouting station. But the chief discounted it as settler hysteria. Brown then thought it his duty to quiet the alarm that he had started, as quickly as possible, so he got a fresh mount and headed back toward Fort Wadsworth (now in South Dakota). A huge storm came up, making it almost impossible for Brown to find his way back. Exhausted and near death, he finally made his way to the fort's gate where he declared with some embarrassment that his warning had been false. All was well. In Browns Valley, a state monument was raised in 1929 to the man who has been called Minnesota's Paul Revere.

The "Blueberry War"

⭐ Settlers near Brainerd had lynched two Indians for the rape and murder of a young girl in 1872. So they were particularly leary when, on July 23, someone saw a group of Indians moving quietly through the woods—the sight spelled an incipient Indian raid. Chaos and fear grew, until the National Guard had to be called out to calm things down. The Indians had only been picking blueberries.

Extending the hand of friendship

⭐ False fear of an Indian massacre spread among settlers in the Roseau Valley on January 28, 1891, when Sheriff Oscar Younggren of Kittson County sent a telegram to Governor Merriam, requesting 300 rifles with ammunition. "They say Indians at Lake of the Woods are threatening ghost dances, and an outbreak is imminent," he wired. When the sheriff ventured out to investigate, fleeing settlers filled the roads. The sheriff later learned that the Ojibway Indians had only gathered for their annual ceremonial dance, and meant no harm. When the settlers finally returned to their homes a few days later, they discovered that their abandoned livestock had been well cared for by the Indians.

⭐ The last Indian battle fought in the United States took place not in the Wild West but at Minnesota's Sugar Point on Leech Lake in 1898. A U.S. marshal was sent to bring back an Indian named Bug-ah-na-ghe-shig ("Hole-in-the-Day"), a.k.a. "Old Bug," to give testimony in a federal case against illegal liquor dealing. However, "Bug" refused to come because the previous year, after testifying in a similar case, he had been left to walk home over 100 miles. The marshal ordered the man arrested, but 17 of his friends defended him. Federal troops were called out and the whole band was arrested. Major Wilkins and six privates of the U.S. Army were killed by the Indians before they were arrested.

Last of the Indian battles

Reservations today

Only those tribes of Dakota Indians who had remained friendly to the whites were allowed to remain in the state, so, the Dakota, or Sioux, Indians have only four reservations in Minnesota today:

1. Upper Sioux in Yellow Medicine County
2. Lower Sioux in Redwood County
3. Prior Lake in Carver County
4. Prairie Island in Goodhue County

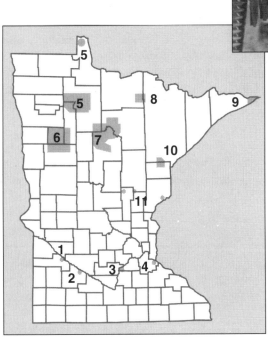

Chippawa powwow at White Earth Reservation

The Chippewa bands have seven major reservations:

5. Red Lake in Beltrami and Clearwater counties and also scattered throughout Roseau, Lake of the Woods (including Northwest Angle), and Koochiching counties
6. White Earth in Mahnomen, Becker, and Clearwater counties
7. Leech Lake in Beltrami, Cass, Hubbard, and Itasca counties
8. Nett Lake in Koochiching and St. Louis counties
9. Grand Portage in Cook County
10. Fond du Lac in Carlton and St. Louis counties
11. Mille Lacs located in three counties—Mille Lacs, Aitkin, and Pine

THE PIONEERS

Swallowing up the land

⭐ Minnesota's first large wave of settlers entered the territory in 1848 when a land office was opened at St. Croix Falls. Most settlers were lumbermen from Maine, farmers from the Mid-Atlantic states, and tradesmen and craftsmen from large eastern cities. Land could be had for $1.25 an acre, proof of occupancy, and cultivation. By the end of 1854, about 500,000 acres of land were occupied; by 1856, more than 1 million acres were owned by settlers; and by 1858, another 2.5 million acres had been sold.

The first Swede

⭐ Though Swedes and other Scandinavians now make up a large part of Minnesota's population, it wasn't always that way. Nils Nyberg, a shoemaker, was the first known Swede to make his home in Minneapolis territory. He settled in St. Anthony in 1851, and was always called the "foreigner." Nyberg, with his fair coloring, was considered a curiosity until after the Civil War, when the Scandinavian population began to increase in Minnesota.

Ancient runes

⭐ It was a normal workday in 1898 when Kensington farmer Olof Ohman started to remove a tree from a swamp-surrounded knoll on his property. Tangled within the roots of the tree he found a large stone, on which his 10-year-old son uncovered some incised marks that looked like runes, or old Scandinavian writing. The following year, the Kensington Runestone, as it came to be called, was translated and found to contain the message below.

Excitement died when Scandinavian scholars claimed the stone was a hoax. The large stone (30 inches long, 3 to 6 inches thick, and 15 inches wide) lay in Ohman's farmyard until some years later when Hjalmar Holand of Ephraim, Wisconsin, became fascinated. He spent the remainder of his life trying to persuade the world of the stone's authenticity. However, even when the Smithsonian Institution put it on display, no claims were made for it. The stone now resides in the Kensington Runestone Museum at Alexandria.

Three large stones located on the shore of Big Cormorant Lake support the possibility that Vikings were in Minnesota so early. The three huge granite boulders are known as the anchor stones. Each stone has a hole an inch wide and about nine inches deep cut into it. Also increasing the odds is the discovery of the Vinland Map in 1965 and of ruins of Norse settlements in Newfoundland.

> *"8 Goths and 22 Norwegians on an exploration journey from Vinland westward. We had camp by 2 skerries [rocky inlets] one day's journey north from this stone. We were out to fish one day. After we came home, we found 10 men red with blood and dead. AVM [Ave Maria] save us from evil. We have 10 of our party by the sea to look after our ships 14 days' journey from this island. Year 1362."*

Scandinavian novels

Novels that tell the stories of Scandinavian immigrants in Minnesota include:

Norwegians - *Big Ember* by Edward Havill (1947)

Danes - *Circle of Trees* by Dana Faralla (1955)

Swedes - *Unto a Good Land* by Vilhelm Moberg (1954) and its sequel, *Last Letter Home* (1961)

Don't forget Rölvaag's book, *Giants in the Earth* (see p. 97)

⭐ It was hard sometimes to attract women to early Minnesota, but "personals" were used then as they are today. An early ad in the *Pelan Advocate* read: "Girls, here's your chance! A handsome young man with a good income offers a good home to the right party. Address all communications to Box _ _, Pelan, Minnesota."

Want ads

SLAVERY AND THE CIVIL WAR

⭐ Dr. John Emerson, an army physician from St. Louis, took his personal slave with him when he was transferred first to Illinois and then to Fort Snelling in 1836. There the slave, named Dred Scott, married and had a child. However, Dr. Emerson died and the slave became the property of Emerson's widow. She forced him to return to Missouri with her. Dred Scott, encouraged by abolitionists, sued for his freedom on the basis that both Illinois and Minnesota (actually part of Wisconsin Territory at the time) were free territory. Loath to lose her property, Mrs. Emerson fought in court and won—her ownership was confirmed. However, Dred Scott's backers took the case all the way to the U.S. Supreme Court. The court, under Chief Justice Taney, ruled in 1857 against Dred Scott, returning him to his owner.

The dreaded Dred Scott decision

⭐ Southern families vacationing on the Minnesota lakes often brought their nurses, maids, and valets with them to ensure their comfort. Although antislavery sentiment was always high in Minneapolis, there was no real problem until Colonel Christmas brought his slave, Eliza Winston (widow of a free Negro who died in Africa) to Lake Harriet in August of 1860. Eliza mentioned to an acquaintance that the property her husband had owned in Memphis had gone to the Christmas family. Her complaint made its way to Minneapolis abolitionists who charged the Christmas family with holding Eliza illegally. The sheriff and 20 armed abolitionists went to the lake where Christmas surrendered Eliza peacefully. Eliza was a free woman and could go where she wanted. She was paraded through the streets like an abolitionist "trophy."

A challenge to slavery

The Minneapolis hotel owners weren't so happy—thousands of southerners came north to vacation every year, and the abolitionists were threatening business. Christmas had given Eliza $10, and she was sent to Canada. When she wrote to her Minneapolis friends for money, they refused—she had served their purpose and was quickly forgotten. Her former master was the only person who helped Eliza financially.

Charge those lines! ⭐ It could be argued that perhaps 262 Minnesotans from the First Minnesota Volunteer Regiment at Gettysburg won the Civil War. After Gettysburg, the South never regained the upper hand, and Minnesota soldiers, although small in number, had a big part in that outcome.

On July 2, 1863, General Winfield Hancock, observing an approaching Confederate force, ordered the men to charge it. Other units started out, but only the Minnesotans hung on until the conclusion of the bloody battle. By tradition (solidified by a poem by MacKinlay Kantor), there were 262 Minnesota men in the charge, but later research puts the number at 335. Even so, they were outnumbered and their line was thin. They attacked with such ferocity that the Confederates were surprised and had to regroup. Union reinforcements arrived, held the position, and eventually won the Battle of Gettysburg.

The Monitor, the Merrimack, and the Minnesota ⭐ The United States frigate *Minnesota*, launched in 1855, played a role in the Battle of the *Monitor* and the *Merrimack* during the Civil War. On March 8, 1862, the *Virginia* (which was the new name the

Confederates gave to the old *Merrimack* when they covered it with iron sheeting) single-handedly took on a fleet of wooden Union vessels, including the *Minnesota*, which ran aground. The next morning, as crowds watched from the shore, the *Virginia* turned its guns on the *Minnesota* again, in the opening salvos of the great battle of the iron-clad ships. The *Minnesota* survived the encounter and remained in use until the late 1890s. Its bell and wheel are in the Minnesota Historical Society Museum.

History the painless way

Minnesota children's writer Maud Hart Lovelace (see p. 100) also wrote several adult novels about Minnesota history, including:

The Black Angels (1926) - touring entertainers in Minnesota.
Early Candlelight (1929) - life at early Fort Snelling.
Gentlemen from England (co-authored by husband D.W. Lovelace, 1937) - Minnesota in the 1860s and 1870s.
One Stayed at Welcome (1934) - 1950's Minnesota.

Or take a look at:

Burning by Richard Snow (1981) - fire in a Minnesota town in the 1890s.
Candle in the Mist by Florence Means (1931) - 1870s Minnesota.
O River, Remember by Martha Ostenso, 1943 - immigrant families in the Red River Valley.
The Oxcart Trail by Herbert Krause, 1954 - life among the settlers and traders.

GUBERNATORIAL GOSSIP

⭐ Just as Minnesota would later start functioning as a state before it officially became one, its first territorial governor, Pennsylvanian Alexander Ramsey, started governing the territory in 1849, months before the U.S. Senate got around to confirming the Republican's appointment. Unlike most territorial governors, Ramsey liked the area he governed and decided to link his own future with it. After the territory became a state, he was elected the second governor and later represented Minnesota in the U.S. Senate.

Getting a head start

⭐ One of the important names in early Minnesota is Henry Hastings Sibley, who arrived in Mendota in 1834. Later to become one of Minnesota's most prominent early citizens, he was the resident partner and manager of Astor's American Fur Company. In 1848, when the first land office opened and land went on sale, he bought the site of St. Paul and gave it to the people who had already settled there without ownership. At a convention held to establish the Minnesota territory on August 26, 1848, Sibley was named to represent the people of Minnesota in the U.S. Congress, though he was still formally a delegate from the Territory of Wisconsin, which had disappeared when Wisconsin became a state. Ten years later, he beat Republican Alexander Ramsey in the race to be the first governor of the new state, though he won by only 240 votes out of 35,340 (after numerous votes were thrown out on both sides for being fraudulent).

The first state governor

⭐ The first native of Minnesota to become governor was the flamboyant John A. Johnson, born in St. Peter, son of a drunk and a washerwoman. After serving first as a state senator, he ran for the governorship in 1904. When his adversaries tried to make political hay out of his poverty-stricken background, he just acknowledged the truth of it and the voters elected him by a wide margin. Because of his immense popularity, his three terms—all of them as a Democrat trying to work with a Republican legislature—were very successful. He was being heralded as a potential presidential candidate in 1909 when he suddenly died. A statue of Johnson stands in front of the State Capitol building.

From poverty to possible president

⭐ The 1963 gubernatorial election was so close that a recount of votes was called for to see whether Karl F. Rolvaag or the incumbent governor, Elmer Andersen, had won. Usually recounts happen pretty quickly, but this one dragged on and on, while Andersen stayed in the governor's chambers and Rolvaag was relegated to a small office in the Capitol's basement. Finally the courts decided that Rolvaag had won by 91 votes and he was allowed to move upstairs.

The governor in the basement

⭐ Rudy Perpich, son of a Croatian immigrant to Minnesota, was first elected governor in 1982. He set several records for the state's governors. He was Minnesota's first Roman Catholic governor, the longest in office (eight years and he wanted to go for more), first from the Iron Range, and first to win, lose, then win again.

Perpich the record breaker

QUEST FOR THE WHITE HOUSE

HHH

Hubert H. Humphrey, who was born in South Dakota, had been a pharmacist and a college instructor by the time he was elected mayor of Minneapolis in 1945. Kevin Duchschere, writing in the *Minneapolis Star Tribune*, noted that Humphrey "would almost single-handedly transform Minneapolis's image from a corrupt backwater of crime and bigotry into a progressive city of clean and efficient government." A fighter from the beginning for civil rights, Humphrey had enough influence by 1948 to get civil rights planks into the Democratic Party platform. Elected to the U.S. Senate, he began to put some of his ideas into play in the national arena. In 1964, he was elected vice president at the urging of his president, Lyndon B. Johnson. In 1968, after Johnson dropped out of the election, Humphrey overtook another Minnesotan, Eugene McCarthy, to be the Democratic candidate for president. He lost to Richard Nixon and returned to the Senate where he served until his death in 1978.

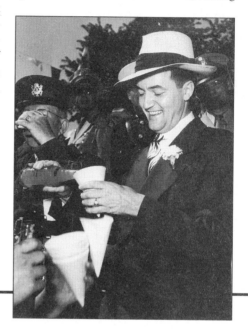

Walter Mondale

Walter F. Mondale, a native of the town of Ceylon, became active in politics while at Macalester College. Serving as the state's attorney general, he helped Humphrey get elected to

the Senate and then was appointed (then elected) to fill his position in that august body when Humphrey resigned to run for the vice presidency with Lyndon Johnson. He himself resigned for the same reason in 1977, to run with Jimmy Carter. After serving as VP for one term, he and Carter lost the 1980 election to Ronald Reagan. In 1984, Mondale ran for the presidency. He chose Representative Geraldine A. Ferraro of New York as his running mate for the Democratic Party. Ferraro is the first woman ever to be selected to run for vice president on a major party ticket. However, the two of them were firmly trounced by Reagan and Bush.

⭐ Progressive Republican Harold E. Stassen was governor of Minnesota from 1939 to 1943, during which time he modernized state government. He has run for the presidency of the United States every four years since 1948. In 1987, at age 80, he again appeared on the ballot.

Perennial candidate

ALL THE PRESIDENT'S MEN

Presidential Cabinet officers from Minnesota:
Secretary of State
    Frank B. Kellogg under Calvin Coolidge 1925 (see p. 52)
Secretary of the Treasury
    William Windom under James Garfield 1881 and Benjamin
       Harrison 1889
Secretary of War
    Alexander Ramsey under Rutherford B. Hayes 1879
Attorney General
    William D. Mitchell under Calvin Coolidge 1929
Secretaries of Agriculture
    Orville L. Freeman under John F. Kennedy and Lyndon B. Johnson
       1961
    Bob Bergland under Jimmy Carter 1977
Secretary of Commerce
    Maurice H. Stans under Richard Nixon 1969
Secretary of Labor
    James Day Hodgson under Richard Nixon 1970

MINNESOTANS IN WASHINGTON

⭐ General James Shields of Illinois, who first made his name serving in the Mexican and Civil wars, later made it into national politics from four different areas! He served as governor of Oregon Territory, and then as a senator—first from Illinois (1849-55), then from Minnesota (1858-59)—and many years later, perhaps suffering withdrawal pains, he ran for the Senate from Missouri in 1879 and was elected.

One senator: four different states

⭐ William O. Douglas was born in Maine (a town in Minnesota, not the state), where his father was a missionary. His father took him west where he grew up in California and Washington, years that gave him a lifelong interest in preserving the natural world and in mountain climbing. Becoming first a professor at Yale Law School and then chairman of the Securities Exchange Commission, he was appointed to the U.S. Supreme Court by Franklin Delano Roosevelt in 1939. He served longer on the court than any other justice—36 years. Always controversial, Douglas was a strong supporter of individual rights and society's disadvantaged.

Longest time on the bench

Chief justice

⭐ St. Paul-born Warren Earl Burger received his legal training and his initiation into Republican politics in Minnesota. President Eisenhower started Burger on his ascent in the federal court system in 1953, and 16 years later Richard Nixon appointed Burger to be chief justice of the U.S. Supreme Court. Though he was expected to be conservative, Burger upheld a number of civil rights issues, as well as *Roe v. Wade*. He retired from the court in 1986.

Other justices from Minnesota

⭐ **Pierce Butler,** born near Northfield, was named to the U.S. Supreme Court by Warren Harding, 1922-39. **Harry Blackmun**, an attorney in Rochester, was named by Richard Nixon in 1970. He is best known for writing the majority opinion in *Roe v. Wade*, granting women the right to abortion.

Burning a cross

⭐ When the U.S. Supreme Court decided (by a very narrow margin) that burning the American flag was a protected gesture of free speech, many people were aghast. They were just as horrified in 1992 when the court ruled that Robert A. Viktora, a teenager who burned a cross on the lawn of a house belonging to an African-American family in St. Paul, was protected by the First Amendment.

Minnesota's only woman sent home

⭐ Minnesota has sent only one woman to Congress—Coya Cjesdal Knutson, Democrat, elected in 1954. A teacher whose major political concern was the preservation of the family farm, she became the first woman appointed to the House Committee on Agriculture. However, in running for re-election in 1958, Knutson had the misfortune to have an alcoholic and resentful husband. He published a public letter to her headed "Coya, Come Home." It accused her of letting her home life be ruined and implied that she was having an affair with her young administrative assistant. She was the only incumbent Democrat to lose her seat in the 1958 election. Coya Knutson returned home, got rid of her husband, and, in 1977, made another unsuccessful bid for congress.

The "Bloody Fifth"

⭐ The Nelson-Kindred fight was no boxing match with gloves, but it was one of the bloodiest political fights in Minnesota history. When the new Fifth District was created in Minnesota in 1881, Charles F. Kindred, a wealthy railroad man, and Knute Nelsonwanted to be its congressman.

Kindred loyalists tried to keep Nelson's men from reaching the convention hall. But somehow, two sets of delegates—Kindred's and Nelson's—managed to arrive at Detroit Lakes on July 12, 1882, for the district convention. The Kindred delegates booked all the hotel rooms except one, which they saved for Nelson, and took possession of the meeting hall. Not to be outdone or undone, the Nelson delegates put up a circus tent across the street. Fistfights and rumors rocked the town. Nelson, who managed to rise above the slings and arrows of Kindred-inspired rumor, came out on top with 16,956 votes to Kindred's 12,238. Knute Nelson eventually went on to be elected governor in 1892 and U.S. senator from 1895 to 1923. A native of Evanger, Norway, Nelson is heralded as the first Scandinavian-born governor of an American state.

MINNESOTANS AT WAR

⭐ Captain Franklin van Valkenburgh, commanding officer of the USS *Arizona* at Pearl Harbor, was a native of Minneapolis. On December 7, 1941, when the Japanese attacked Pearl Harbor in the Hawaiian Islands, starting the U.S. involvement in World War II, Captain van Valkenburgh tried valiantly to fight back from the bridge of his battleship. But then a munitions magazine exploded, and he died, along with 1,102 other men, when the ship capsized. The *Arizona* was allowed to remain unsalvaged in the waters of the harbor as a permanent memorial to the 2,400 people who died on that day of treachery. Captain van Valkenburgh was awarded a posthumous Congressional Medal of Honor.

The USS Arizona at Pearl Harbor

The Medal of Honor

The Congressional Medal of Honor is America's highest reward for bravery in combat. Only 3,398 people have been given the medal since it originated in the Civil War, and half of those were from that war. President Truman said, "I'd rather have this medal than be president." The action for which it is given must present clear risk to life, be a voluntary act beyond normal duty, and be witnessed by two other people. Those men whose names are followed by an asterisk (*) were rewarded posthumously. Their place of birth is given in parenthesis.

WORLD WAR I
Sgt. Louis Cukela
  two medals, Navy and Army, (Minneapolis)
Capt. George H. Mallon (Minneapolis)

WORLD WAR II
1st Lt. Wilibald C. Bianchi (New Ulm)*
Pfc. Mike Colalillo (Duluth)
Maj. Henry Alexius Courtney, Jr. (Duluth)*
Capt. Richard E. Fleming (St. Paul)*
Cpl. Louis James Hauge, Jr. (Ada)*
Pfc. Lloyd C. Hawks (Park Rapids)
Pfc. James Dennis La Belle (Columbia Heights)*
2d Lt. Donald E. Rudolph (Minneapolis)
Pvt. Richard Keith Sorenson (Anoka)
Capt. Franklin Van Valkenburgh (Minneapolis)

KOREA
Lt. Col. John U.D. Page (St. Paul)*

VIETNAM
Spec. 4 Michael R. Blanchfield (Minneapolis)*
Spec. 4 Kenneth L. Olson (Paynesville)*
S/Sgt. Robert J. Pruden (St. Paul)*
S/Sgt. Laszlo Rabel (Minneapolis)*
Lt. Col. Leo K. Thorsness (Walnut Grove)
Spec. 4 Dale Eugene Wayrynen (McGregor)*

TALLY OF WAR DEAD
1,430 Minnesotans died in World War I
6,284 Minnesotans died in World War II
688 Minnesotans died in Korea
1,053 Minnesotans died in Vietnam

PUBLIC MEN

Third parties

⭐ Ignatius Donnelly, one of Minnesota's most colorful figures (see p. 96), was also one of Minnesota's best-known third-party politicians. As a Republican representative during the Civil War years, he was known for his sense of humor. While giving a speech in Stillwater, someone threw a cabbage at him, to which he responded, "Gentlemen, I only asked for your ears. But somebody has given me his whole head!" In the 1880s, Donnelly left the Republican Party to fight against the railroad and business monopolies. He formed the People's Party in 1891 and succeeded in winning a number of state elections, but the party faded by 1896. The People's Party was just one of many third parties established in Minnesota, and because of that tradition, Minnesotans are some of the most independent voters in the union.

The Lone Eagle's father

⭐ One of the best-known names in American history is Charles A. Lindbergh, the man who made the first solo flight across the Atlantic Ocean (see p. 133). But in Minnesota, his father was a well-known figure long before that 1927 flight. Swedish-born Charles A. Lindbergh, Sr., a resident of Little Falls, was elected to the U.S. Congress as a Progressive Republican in 1907. He remained in Congress for 10 years, until he ran for the governorship in 1917. He lost because he had dropped his Republican label to join the party formed by militant farmers, the Nonpartisan League, and because he had been too outspoken against America becoming involved in World War I. In 1930, the Lindbergh family gave the state Charles Senior's farm at Little Falls as a state park. Charles Junior grew up there while his father was in Congress.

A Nobel Peace Prize for a Minnesotan

⭐ A New York boy spent his childhood in St. Paul and Mantorville and went on to help establish peace in the world. Frank B. Kellogg was trained as an attorney and became a U.S. senator in 1917. In 1923 he was named U.S. ambassador to Great Britain and then was named secretary of state by President Calvin Coolidge. As more and more citizens of the world were decrying war as an instrument of a nation's diplomacy, Kellogg and French foreign minister Aristide Briand developed an agreement signed by almost every nation which, they hoped, would keep nations from ever going to war again. Unfortunately, no means of enforcing the agreement were built into it. However, Kellogg was awarded the 1929 Nobel Peace Prize for his efforts (Briand had won the award in 1926 for the Pact of Locarno).

The Berrigans

⭐ Daniel and Philip Berrigan are two Roman Catholic priests born in the Minnesota town of Virginia and raised in Syracuse, New York, who led the Catholic protest against the Vietnam War in the late 1960s. Their protests began in 1965 when they were the only priests to sign the "declaration of conscience" which was signed by Martin Luther King, Jr., and Benjamin Spock. In May 1968, they led seven others in a break-in at the Catonsville, Maryland, draft board offices. That began their frequent sojourns in prison for their activist work. Father Philip Berrigan married a former nun and the two were excommunicated from the Catholic Church. After the Vietnam War ended, they turned their attention to nuclear weapons. They were arrested on September 9, 1980, at King of Prussia, Pennsylvania, for leading a group of six others in smashing the nosecones of Minuteman missiles. That time they were sent to prison for longer than the few weeks they had previously received.

★ Bruce Laingen, originally of Odin, was chargé d'affaires in Tehran, Iran, in November 1979 when the U.S. Embassy was taken over by fundamentalist Muslims. He and 51 other hostages were held by the Ayatollah Khomeini and his revolutionaries for 444 days. They were released on January 20, 1981, the day that President Ronald Reagan was inaugurated.

Prisoner of Iran

PUBLIC WOMEN

★ Women were given the right to vote for school affairs in 1875. This was the first time women in Minnesota were allowed to vote.

Some women's firsts

Two women—T.A. Jenkins and C.G. Carleton—came from the town of Wyoming to Minneapolis on June 7, 1892—the first women to attend a national political party convention as delegates. The Republican Party was meeting to nominate Benjamin Harrison.

G.F. Kaercher of Ortonville became the first woman elected clerk of a state supreme court in 1922.

Rosalie E. Wahl was the first woman appointed to the Minnesota Supreme Court. The St. Paul law professor was appointed in 1977.

Joan A. Growe became Minnesota's first woman secretary of state, elected in 1975. She ran for the Senate in 1984 but lost to incumbent Rudolph Boschwitz.

"Have assumed charge"—first woman ambassador

Eugenie Anderson (born Helen Eugenie Moore in Adair, Iowa) married a Carleton College art student who owned a large farm at Red Wing. She settled onto the farm happily, until the horrible stirrings of World War II began to make themselves felt. She worked to keep Minnesota from turning isolationist, and after the war, she campaigned for Harry Truman for president and Minneapolis mayor Hubert H. Humphrey for the Senate. When they took office in 1949, she was rewarded with the position of ambassador to Denmark, the first woman to attain the rank of ambassador in the United States. On reaching Denmark, she cabled the State Department: "Have assumed charge. Anderson." Two years later she became the first American woman to sign a treaty when she signed for the United States in an agreement of commerce, navigation, and friendship with Denmark. She served in Denmark for almost four years. In 1962 she was named by President Kennedy to be ambassador to the eastern bloc nation of Bulgaria.

Ahead of her time

⭐ Jane Grey Cannon Swisshelm challenged both slavery and the lack of women's rights long before most people. The young Pennsylvania woman had met James Swisshelm at a quilting bee, married him, and then had nothing but problems. She wanted to write and make speeches advocating reforms—James wanted her in the kitchen. The marriage foundered for good when James traded his business for two bears, a panther, and a big roll of worthless wildcat currency. Since James wouldn't give her a divorce, she decided she'd head west and simply start over.

She arrived in St. Cloud, to which her family previously had moved, with her baby daughter and secured a job as editor of the local newspaper, the *St. Cloud Visitor,* becoming an ardent abolitionist. In 1858 she went head-on with General Sylvanus Lowry, the town "boss" and former southern gentleman who had brought his slaves to the area. The general had Swisshelm's newspaper office broken into, the presses destroyed, and the type thrown in the river. A warning was left—"If you ever again attempt to publish a paper in St. Cloud, you yourself will be as summarily dealt with as your office has been." She managed to raise enough money to publish again.

Jane Swisshelm later became a nurse in the Civil War, a prominent lecturer, and a prison reformer. Ultimately she was able to get part of her husband's estate at Swissvale, Pennsylvania, and there this progressive woman died in a tiny log cabin.

Minnesota vs. Turkey

According to women's studies historian Marjorie Bingham, a disgusted Minnesota suffragist of 1909 was quoted as saying, after the legislature failed one more time to pass a bill allowing women to vote, that the women of Turkey would get to vote before Minnesota's women did. She was right—a number of Turkish women voted in 1910. Ten years later, Minnesota women hoped to get the same privilege when 20,000 women sent a "Monster Petition" to Congress. It had no effect. It wasn't until 1919, when the Nineteenth Amendment was ratified, that Minnesota's women finally caught up with the Turks.

The impersonation

Lucy Ann Lobdell of Delaware County, New York, learned from lumberjacks and hunters to do all the things the men did. Her reputation as a superb markswoman made Henry Slater challenge her to a shooting contest—if she lost, she had to marry him. When she lost, she kept her side of the bargain and married Slater, who treated her badly. She left him, headed west, and arrived in Minnesota in the summer of 1856, using the name La-Roi Lobdell. For almost a year, she hunted and trapped with Ed Gribbel—even slept under the same blanket with him—without him knowing she was a woman. In 1857 she became the hired "man" on a farm at Manannah and did all the work a man would do. When her true sex was discovered, charges were filed stating that "one Lobdell, being a woman, falsely personate a man, to the great scandal of the community, and against the peace and dignity of Minnesota." Lucy, or La-Roi, entered a plea of "not guilty" and was vindicated. The court upheld that women "had the right to wear masculine clothes . . . since the time of Justinian and there was nothing that could be done by way of punishment." But public opinion wasn't so kind. She was treated as a pariah and sent back to New York with her rifle at the expense of Meeker County. She lived in poverty subsisting on berries and roots and was buried in a potter's field when she died.

MUNICIPAL MINNESOTA

The civilization (or citification) of Minnesota started with Fort Snelling, which was established in 1819. It was the site of the state's first school, first theater, first circulating library, first hospital, and first Protestant church. The school was opened in 1823, just two years after the fort was built, for the use of the army. And, of course, the city of Minneapolis grew up around the fort.

Many people feel that Minnesota author Sinclair Lewis defined small-town America in his novel *Main Street*. A sociologist, Edmund deS. Brunner, wrote in 1927 that Lewis's *Main Street* "has an importance beyond its size. To the city, it is the representation of rural America; to the farmer, it is the interpreter of the city. Both need it; neither fully understands it."

Certainly, Minnesota has some of both, and these days the two talk to each other, and invite everyone else to come and see what the state can offer.

- Names and Nicknames
- Celebrations
- County Squabbles
- Wicked Ways
- Fire in the Forests
- Up North
- Minnesota's Immigrants
- The Twin Cities
- Winona and Wabasha
- Cities at Random

NAMES AND NICKNAMES

An assortment of nicknames

Alexandria - Bass Capital of the World; Home of the Runestone (see p. 44)

Anoka - Halloween Capital of the World

Barnum - An Arrowhead Egg Basket (chicken farms in Arrowhead country)

Bemidji - Paul Bunyan's Playground

Bena - City Where the Partridge Finds a Refuge

Brainerd - Hub City; Paul Bunyan's Capital (a 27-foot animated Bunyan statue)

Buhl - Springs of Health and Pits of Wealth

Carlton - Birthplace of the Northern Pacific (first spike driven)

Cass Lake - Capital of the Chippewa Nation

Crookston - City with the World's Largest Ox Cart (located in Pioneer Museum)

Duluth - Center of the Universe; Hay Fever Relief Haven of America (which goes along with "Air Conditioned City"); Zenith City of the Unsalted Seas (a poetic journalist at work)

East Grand Forks - Potato Capital of the World

Ely - City where the Wilderness Begins

Faribault - Nation's Peony Capital; Athens of the Northwest

Gilbert - The Village of Destiny

Grand Portage - Oldest Settlement in Minnesota (see p. 37)

Hibbing - Town that Moved Overnight; Iron Ore Capital of the World

Longville - Turtle Center of the World

Mabel - America's Steam Engine Capital

Minneapolis - City in Touch with Tomorrow; Sawdust City; City of Flour (hope they don't mix up those last two!)

Northfield - City of Cows (a.k.a.: America's Holstein Capital)

St. Cloud - Busy Gritty Granite City (first quarry opened 1868)

Sibley - The End of the World

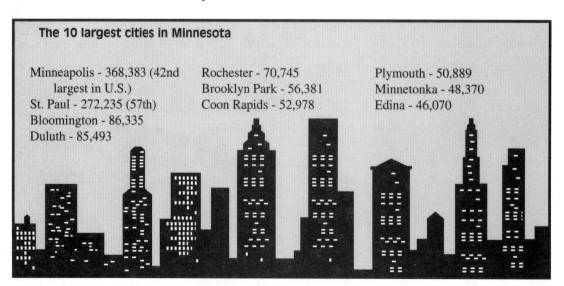

The 10 largest cities in Minnesota

Minneapolis - 368,383 (42nd largest in U.S.)
St. Paul - 272,235 (57th)
Bloomington - 86,335
Duluth - 85,493

Rochester - 70,745
Brooklyn Park - 56,381
Coon Rapids - 52,978

Plymouth - 50,889
Minnetonka - 48,370
Edina - 46,070

Naming nuggets
- In the mid-1800s, the towns of Manton, Minnesota, and La Crosse, Wisconsin, were rivals. Manton changed its name to La Crescent, the symbol for Muhammad and Islam, because it was thought—mistakenly—that LaCrosse was named after the cross, a Christian symbol.
- Charles Patterson, fur trader, built a trading post in 1783. The Indians called him "sacred hat man" because he always wore a bearskin hat and the bear was sacred to them. Over the years, "sacred hat" evolved into "sacred heart" and became the town's name.
- The founder and name-giver of Northfield, John W. North, didn't like to hang around long. He founded Northfield in 1855, Washoe City, Nevada, in 1861, and Riverside, California, in 1870.
- Ivanhoe is named for Sir Walter Scott's novel of the same name and its streets are named after the characters in the book.
- When Crookston was first settled, it was known as Hawley. But a post office already existed by that name so the postmaster ordered a new name. Davis, Ames, Aetna, and Crookston were suggested. Crookston—derived from William Crooks, chief railroad engineer—was chosen with a coin flip.
- Not terribly exciting, but everybody asks—Albert Lea was named for a lieutenant who published maps of this area of southeastern Minnesota in 1835 after returning from a military expedition.

CELEBRATIONS

State fair

The first agricultural fair in Minnesota took place in Hennepin County in 1855, and only four years later, the first Minnesota State Fair was held. One of the main purposes of the fair at first was to show the world that crops could indeed grow in what outsiders often regarded as the completely useless climate of Minnesota. In 1885, the fair's location settled in St. Paul. Very early, awesome entertainment became an important facet of the state fair. In 1925, the planned appearance of the U.S. Navy dirigible *Shenandoah* at the state fair led to disaster.

Death of the Shenandoah

During the 1920s and '30s, dirigibles were all the rage. Everyone had to have one. The U.S. Navy built two of the giant airships. *Shenandoah*, meaning "Daughter of the Stars," was built in 1923 and then was moved all around the country as a way of showing off the Navy. One flight to California was made with the giant craft maneuvering through passes in the Rocky Mountains.

The flight from Lakehurst, New Jersey, to St. Louis and then on to Minnesota for the state fair in 1925 was not supposed to be particularly tricky. However, during the early morning hours, *Shenandoah* hit a thunderstorm over Ava, Ohio. Because maintenance funds had never been approved, some of the craft's structures were weakened and could not withstand the battering by the line squall. The dirigible began to break up. First the tail broke off. Then, bit by bit, for three hours, the craft fell apart and the helium chambers opened up. The pilot, Lt. Commander Zachary Lansdowne, died along with 13 of the 40-man crew.

Celebrating winter

After several newspaper correspondents visited St. Paul in 1885, they wrote that Minnesota was the second Siberia and no human should live there. Minnesotans struck back with plans for a huge winter carnival "to correct the wrong impressions generally held that St. Paul and Minnesota are a hyperborean region where existence is a burden during the winter months." The businessmen decided to build on the tradition started by the voyageurs of getting together for riotous feasting and storytelling during the winter. The first carnival opened on a cold February 1, 1886.

Thousands from throughout the United States and Canada joined the festivities, which included a parade and competition in such winter sports as skating, tobogganing, curling, snowshoeing, and horse racing on the frozen river. The public was invited into an ice palace, built at a cost of $5,210 by 200 men. Because one of Minnesota's major industries at the time was ice-cutting, the 100 tons of ice used for the palace were inexpensive and plentiful. The ice palace stood 140 feet long and 106 feet high and had Gothic archways, towers, turreted walls, and battlements. King Borealis and Queen Aurora were crowned.

The carnival was held regularly until several unseemly warm winters struck. Then, starting in 1916, it became an annual event. The name King Borealis was changed to *Boreas* because it was easier to pronounce. But the carnival has gone on every year since, with sporting events, food, dancing, and many welcome visitors.

America's Icebox

Known for its very cold winter temperatures, International Falls (see p. 31) celebrates its freezing conditions with Icebox Days in late January. Over 35 events highlight the cold—there's smoosh racing, Sleet Feet Obstacle Course, outdoor chess, beach parties, Freeze yer Gizzard Blizzard Run, softball and broomball on the lake, Voyageur Loppet, and jam pail curling.

So much for Paul!

Many logging communities celebrate Paul Bunyan in one way or another. In fact, several towns have giant Paul Bunyan and/or Babe the Blue Ox statues and offer the public Paul Bunyan Days as bits of authentic North Woods folklore. Kelliher even shows off what purports to be Bunyan's gigantic grave. Bemidji's statue stands 18 feet tall (see p. 124). However—and that's a big "however"—Minnesota historian Theodore C. Blegen writes: "There is scarcely a shred of evidence that the lumberjacks were familiar with Paul Bunyan, told stories about him, or indeed had ever heard of him." But let's not let a bit of reality interfere with Minnesota civic pride and celebration!

In 1978, the town of Olivia held its annual Corn Capital Days as usual, but at the head of the parade was attention-getting singer Olivia Newton-John. Even without Olivia (the woman, that is), you can't miss the town—there's a giant green-and-yellow fiberglass ear of corn on the fest site.

That's corny!

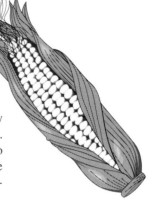

In Rochester, the entire water tower is shaped and painted like an ear of corn (probably better than a pancreas or a kidney!).

Days for eating

Minnesotans could get fat on the special days that many towns celebrate to advertise themselves. Among the most prominent is Kolachy Day in Montgomery, which the Bohemian population started in 1929. King Turkey Days in Worthington are held each year in September to draw attention to the turkey farmers of the area. It features a race by the puzzled birds through the center of town and attracts major political figures to speak.

Among the other days meant for gorging:

Sugar Day, in Chaska
Corn Carnival, in Cokato
Raspberry Day, in Hopkins
Sauerkraut Day, in Springfield
Watermelon Day, in Vining.

But what does one eat at Luverne's Buffalo Days? At least the town does have its annual Hot Dog Night.

Can Ball of Twine Days be far behind?

Darwin's not large, not even remotely so, with fewer than 300 residents. But that doesn't stop it from being grand in the hearts of trivia lovers everywhere. For Darwin possesses—as certified by the *Guinness Book of World Records*—the World's Largest Ball of Twine. Seems Meeker County farmer Francis Johnson just couldn't bear to throw anything away, not even the smallest bit of baler twine, so he just kept rolling it all together, and just kept rolling, until sometime in 1979 when he quit and put his creation on display. It stands 11 feet high, almost 13 feet in diameter, and weighs 11 tons. In 1991 the Darwin Community Club, in an effort to improve the economic chances of the fading community, brought the gargantuan ball to a new home under a gazebo by the water tower. Though the last town restaurant had closed months before, the village also opened a new eating place, the Ball of Twine Inn, where visitors can also see another prize from Johnson's huge collection of odds and ends—an 8-foot pliers that keeps opening into smaller and smaller pliers until 27 are opened. Boggles the mind!

COUNTY SQUABBLES

Butter's better

The towns of Caledonia, Brownsville, and Houston all vied for the county seat during the election of 1855. The residents of Houston campaigned for their town with posters showing Brownsville buried by an avalanche from Wildcat Bluff. Brownsville citizens used cartoons of Houston under an annual spring flood. Caledonians used a positive campaign gesture—they gave voters free hard-boiled eggs and a pioneer delicacy, butter—and Caledonia ran away with the election.

And the race is on!

The neighboring towns of Albert Lea and Itasca were both vying to be declared the county seat, so interest was high when the Itasca promoters challenged Albert Lea to a horse race. The residents of Albert Lea were mighty proud of their sheriff's horse, Old Tom, but they didn't want to leave anything to chance. During the night before the race, they kidnapped Itasca's horse and raced it against Old Tom out on the prairie. Old Tom won handily, and the men knew it was probably safe to bet everything they had on him. The next day, the Itascans readily covered all Albert Lea's bets, but they shouldn't have. Not only did they lose the race and their money, but they no longer had the wherewithal to fight for the county seat. Albert Lea won that position and Itasca became a ghost town.

Who's got the safe?

When the Marshall County commissioners voted to move the county seat from Warren to Argyle, it was no simple task. The commissioners directed the sheriff to take the county safe containing the county's legal documents to Argyle. For 10 years, citizens loyal to each town would steal the safe and place it in one town or the other. Then the opposition would steal it back. Argyle's local paper said county government had turned into a "game of 'Who's got the safe?'" Whichever town had the safe with the documents would set up county government until the rival town could steal the safe back. The dispute was finally settled when the voters chose Warren as the county seat by 303 votes.

WICKED WAYS

Moorhead cleaned up

Moorhead was congratulated for its revision from a sinful city to an upstanding one in a brief editorial in the *Minneapolis Tribune* on May 13, 1878. It compared the current city to its previous ways, stating, "Moorhead was the wickedest town in America. Dance houses, gambling dens and harlotries flaunted their signs openly upon the streets, and vaunted their legitimacy as matters of business. In place of the wicked Moorhead of six years ago we have now a staid and sober village of 500 or 600 reputable people. The school house has usurped the place of the dance house; flouring mill of the gambling hall and the harlotry 'gone west' or slunk back to the filth and darkness of the large eastern cities."

Anoka's year-long "saloon war" of 1858 rivaled Carry Nation's later conquests! It all started when Daniel Dudley set up the first bar in Anoka and aroused the town's temperance sentiments. One night a masked mob broke in, tied Dudley up, and smashed his inventory. Dudley had a dozen men arrested, but all went free on bail. When the case came to court, most of the accused didn't bother showing up. After numerous postponements, the trial began. Aggravated by the proceedings, defendant Benjamin Shuler rose in court one day, fired the attorneys, and made a motion that the whole proceeding be adjourned. The judge, unable to regain control, was powerless as the motion carried and the defendants left the court.

The Anoka fray

Dudley reopened his business more discreetly and all was well for some months until a mysterious fire destroyed his saloon. Dudley, sure that the culprits were members of the Methodist church, struck back. The new Methodist church was just about ready for dedication when it was destroyed by a fire "of unknown origin." Dudley moved his business into a barn and boldly sold whiskey by the jug. He was arrested and jailed for stealing a hog but was released when his lawyer pointed out he'd already been in jail longer than the prescribed sentence for stealing. The saloonkeeper's luck later ran out when he was convicted of forgery and sent to prison in Stillwater. Peace reigned in Anoka once more.

Eugene St. Julien Cox was a Swiss immigrant who settled in St. Peter to practice law and soon was named a legislator and a judge. He was very well liked—one of the original "good old boys." But Cox had one fatal flaw—some of his best friends were barflies and saloon keepers. After several weeks on the bench, it was reported that Cox had tried some cases while intoxicated and even sent the defendants down to the saloon to bring back beer. Gossip brewed over several years until finally a Republican county official (Cox was a Democrat) and a minister sent a detailed complaint to the Minnesota House, which issued twenty articles of impeachment. The defense argued that Cox hadn't committed any impeachable offense, but the legislature wasn't convinced. The most difficult task of the trial was to get an accurate definition of "drunkenness." One attorney said it was "a confusion of thought, sometimes accompanied by nausea, delirious excitement, and a tendency to sleep in the secondary stages." Many witnesses admitted that Judge Cox had gone into court under the influence of alcohol, but that he'd been able to do his duty. Ten saloon keepers gave testimony on his behalf.

Justice at the bar

The Senate wasn't swayed by the judge's eloquent closing speech and he was removed from the bench by a vote taken on March 22, 1882. He was also banned from public office for three years. His Democratic friends, loyal drinking buddies to the end, succeeded in getting his impeachment reversed and the proceedings taken out of the record by a legislative resolution passed in 1891. The judge left Minnesota shortly thereafter and died in Los Angeles.

When St. Paul lost its saintliness

When many cities suffered from crooks taking over during Prohibition, the police chief of St. Paul, John J. O'Connor, decided to take the matter in hand. He offered the crooks safe haven in St. Paul, on the strict stipulation that they go elsewhere to carry out their crimes. However, the deal ended when the Barker-Karpis gang kidnapped brewer William Hamm in 1933 and then banker Edward Bremer in 1934 (see p. 117). The news media then exposed the arrangement and worked to clean up St. Paul.

Public Enemy No. 1 in St. Paul

In the spring of 1934, "Public Enemy No. 1" John Dillinger was living with Evelyn "Billie" Frechette under the name Carl Hellman in St. Paul's Lincoln Court apartments. Recruiting a new gang (including "Baby Face" Nelson), he rather messily robbed banks in Sioux Falls, South Dakota, and Mason City, Iowa, taking hostages both times. Then the FBI located Dillinger and arranged a trap at his apartment building. On March 31, they pounced, but Dillinger escaped with only a small bullet wound in his leg. After a quick trip to Chicago, during which Billie Frechette was arrested, he moved to Manitowish Waters, Wisconsin. Dillinger's last Minnesota episode occurred on April 22, when the FBI caught up with him at the hideaway, and he managed to get away, escaping toward St. Paul. When his car was damaged by machine-gun fire, he stopped a motorist, stole his car, and held the family of Roy Francis hostage briefly. He got as far as Chicago, but the FBI was in close pursuit and he was apparently shot at the Biograph Theater on July 24, 1934.

The Minneapolis gang

They were called the "Ames gang" and they made Minneapolis one of the most corrupt cities in the country. Albert Alonzo Ames began as a doctor in Minneapolis who always took care of those who couldn't pay by adding their charges onto his wealthier patients' bills. The original "goodfella" of medicine, he was pushed into running for mayor by many who thought he would let the city be "wide open." They were right. For four terms Ames rivaled New York's Boss Tweed for corruption. His chief of detectives was a known gambler who opened the city to criminals who would give the Ames administration a cut of the action. The whole city was divided into areas and a trusted lieutenant put in charge of "collecting" protection money. In 1886, Ames ran for the governorship but lost to Andrew McGill, who wanted saloons to have to pay large licensing fees.

Despite such fees, Mayor Ames became very rich . . . but eventually there was rumbling in the ranks below, which brought the whole scheme down. Some of the "gang" thought they weren't getting enough and began fighting and stealing from each other. By the time a grand jury met in April 1902, some of the Ames gang and others who had paid for protection but didn't get it were so upset that they testified against the mayor. The chief of police, Fred W. Ames, and his assistants were indicted and eventually sentenced to jail. Mayor Ames fled Minneapolis on a train one night, but was later arrested and brought back to be tried. However, no jury would convict him.

FIRE IN THE FORESTS

The Chisholm fire

Small brushfires had been burning around Chisholm for several weeks before Saturday, September 5, 1908. Most people were convinced that there was no danger since they were protected by Long Year Lake, but the wind shifted and with destructive swiftness the fire engulfed Chisholm. Many of the 6,000 residents ran from town as fast as they could and watched the destruction from a hill to the southwest. No one was killed and the task of rebuilding began on Monday. The editor of the town newspaper declared, "Our office will be found in the street." The citizens of Minnesota contributed about $250,000 to help the town absorb the $2-million loss. This fire, one of a long series that devastated parts of Minnesota, caused the state to begin a ranger service to spot fires before they got too far along to fight.

One disappeared . . .

Don't look in Rice County anymore for the thriving village of Walcott—or even a non-thriving village. No signs of its 50-year existence were left after an 1895 fire that completely wiped out the town. Apparently it started in a flour mill, and the town was never rebuilt.

. . . and one came back

Virginia is one of the main towns of the Mesabi Range, with a population today of almost 10,000. But it's a miracle it ever got so big, because it completely burned down, twice in its history, once in 1893 and again in 1900.

Good-bye Hinckley

After the dry summer of 1894, a forest fire roared through the western part of Pine County on September 1, killing more than 400 people as it completely wiped out the town of Hinckley and several other communities. Two freight trains carrying Hinckley residents escaped the fire, but the town was burned to the ground. The train traveled backward for six miles to Skunk Pond where it picked up 100 Hinckley residents who had stayed in the pond while the fire burned around them. A monument to the fire's many victims stands in the Hinckley cemetery.

One of the worst fires in American history occurred on October 12, 1918. About 75 separate fires, driven by 70-mph winds, merged to destroy 2,000 square miles of timberland north of Duluth. Estimates of people killed vary from 400 to 1,000, and 2,000 were burned badly, with 13,000 left homeless. Almost $25 million of property was lost. Cloquet was the hardest hit, losing its entire business and residential sections. As it rebuilt, it began to call itself the "Modern Phoenix." Moose Lake was also destroyed, and now a 28-foot granite spire in Moose Lake Cemetery commemorates the dead.

The Cloquet fire

UP NORTH

Help for hay fever victims

Duluthians have been known to describe their city's climate as "nine months of winter and three months of poor sledding." They insist that their winter climate is no "worse" than the rest of the state's, but they are extremely happy when winter is over and Lake Superior's waters thaw. Mark Twain joked that "the coldest winter he ever spent was a summer in Duluth." These same attributes, however, made the Hay Fever Club of America choose Duluth as its headquarters at the beginning of the century. Hay fever sufferers come from all over to enjoy Duluth's summers.

Growing pains

The Duluth region was a popular spot for fur traders, lumbermen, and explorers for years before George P. Stuntz became the first true settler in the area in 1853. Others followed, and by 1856 the village was made the seat of St. Louis County. A national financial crisis in 1857 seriously slowed the town's growth—many people left, and for 10 years there was not an open store on the Minnesota shore of Lake Superior. A scarlet fever epidemic in 1859 cleared out more residents and by 1865 there were only two occupied homes in Duluth. It had become a virtual ghost town. The next year, though, geologists found iron ore and gold-bearing quartz in the area and in 1869, the town went from 14 families in January to a population of 3,500 by July.

By 1870, Duluth regarded itself as a "City of Destiny." But again, it met with hardships in 1873 when banks failed and jobs dwindled. The population dropped back to only 1,300. Duluth had to sacrifice its legal status as a city and revert back to being a village. However, Minnesota's natural resources paid off again, this time with lumber. By 1886, the population had climbed to 26,000 and Duluth was on its way into the future.

Duluth overlooking Lake Superior

A congressman from Kentucky, J. Proctor Knott, was desperate to make a speech to the House of Representatives so that he would look good for the folks back home as election time approached in 1871. A bill came before the House to provide land to build a railroad from Bayfield to Superior, Wisconsin. Somehow, Knott got the idea that the railroad would end in Duluth—a place he knew little about except that it didn't need a railroad. Knott, so excited at this opportunity to look good, forgot his prepared remarks and launched into speech:

"Duluth! 'Twas a name for which my heart had panted for years . . . But where was Duluth? I rushed to my library . . . examined all the maps I could find . . . but I could nowhere find Duluth."

When Knott reached the end of his half hour, the laughing congressmen demanded he continue his entertaining harangue. He concluded by expressing, with deep regret, that he could not vote for the bill to build a railroad to Duluth because his constituents didn't support it. The bill didn't pass. Knott was thereafter thought of as a humorist and not a statesman; and Duluth, grateful for the free advertising, offered Knott the best lot in town to thank him.

The "Glories of Duluth"

Fastest bridge in the world

A sand spit called Minnesota Point, five miles long, curves out into Lake Superior, protecting the Duluth harbor, formed by the estuary of the St. Louis River (see p. 26). The Aerial Lift Bridge, which connects Minnesota Point with the mainland in Duluth, was built in 1930 by the Kansas City Bridge Company. It is 510 feet long and has a vertical clearance of 138 feet. The 900-ton lift is counterbalanced by two 450-ton concrete blocks. The bridge rises 120 feet in 55 seconds, and is capable of even greater speed. It is the fastest bridge in the world.

Residents of the Mesabi Range may have thought they were settled, but the positions of their homes and towns were subject to the will of the managers of the strip-mining companies. The first town that had to be moved was Eveleth, which was moved in 1898 when ore was discovered under the town. In 1909, Sparta was moved to Gilbert, leaving behind nothing but a pit. But Hibbing bore the brunt of the problems.

Towns on the move

Hibbing was settled by Frank Hibbing who discovered iron ore and built a town right on the spot. In the early days there were 60 saloons in town—many of them equipped with gambling machines and other games of chance. But Hibbing added something extra—sports. J.F. Twitchell, the first mayor of Hibbing, organized the first athletic club and almost single-handedly made Hibbing the sports capital of Minnesota. By 1910, it became apparent that the town would have to be moved so that the ore deposits beneath it could be mined. Surrounded on three sides by dangerous chasms, the residents fought back. They sued the Oliver Iron Mining Company, but all it did was delay action until 1919. Hibbing was moved about a mile to the south to a small village known as Alice. This move started what became the Greyhound Corporation (see p. 129).

Moving a town

The Bemidji Bunyan

The old timers in Bemidji might tell you they remember when young Paul Bunyan was born. Five storks had to transport the huge child in relays to his parents. By the time he was a year old, he had to use wagon wheels for buttons. Not only did Bunyan grow fast, but his pet ox, Babe, also grew so fast that wherever she stepped a lake was formed and that's why Bemidji has hundreds of "footprint" lakes. To commemorate the town's logging past, Paul Bunyan and Babe statues were erected in downtown Bemidji in 1937 with Paul standing 18 feet tall and weighing over 2 tons (see p. 124).

MINNESOTA'S IMMIGRANTS

Grasshopper day

The Irish have Saint Patrick, but the Finnish have Saint Uhro and on March 13, Finnish-Americans all over Minnesota celebrate the patron saint who drove grasshoppers out of Finland with a mysterious chant. The grasshopper legend came to light in the 1950s and the Saint Uhro's Day festivals began with parades of green and purple and a grapes-and-grasshoppers meal. The town of Menahga has a statue of Saint Uhro holding a pitchfork with a grasshopper impaled on its lethal-looking tines.

One lone Swede

A shoemaker named Nils Nyberg was the first Swede to settle in St. Anthony. Swedes were called "foreigners" for a long time and were often looked upon with curiosity. The story is told about a Swede who came to town in the 1850s carrying all his belongings in a piece of red plaid cloth. When the stranger questioned blacksmith John Wilson, Wilson couldn't understand him and thought he was French. He sent for a Frenchman, then a German, and no one understood him. Then someone in the crowd that had gathered remembered the "foreigner," Nils Nyberg, and ran to get him. When the stranger heard Nyberg's Swedish he was overcome with joy at finding one person in town who could understand him.

Census of Immigrants

The 1910 census shows that there were 25 different ethnic groups living on the Iron Range. The largest group was Finnish, but others were:

Belgian	German	Russian
Bohemian	Greek	Serbian
British	Hungarian	Slovak
Bulgarian	Irish	Slovene
Canadian	Italian	Swedish
Chinese	Montenegrin	Swiss
Croatian	Norwegian	Syrian
Danish	Polish	
French	Romanian	

The sheet people

Because the Finns were a clannish group, they were often suspected of doing strange things. In the community of Esko, they clung to their Old World traditions. A farmer in the area—who was not Finnish—spread a rumor that the Finns were worshiping pagan gods and practicing magic. He said that whole families wrapped themselves in white sheets and went into a square building where they worshiped their gods and asked for good crops, rain, and bad luck for their neighbors. The Finns did wrap themselves in sheets, but it was for the purpose of taking baths in their steam bathhouses called saunas.

THE TWIN CITIES

Busy people

The Stevens house, built in 1849 by John H. Stevens, was the site of many Minneapolis "firsts." Hennepin County was organized in its parlor, as was the first agricultural society, school district, singing school, courts, and literary society. The name "Minneapolis" was first conceived there and Mary Stevens, the first white child born—but presumably not conceived—on the west side of Minneapolis, was born in the house on April 30, 1851. The historic house was purchased by the Board of Park Commissioners in 1896, mounted on wheels, and pulled by relays of children to its present site in Minnehaha Park.

Minneapolis skyline from St. Anthony Falls

Fort Snelling

Fort Snelling, after serving as the basis of the state of Minnesota, was sitting there doing nothin' in 1958, when plans were made to bulldoze it to make way for a huge highway cloverleaf. The public quickly protested the loss of the 140-year-old fort. The Minnesota Historical Society, which had never previously been much into preserving historical sites, was put in charge of the fort and gradually turned it into an education center dealing with the state's early history. In 1961, it became Fort Snelling State Park. And by 1978, it had been restored to its 1825 condition.

Oddly enough, Fort Snelling had been lost to the people once before. When it was going to be closed in 1857, pioneering Minneapolis figure Franklin Steele bought it for $90,000. However, he had financial difficulties and failed to make later payments, just in time for it to revert to the federal government for use during the Civil War.

St. Paul in a Pig's Eye

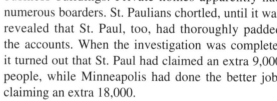 St. Paul was actually founded by a very "ugly" bootlegger—a Canadian voyageur named "Pig's Eye" Parrant. Some say he had only one eye; others say he had two but one wasn't any good. Whatever the case, one historian said that one eye gave "a kind of piggish expression to his sodden, low features." Chased out of Sault Ste. Marie, he came to Minnesota Territory, and in 1838 decided that selling rum would be more lucrative and easier than farming or establishing a factory. He set up "shop" just outside Fort Snelling in a cave that was accessible to river traffic. His "speakeasy" was an instant success with the Indians and soldiers even though Major Lawrence Taliaferro ordered him to cease and desist. A family of Swiss immigrants—the Abraham Perry family—built a cabin nearby. Parrant's establishment became known as Pig's Eye and was the first "building" in what is present-day St. Paul. Parrant stayed in the cave a year, moved his claim into present-day St. Paul, and then to an island downstream which is still called Pig's Eye. Lucky for the city that Lucian Galtier came to the same area in 1841 and built the Chapel of St. Paul or the state's capital might have been called Pig's Eye.

Which was the better liar?

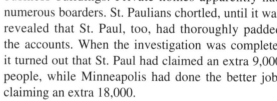 Rivalry between St. Paul and Minneapolis has been fierce at times. It came to a peak in 1890 when the new 10-year census was being taken. Each city wanted to come out the biggest. But the result when it emerged from the counting process was Minneapolis 182,967, St. Paul 142,581. St. Paul was shaken to the bottom of its city hall, and immediately accused its twin city of padding the numbers—which it had. Investigators found that hundreds of nonexistent people were living in business buildings. Private homes apparently had numerous boarders. St. Paulians chortled, until it was revealed that St. Paul, too, had thoroughly padded the accounts. When the investigation was complete, it turned out that St. Paul had claimed an extra 9,000 people, while Minneapolis had done the better job, claiming an extra 18,000.

Nicollet Mall

The trail that ran through Minneapolis to Fort Snelling eventually became Nicollet Avenue. By the 1950s this avenue was known as the best shopping area in the Upper Midwest. But in 1955 General Mills moved its main offices to Golden Valley and the next year Southdale Mall opened in Edina. Leslie Park, a prominent owner of Minneapolis real estate, wanted to stem the deterioration of the downtown district so he proposed Nicollet Mall to the city council in 1956. Construction began in 1966 and was completed in November 1967. The new mall was featured on " The Mary Tyler Moore Show" when it premiered in 1970. Two TV movies and six feature films have been filmed there including *Purple Rain*, *Old Explorers*, *Drop Dead Fred*, and *Ice Castles*.

Minneapolis Star columnist Jim Klobuchar wrote after the mall's opening in 1967 that "there is some question . . . as we view affectionately this exciting new shopping thoroughfare, whether it more closely resembles a dream or a hangover."

🏠 The Foshay Tower, for many years the tallest, most conspicuous building in Minneapolis, stands 447 feet tall. It was modeled after the Washington Monument, which financier Wilbur B. Foshay admired. The tower was built to house Foshay's huge public utility empire. It was dedicated in lavish ceremonies on August 30, 31, and September 1, 1929. More than $100,000 was spent on the celebration, which included special dinners and a visit by John Philip Sousa. Sousa wrote "The Foshay Tower Washington Memorial March" for the occasion. Unfortunately, Foshay's empire crumbled shortly thereafter.

The tower

WINONA AND WABASHA

The willful Winona

A character in Mark Twain's *Life on the Mississippi* describes Maiden Rock at Winona as "Perhaps the most celebrated, as well as the most pathetic, of all the legends of the Mississippi." The legend involved We-no-nah, a Dakota Indian maiden who was being forced by her parents to marry a young man she didn't love and to forsake the one she did. Rather than give in, she threw herself off a rock.

However, the ever-iconoclastic Twain decided that she actually threw herself onto her parents who were standing on the rocks below, killing them, and then disappeared with her lover. Regardless, legend also says that We-no-nah's name became Winona, the town. However, later historians have attributed the name to a generic Winona, since it was the name usually given to first-born girls. Winona comes back to life in a pageant (pictured at right).

🏠 Orren Smith was captain of the steamboat *Nominee*, which traveled between Galena and St. Paul. In the fall of 1851, the captain left his ship's carpenter and two other men on the shore with instructions to build a town that could supply him with wood—from the Wisconsin side of the Mississippi. Winona was founded, then, at 10 P.M. on the night of October 15, 1851, when the three men disembarked the *Nominee*. Originally named Montezuma after the Aztec king, the town was platted in 1852 but its name was later changed to Winona. The first lumberyard was established in 1855 and before long Winona had 2,000 loggers, 10 sawmills, and 1,500 mill workers. But by the fall of 1915, the last lumber raft left Winona down the Mississippi behind the *Ottumwa Belle*. Lumber was replaced by wheat shipping.

Can't usually be so specific

Wabasha steamboats

The age of the steamboats hasn't really ended, at least not for Wabasha. The wonderful old *Delta Queen* and the newer *Mississippi Queen* dock at Wabasha on the journeys they make between New Orleans, Cincinnati, and Minnesota. They are the only overnight paddlewheelers still functioning on the Mississippi. Originally called Cratte's Landing, Wabasha was named for Sioux chief Wa-pa-shaw. When Mark Twain visited the town on the journey that became his book *Life on the Mississippi*, he called it "beautiful Wabasha, City of the Healing Waters."

Spend a cozy night

You can request a cat for a night at Wabasha's Anderson House hotel. The rent-a-cat tradition started in the 1970s when a gentleman guest said that "he had been on the road so long, even his wife's cat would be welcome as a companion . . . so we delivered a cat to his room, complete with food and litter box." The guest declared that night the best he'd spent in 25 years of traveling. Now one of 15 cats can be reserved with a room. The Anderson Hotel, originally opened in 1856, is Minnesota's oldest operating hotel. Owner John Hall explains his philosophy of old-fashioned service: "We have a cookie jar at the front desk, hot bricks for the bed, and we'll shine your shoes if you leave them out. We want you to feel at home. . . "

CITIES AT RANDOM

Royal Minnesotan would rather dig potatoes

August Boyn von Lazar of Princeton in Mille Lacs County went to Serbia in the summer of 1875 with his family Bible under his arm and introduced himself to the Minister of Finance, Chedomille Mijatovich, as a direct heir to throne of Serbia. Inside the family Bible, von Lazar's genealogy showed that he was the great-grandson of the last-known heir to the Serbian throne, Milosh Obilitch (or Kobilic). The Bible also contained directions to the location of Obilitch's treasure, which the last Serbian czar buried before the Turks invaded. Von Lazar searched without success in 1875 and 1876, and returned again in 1877, when he became convinced that he had located the treasure vault. He was afraid to open it without protection from troops, which Mijatovich refused to send until after the vault was opened and the treasure found. Von Lazar wasn't heard from again until he turned up in Belgrade so ill that he couldn't communicate. He died with his secret and the treasure was never found. His son, John Boyn, never continued the search. He said he "couldn't go digging for treasure in foreign parts when there was so much stump-digging to be done in the potato belt of Minnesota."

A matter of prison

Appleton, in western central Minnesota, was in serious need of jobs for its people. People were moving away in droves, and even the high school had to be shut down. In 1991, the residents voted to build a private medium-security prison that they could rent out to other municipalities as the need arose. They're taking a chance on their Prairie Correctional Facility, however, because it had to be built and staffed before it could be offered. The result is a 472-bed facility in which guards are already at work, guarding nothing. Hang on for later news.

Askov, on the other hand, has never even had a jail because it never needed one. Founded in 1887 through the Danish People's Society, Askov became a flourishing "cooperative" community whose fame spread to Europe. It has been known as the "Rutabaga Capital of the United States."

Floating loon

Rothsay may have its prairie chicken (see p. 22), but Virginia has the world's largest loon—and it floats! The 20-foot bird is located (at least in summer) just where a loon should be—on the water of Silver Lake. If someone hasn't come and cut its tether, it bobs gently on the water, greeting visitors.

The Brainerd revolution

An early traveler painted a romantic picture of Brainerd: "We first saw Brainerd at night and the view was pleasant and novel. The winds sang through the tops of the pines and the lights from the homes twinkled amongst the many trees . . . the whole place seemed like a fairy tale." Apparently things had settled down since the town was first settled by railroad agent "Pussy" White in 1870. Brainerd became a haven for lumberjacks and railroad men out to have a good time. Gambling games such as "high dice," "mustang," and "chuck-a-luck" were popular. Life in Brainerd became a little more serious when iron ore and paper mills began to dominate the area, but then the tourists started coming again to enjoy the 500 lakes in the area. Brainerd is called the "Capital of the Paul Bunyan Playground." It boasts the largest animated statues of Paul and his Blue Ox, Babe.

Robbing Paul to pay Peter to pay Paul

In 1873, just before Minnesota became a state, the St. Peter Company was organized to rob St. Paul and move the capital to St. Peter. Territorial Governor Gorman and other officials owned stocks in the company so the task seemed doable. In fact, everyone was so positive the capital would be moved that lots sold for as much as $1,500. It would have happened if Joe Rolette of Pembina hadn't stepped in and stolen the copy of the bill to make St. Peter the capital. The bill actually did pass and was held in committee waiting for the governor's signature. But Rolette stayed in hiding in an attic until the legislature adjourned. According to the constitution, the legislature could only be in session a certain number of days. The governor did sign a copy of the bill, but the territorial supreme court said the bill wasn't legal because there wasn't any evidence to show that the paper that was signed was actually the bill that passed.

Though it failed to the capital, the St. Peter Company, which for almost 75 years was referred to as a "benevolent despot," succeeded in getting the Nicollet County seat moved to St. Peter. It also got the state's first insane asylum, St. Peter Regional Treatment Center. The center continued in use (though in later years as just a warehouse for patients) and is now a museum.

Garden City bequest

Upon his death in July 1936, the town of Garden City inherited $400,000 from a London millionaire, Sir Henry Wellcome. In his will he stated that the money was for construction and maintenance of an auditorium/library and an athletic field. The millionaire had come to Garden City in 1865 with his father and lived in town as a boy. He later moved to Rochester, then Chicago, Philadelphia, and back to London where he made a fortune in pharmaceuticals. Knighted in 1932 by King George V, he always held a fondness for the little town of Garden City and visited it whenever he was in the United States.

Fergus Falls

James Whitford led an expedition financed by a Minnesota Scot named James Fergus. In 1857 Whitford laid out a new town site, Fergus Falls, but it wasn't incorporated until 1872. The town's first postmaster was a German who couldn't read English. He solved his mail-sorting problem by simply pouring the mail on the floor in a pile and letting the citizens find their own. Today, Fergus Falls is called "City Beautiful in the Land o' Lakes."

Build and they will come

The town of Nininger was platted on the Mississippi River, 35 miles south of St. Paul, in 1856 by John Nininger. A young lawyer, Ignatius Donnelly (see p. 96), and his partners had dreams of turning it into one of the great cities of the world. Donnelly particularly did a super job of selling its potential charms to easterners, citing (potential) libraries, theaters, symphonies, and other cultural advantages. And the people came. The city flourished briefly, growing to nearly 1,000 residents. However, it quickly faded nearly out of sight when the steamboats decided to make Hastings the stopping place and the banks stopped their loans in the financial panic of 1857. Little was left after 1858 except Donnelly's grand house, his unrealized dream, and ghosts.

A bit late

Other towns vying for the St. Croix regional land office made fun of Sunrise City. The *Stillwater Messenger* said the town's name should be changed to "Sundown," because "The sun doesn't rise there until three or four weeks after it makes its appearance at other places." But Sunrise City still got the land office and grew, at least until it failed to get the railroad station. About the only thing Sunrise City is remembered for now is that actor Richard Widmark was born there.

Some fictional towns

Of course, Sinclair Lewis's novel *Main Street* is set in the narrow-minded town of Gopher Prairie (see p. 94), which didn't thrill his hometown folk of Sauk Centre, who easily recognized themselves, but some other fictional towns are less easily identified.

Lake Wobegon is located in a township lost from the government land survey (see p. 99).

Frostbite Falls is the Minnesota hometown of Rocket J. Squirrel and Bullwinkle J. Moose.

Dr. Paul Christian of radio, TV, and movies lives in the fictional town of Rivers End.

MINNESOTA MISCELLANY

Education was important in Minnesota from the beginning. As early as 1849, the territorial legislature decided that education should be free to everyone from 4 to 21. But that wasn't so easy to achieve on a frontier. When it became clear that there was going to be a continuing problem, the state funded three normal (teacher-education) schools. The first one opened at Winona in 1860, making it the oldest normal college west of the Mississippi.

The life of the mind and the spirit has remained of prime importance to Minnesotans. Education, adventure, research, religion, and wit all contribute to the joyous life.

- Adventure
- The Learning Way
- Minnesota Medicine
- The Scientists
- Organizing to Achieve
- Spiritual Minnesota
- A Duet of Duels

ADVENTURE

Today's polar man

❖ A science teacher from Ely can't seem to leave the Earth's polar regions alone. Will Steger grew up in the Minneapolis suburbs but spent his summers in the Yukon and Alaska. While running a wilderness program in the Boundary Waters and having done considerable solo Arctic travel, he conceived the idea of going to the North Pole on foot. No one since Robert Peary in 1909 had arrived at the North Pole assisted only by sled dogs. Steger joined up with Paul Schurke, an outfitter in Ely, and they put together a team of 7 men, 1 woman, and 49 dogs that made the journey in 1986 (see below).

Steger's journey to the North Pole convinced him it was time to try the Antarctic, but he wanted to do more than just reach the South Pole. He chose to cross the entire Antarctic continent, from the Pacific Ocean to the Atlantic. The International Trans-Antarctic Team was made up of 6 men and 36 dogs. They spent the better part of a year—220 days— on the journey. On March 3, 1990, they arrived at a welcome finish line created by the Soviets.

First woman at the North Pole

❖ A St. Paul physical education teacher, Anne Bancroft, was the first woman to reach the North Pole overland. She was the only woman in a party of 7 people to accompany Ely's Will Steger through the Arctic. Determined not to be a mere token woman, Bancroft learned to handle the dog team. On March 8, 1986, they took off from a point 500 miles from the pole. They averaged 20 miles a day, living primarily on pemmican, butter, cheese, peanut butter, and oats. But it wasn't all primitive. As the load lightened, spare dogs were airlifted out. Also, they carried homing devices that talked to satellites. They arrived at the North Pole on May 22, when Anne Bancroft became the first woman ever to reach it.

Viking adventure

A teacher, Robert Asp, built a full-scale replica of a Viking ship in Hawley at an old potato

warehouse next to the city hall. The 76-foot ship was taken to Lake Superior at Duluth and, although Asp died of leukemia in 1980, his children and some Norwegian sailors sailed his ship, the *Hjemkomst* (meaning "homecoming"), to Norway in the summer of 1982, thus fulfilling his lifelong dream. The ship has been preserved and is displayed at the beautiful Heritage Hjemkomst Interpretive Center on the Red River of the North at Moorhead.

THE LEARNING WAY

◆ Harriet Leavenworth was the wife of the first commander of Fort Snelling. Lake Harriet in Minneapolis was named for her. In 1836, one of the earliest schools in Minnesota opened there, the Lake Harriet Mission School for Sioux Indians. It was founded by Rev. Jedediah D. Stevens and taught by his niece, Lucy.

Harriet #1

◆ Vermont schoolteacher Harriet Bishop answered the call for young women to come to the frontier to open schools, at the request of the Board of National Popular Education. She landed in St. Paul and opened her first school, in an old blacksmith's shop, in 1847. Much of what we know now about life on the early Minnesota frontier comes from the book she wrote 10 years later, called *Floral Home*, although she tended to put a romantic overtone on everything.

Harriet #2

◆ Martin McLeod, a Canadian-born fur trader, loved books even more than he loved furs. In 1849, he sponsored a bill to create schools that would be open "to all persons between the ages of four and twenty-one years, free." Minnesota was the first state (even before it was a state) in the nation to pass such a law. Two years later, Dr. Edward D. Neill became the territorial superintendent of schools, as well as secretary of the State Historical Society. However, only primary schools—which functioned just three months a year—were instituted at first, even just for basic readin' and writin'. Not until 1860 did the town of St. Anthony authorize a central high school. Neill later went on to found Macalester College, first as a preparatory school and then as a college in 1885.

Ahead of the pack

Did 'ja' know? Minnesota has the highest high school graduation rate in the nation. Ninety percent of those who start high school finish, and 66 percent of those go on to college.

What a career!

Francis Vivaldi, an Italian nobleman who was forced to leave his native Italy, established a school for the Winnebago Indians at Long Prairie in 1851. He became a priest, got married, deserted his wife, and after years of penance became a priest again. President Lincoln later appointed him consul in Argentina and Brazil.

◆ The St. Anthony Board of Education authorized a high school for "instruction in the higher English branches" in 1860, but it didn't get started and the first public high school in Minnesota opened at Winona in 1861. Within a year it had 35 pupils.

First high school

Never too late

Caledonia residents for fifty or more years, Joseph and Laura Scholl celebrated their retirements in 1992 by completing the work for their high school diplomas. They had both had to abandon pursuit of their diplomas as teenagers when each was an oldest child on a family farm and had to give up school to get to work. The schooling took two years, during which they were encouraged by their children, who already had college degrees.

An awkward birth

◆ The charter for the University of Minnesota was signed by the governor on February 25, 1851. The charter called for the university to be built "at or near the falls of St. Anthony." A preparatory school was opened that fall and it even had its own building, but the school did not actually start college education until the autumn of 1869.

First college

◆ Even though the University of Minnesota existed on paper, Hamline University in Red Wing (though Faribault and St. Paul had both tried to get it) became Minnesota's first private college when it was opened by the Methodists in 1854. Founded as a co-educational school, it was the only college to actually function as a college during the 1850s. But the Civil War and other problems forced its closing in 1869. However, 11 years later, St. Paul got its way when Hamline was reopened in that city. In 1882, the boys of Hamline played against the U. of M. in the university's first intercollegiate football game.

The first president

Even though it had existed on paper for 17 years, the not-quite University of Minnesota failed to get itself out of its financial problems until 1868 when, at the urging of John S. Pillsbury, a new organization act was passed, finally establishing the university. A New York-born professor from Ohio's Kenyon College, 36-year-old William Watts Folwell, became the first president. An Irishman with a keen sense of humor, Folwell found 154 students—including 57 women—and 8 male faculty members. "Experience has proven that men and women students can associate freely without danger," Folwell stated. When he was inaugurated in 1869, he spoke of his vision of a great institution with libraries, research facilities, museums, and laboratories.

After Folwell retired from the presidency in 1884, he continued to teach political science and served as the librarian until 1907. He lived to be 96. His four-volume *History of Minnesota*, published between 1922 and 1930, is still a standard reference.

Folwell's fulfillment

◆ The first public junior college in the state opened at Rochester in 1915, forty-five years after William Folwell, president of the U. of M., introduced the idea of having high schools and academies extend into the junior college level.

The dean of women educators

◆ Ada Comstock was born in 1876 in Moorhead, on land that her New England father had acquired from railroader James J. Hill. He eventually became a regent of the University of Minnesota, which Ada started attending in 1892. After serving as a rhetoric teacher, in 1907 she became the first dean of women at the University of Minnesota, the only female administrator. As dean, she took on such added responsibilities as finding jobs and better housing for all students and greater opportunities for women. In 1912, she was asked to become the first dean of Smith College, from which she had earlier earned a degree. With the departure of Smith's president, Ada ran the college (1917-18) but was refused the title of acting president because she was a woman. When the American Association of University Women (AAUW) was founded in 1921, Comstock became the first president. She assumed the presidency of Radcliffe College in 1923, and through her genius for administration opened new opportunities for women scholars, turning Radcliffe into a leading graduate center for women all over the world. Shortly after retiring from Radcliffe in 1943, she married Wallace Notestein, Yale professor emeritus, whom she had first met—and, apparently, loved—at the U. of M. 33 years before.

Claiming his own

◆ Minneapolis-born Allan Paul Bakke was twice refused admission to medical school at the University of California in the 1960s. He sued on the grounds that the school was using "reverse discrimination" and admitting African-Americans with lower grades because of the school's need to meet quotas. In 1978, the U.S. Supreme Court ruled narrowly in Bakke's favor, calling for maintaining affirmative action programs but ruling against minority quotas. Civil rights activists who had worked so hard to get quotas were not pleased.

MINNESOTA MEDICINE

Minnesota's own petrified man

He was in jail, but not for a crime . . . he was put there for safe-keeping. He was the famous Petrified Man of Bloomer, discovered in 1896 in the ground at Bloomer and thought to be the body of a French voyageur or *courier du bois* of the seventeenth century. When the figure was sold to Peter Bergo for $175, he displayed his "freak" for a fee until he sold it for $1,000. Gradually, anyone who could dream up a reason why the Petrified Man should belong to him put in a legal claim. The sheriff of Grand Forks booked the Petrified Man until the whole thing could be settled. When plaster molds were found in Crookston, the Petrified Man's origins became clear. He was a hoax, created by a plasterer during a slow business period. Interest in the Petrified Man plummeted in Minnesota, but the figure was sold to a traveling showman who charged admission in other parts of the country where no one knew the real story.

She reached out

◆ Martha Ripley was a New Englander who, at age 37 and after having had three children, decided to become a physician. It was just in time, because the year she got her degree, her husband was disabled and she had to support the family. To be close to his relatives, they moved to Minneapolis in 1883, when she opened her medical practice. She specialized in children's diseases, obstetrics, and women's suffrage. She was known for numerous humanitarian efforts, especially the founding of the Maternity Hospital, which welcomed both unwed and married mothers. She was avid in her work toward a healthy environment for all residents of the area. Dr. Ripley was recognized by a memorial plaque in the Minnesota State Capitol.

Minnesota means Mayo

◆ Dr. William W. Mayo, an English-born surgeon in pioneer Minnesota with headquarters at Rochester, taught his sons human physiology with the use of a Dakota skeleton. Both William James (born at Le Sueur in 1861) and Charles Horace (born at Rochester in 1865) went with their father on his medical rounds instead of playing ball with the other boys. Future surgeon Charles began to administer ether for his father's surgery when he was nine years old.

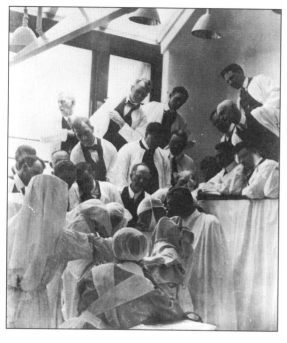

In 1883, a huge tornado struck Rochester, and Dr. Mayo was put in charge of the hospital. The Sisters of St. Francis were so impressed by his skills that they offered to build a hospital if he would run it. St. Mary's Hospital opened in 1889, by which time both sons had returned with their medical degrees. Dr. Mayo Senior was a pioneer in the use of the microscope to help diagnose disease, and his sons were no less innovative. They very quickly acquired a reputation as completely up-to-date and daring physicians and surgeons, to whom people from all over the world came, often as a last resort. Charles Horace's son, Charles William, later joined the group.

In 1915, the Mayos joined their clinic with the University of Minnesota by starting the Mayo Foundation for Medical Education and Research, with a $1.5-million grant. Physicians far and wide come there for training in the medical specialties. A great deal of major medical progress has been achieved at the Mayo Clinic.

Mayowood

Dr. Charles Mayo chose a 340-acre farm (which later grew to over 3,000 acres) as his respite from medicine. Mayowood, as he named his home, was built at an estimated $60,000, and its four stories consisted of 38 rooms. The house was so big that at one time his children kept goats in the basement. The distinguished doctor didn't know they were there for two weeks. Dr. Mayo did bring home a few things from the office. The greenhouse was built out of thousands of pieces of glass. Now we're not talking about your typical glass—Dr. Mayo used thousands of glass X rays revealing numerous body parts to line the interior of the building. The home is now owned and operated by the Olmsted County Historical Society.

❖ Gillette State Hospital for Crippled Children, funded by the state after many years of urging by Dr. Arthur J. Gillette, was founded in 1911 in St. Paul. It was the first such hospital in the nation.

A welcome innovation

❖ Unless you're over 50 years old, you probably have no vision of poliomyelitis as anything more than a nuisance disease against which you need to be vaccinated. But before Jonas Salk invented the polio vaccine, the disease—then called infantile paralysis—was a highly contagious scourge. It killed thousands every year and left numerous others crippled or even in an artificial breathing machine called an iron lung for the rest of their lives. Other than Dr. Salk and Dr. Sabin (who invented the oral vaccine), the person to do the most against polio was Elizabeth Kenny, an Australian nurse (therefore called Sister Kenny), whose work was welcomed in Minneapolis when most of the rest of the world thought she was a crackpot.

Overcoming paralysis

The discovery Sister Kenny made, purely because she used her common sense instead of waiting until a doctor told her to do otherwise, was that by keeping warm moist cloths on a polio victim's legs and using massage to keep the limbs moving, she could keep the legs from becoming permanently paralyzed. Learned medical opinion at the time called for the legs to be immobilized in splints—a procedure that invariably left them

> **Minneapolis feats**
> Among the medical firsts achieved at the University of Minnesota:
> **1952** - first open heart surgery, performed by Dr. C. Walton Lillehei
> **1955**- heart-lung machine developed
> **1958** - cardiac pacemaker developed
> **1966** - first pancreas transplant
> **1968** - tied with the University of Wisconsin for first successful bone marrow transplant
> **1975** - first implantable drug pump for diabetics developed
> **1977-78** - development of first total-body computed tomography (CT) scanner

useless. As word of her success spread, the doctors of Australia and Britain tried to discredit her. But some American doctors invited her to demonstrate in the United States. In June 1940, Minneapolis General Hospital turned over a whole floor to her to start the Elizabeth Kenny Institute for use of her treatment. Using Minneapolis as a base, she traveled to epidemic centers worldwide to teach her methods to others. Sister Kenny never accepted money for the work she did with polio. She lived economically on the royalties she received from a special kind of battlefield stretcher she had invented as a young woman. Minnesota writer Martha Ostenso helped Sister Kenny write her autobiography, *And They Shall Walk*.

❖ The first female to receive an artificial heart was Mary Lund of Kensington on December 18, 1985. The 40-year-old woman had suffered a viral disease that destroyed her heart muscle and was failing rapidly, but no heart was available. Surgery was performed to implant an artificial heart at Abbott Northwestern Hospital in Minneapolis. After remaining in a coma for 15 days, she held her own long enough to be the recipient of the real heart of a 14-year-old girl a month later.

Temporary heart

Writer-surgeon

Dr. William A. Nolan brought the training and work of a surgeon to the notice of the book-reading public. The Massachusetts-born, New York-educated surgeon settled at Litchfield Clinic in 1960. He was as interested in educating the public as in his profession. In 1968, his book *The Making of a Surgeon*, concerning his training at Bellevue Hospital in New York, became a best seller. In 1975, Nolan began to have symptoms that turned into full-blown heart disease. After he had surgery and recovered, he wrote *Surgeon under the Knife*. One of his books for young people is *Spare Parts for the Human Body*.

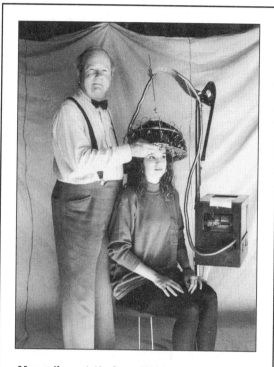

Marveling at their gullibility

Minneapolis has a fascinating Museum of Questionable Medical Devices. Owned by Bob McCoy, it includes this device that studies the bumps on your head. People have paid large sums over the decades for results that depend only on the gullibility of the "clients."

The long fast

In 1880, a Minneapolis doctor, H.S. Tanner, decided to prove his contention that the stomach was simply a nuisance. When doubters doubted that he had cured himself of rheumatism, heart disease, and asthma by fasting for 10 days, he arranged a medically supervised 40-day fast to take place in New York City.

Tanner's fast began in June of 1880 and became front-page news and the subject of all kinds of wagers. Many false reports were printed, such as that Tanner was getting nourishment through a sponge, he'd shrunk two inches, lost 50 pounds, and was delirious. Tanner's fast got more press than Edison's announcement of the electric light and Sarah Bernhardt's tour of the country. The doctor's celebrity status made him the subject of poems, with one memorable one called "With Beef Steak Forty Days Away." At the end of 40 days, New York gave Tanner a celebration that would rival Lindbergh's. He ate his first meal in 40 days— milk and watermelon. Tanner later migrated to California where he started a diet sect and died at age 87 still clinging to his beliefs.

THE SCIENTISTS

Measuring our minds

◆ Known as the MMPI, the Minnesota Multiphasic Personality Inventory, which tests for abnormal personality disorders, is the most widely used psychological assessment test anywhere. Translated into 120 languages and used in 40-plus countries, it was developed by two University of Minnesota professors, Starke R. Hathaway and J. Charnley McKinley, in the late 1930s and early 1940s.The typical "normal" respondent was described as "a 35-year-old Minnesotan who was married and residing in a small town or farming community and who had completed eight years of school." The first test had eight scales: psychasthenia, paranoia, psychopathic deviation, hysteria, hypomania, hypochondria, schizophrenia, and depression. The test includes 566 statements written on a sixth-grade level, which can be answered true, false, or "cannot say." Typical are such statements as "I am strongly attracted to members of my own sex," "I have had no difficulty starting or holding my urine," or "I like repairing a door latch." This test has been taken by many prospective government employees such as Peace Corps volunteers, nuclear power plant personnel, and police officers.

During the 1980s Americans were scoring much higher on MMPI scales that measure depression and paranoia. The test was revised in 1989 and the MMPI-2 was born. This new test has scales to measure drug abuse, anorexia, bulimia, and Type A personality.

♦ Sometime about 1875, somewhere in Minnesota, a child was born who was given the name Charles Hatfield. Not much more is known about his next 25 years, but somewhere in there he acquired a new moniker, the "Rainmaker," and a new address, California. Records indicate that he was hired in 1905 to make rain for Los Angeles. For $1,000 he added 18 inches of water to their reservoirs. But it was 10 years later that he pulled off his biggest precipitation coup. The city of San Diego was feeling the pinch of lack of rain, especially since they had a new reservoir that was less than half full. They offered Hatfield $10,000 if he could fill the reservoir. He and his brother went to the reservoir in the Laguna Mountains and built a tower-like device from which his secret mix of chemicals evaporated into the atmosphere. When only a little rain fell, he mixed up a stronger batch and set to work again. On January 14 it started to rain . . . and it rained . . . and it rained—more than 15 inches in the next two weeks. The city was devastated. Rivers overflowed. Roads were impassable and bridges were washed away. Two dams collapsed, killing people. When the reservoir was full, Hatfield walked into the city to collect his fee. But the lawsuits brought against the city by rain-angry residents amounted to many millions, and he never got paid. However, he did get publicity, and although his results were never so spectacular again, supposedly Charles Hatfield succeeded in making rain more than 500 times during his career.

Viewing society from Minnesota

Philosopher and economist Thorstein Veblen was brought to Minnesota from Wisconsin by his parents at age eight. He received his education at Carleton College where he was constantly criticized, not for being stupid, but for his sharp wit and caustic remarks. After he received his Ph.D., he spent seven years at home, unemployed, and considered a failure by the locals. But all the time he was reading widely and thinking about society. Going to Cornell University, he so  impressed one professor that he was asked to teach at the new University of Chicago. In 1899, he published *The Theory of the Leisure Class*—a study of economic institutions. In it he used the term "conspicuous consumption" for the first time. He was thereafter regarded as a social critic instead of an economist. Unfortunately, it was his social life that continued to get him into trouble: he was forced out of two universities for scandal over marital infidelity.

Two astronauts

Astronaut Robert D. Cabana was born in Minneapolis in 1949. Chosen in 1985 to be an astronaut after some years in the Marines, he has served as a pilot on one mission, in October 1990. He is awaiting another opportunity to go into space.

Astronaut Dale A. Gardner, born in Fairmont in 1948, was originally a navy pilot. He joined the NASA astronaut corps in 1978 and flew on a six-day space shuttle mission in 1983 and an eight-day mission in 1984.

Minnesota's missing link

Outdoors-lover Helen Westring of Bemidji was wandering the woods in 1966 when she was attacked by a hairy, pink-eyed, manlike creature. In terror, she shot it and then stumbled home. Neighbor and showmanship-minded Frank Hansen persuaded Helen to mount the creature in ice, preserving it so that people would pay to come and see it. For two years they did just that, with Hansen declaring he "knew" the creature to be a man from the Ice Age. Several reputable scientists called the creature a "missing link" in North American human evolution. But somewhere in that time, Hansen apparently substituted an Orient-made rubber version of whatever the original creature had been, and the scientists began to back off from their claims. No one now knows what the truth really is.

He watched it all work ❖ Melvin Calvin, born in St. Paul in 1911, was a biochemist gripped by the details of how photosynthesis (the process by which plants make their own food) works. The food-chain base of our entire planet, photosynthesis cannot be duplicated in the laboratory. However, working at Lawrence Radiation Laboratory in California, Calvin and his colleagues succeeded in tracing the action of carbon dioxide, virtually cell by cell, through the plant structure. Calvin was awarded the Nobel Prize for chemistry in 1961.

Cortisone at Mayo ❖ Edward C. Kendall, a Connecticut-born biochemist working at the Mayo Foundation in Rochester, and his coworker, Pittsburgh-born Philip Hench, separated from adrenal gland secretions a steroid chemical that he managed to produce in the laboratory and which he called cortisone. Announcing its discovery in 1949, Kendall said that it appeared to be useful in treating rheumatoid arthritis. At that time it wasn't terribly useful, however, because it cost about $200 a gram to produce. Since then it has been replaced by drugs with fewer side effects. Kendall had previously isolated thyroxine, the thyroid gland hormone, as well as 28 different hormones secreted by the cortex of the adrenal gland. Kendall, Hench, and Swiss researcher Tadeus Reichstein shared the 1950 Nobel Prize for physiology or medicine.

ORGANIZING TO ACHIEVE

❖ The first women's club formed in Minnesota was the Ladies' Floral Club of Austin, in 1869. The club members didn't just work with flowers, they were concerned with civic betterment. Working in the community, the club developed a public library and a rural nursing program.

Women at work

❖ Born to a slave family in Mississippi in 1861, Frederick McGhee graduated from law school in Chicago in 1885 and became Minnesota's first black criminal lawyer and the first black criminal lawyer west of the Mississippi when he opened a practice in St. Paul in 1889. He was also a founder of the Niagara Movement in 1905, which later spawned the National Association for the Advancement of Colored People (NAACP).

Starting the NAACP

❖ Roy Wilkins, director of the NAACP from 1955 to 1977, the most difficult and most productive years in civil rights history, was born in St. Louis, Missouri, and raised in St. Paul. He graduated from the U. of M. and became a journalist. The lynching of three black men in Duluth converted him to activism. He joined the NAACP and worked wherever he was needed for many years. When he was put in charge of the NAACP in 1955, he devoted most of the organization's efforts toward achieving equal rights through the courts. In 1964, the NAACP awarded him their important Spingarn Medal, and four years later, he was given the U.S. Medal of Freedom.

Activist Wilkins

❖ Though their history made them enemies, three Ojibways and a Sioux joined together in Minneapolis in 1968 to form the American Indian Movement, called AIM, to combat racism in the Twin Cities. Founders Ojibways Dennis Banks, George Mitchell, and Clyde Bellecourt, along with Sioux Russell Means took prompt militant political action to bring urban Native Americans to public attention. In 1969, they occupied the empty prison on Alcatraz Island in San Francisco Bay, where they remained for several years. They also occupied other federal buildings in Colorado, Washington, New York, and on Lake Michigan.

Political action for Native Americans

In 1973 ultramilitant factions within AIM occupied Sioux Pine Ridge Reservation, where South Dakota's Wounded Knee Massacre occurred in 1890, demanding revision of historical treaties. Unfortunately, the action turned bloody, and two Indians were killed and a federal marshal was wounded in a shootout. Two years later, in another incident at Pine Ridge, two FBI agents were killed.

Keeping lines open

❖ Another important civil rights leader who began his work in Minnesota is Whitney M. Young, Jr. Born in Kentucky, he came to the University of Minnesota for graduate study in social work and became involved in St. Paul in the Urban League, serving as the director of industrial relations. After a period in the 1950s as Dean of the School of Social Work at Atlanta University, he became executive director of the National Urban League. In 1963, he helped plan the huge march in Washington, D.C. All his work involved the attempt to keep open the lines of understanding between whites and blacks.

SPIRITUAL MINNESOTA

First church

❖ Organized by the Rev. Father Lucian Galtier, the first church building for white settlers in Minnesota was built in 1841. Galtier had come to the area of Mendota the previous year to serve as a missionary to the Dakotas. The "church" Galtier built was a simple shack, which he described as "so poor that it would well remind one of the stable at Bethlehem." It was around this church, dedicated to St. Paul, that the future capital city grew up and took its name. His primitive structure was used as the Catholic church until 1853, when St. Peter's Catholic Church was built at Mendota. It has been in use continuously ever since, the oldest still-used church in the state.

More church firsts

• Less than two years after the Baptist church sent a missionary to the St. Paul area at the urging of a schoolteacher, Harriet Bishop, the first baptism was held in the Mississippi River, on April 6, 1851. Even the fascinated Indians joined the curious crowd that gathered to watch the ceremony.

• The church that Bishop Henry Whipple (see p. 39) built in Faribault between 1862 and 1869 is recognized as the first Episcopal cathedral in the United States, the Cathedral of Our Merciful Saviour.

• The first Russian Orthodox church built in the lower 48 United States was built in Minneapolis in 1888.

Ireland in Minnesota

❖ Archbishop John Ireland was an Irish immigrant who took his name and his heritage seriously. Raised in St. Paul and educated as a priest in France, he became an army chaplain, soon starting the first of several excellent schools for Indian boys. As he gained more influence, he formed the Catholic Colonization Bureau, which worked with the wealthy Catholics in the area to purchase land on which they settled numerous impoverished families brought from Ireland. Spreading out from Swift County, dozens of colonies were established in the 1870s by immigrants who sought only a chance to break free from the poverty that had destroyed them in the Old Sod. Ireland gradually built up St. Paul as one of the most active dioceses in the nation, and he was recognized worldwide for his liberal, immigrant-oriented view of the church (which didn't necessarily please the old-timers who regarded the immigrants as upstarts to be ignored). Named bishop in 1884, Ireland received many financial gifts from St. Paul railroad man James J. Hill, including $50,000 for the construction of St. Paul Cathedral. He became Minnesota's first archbishop in 1888. Several years later he helped to found the Catholic University of America in Washington, D.C.

The Graham crusade

One of the biggest tasks of mail-handling in the nation occurs at the Minneapolis headquarters of the Billy Graham Evangelistic Association. The evangelist's crusades, held all over the world, bring millions of pieces of mail every year. The headquarters building, an old Standard Oil building, was taken over by Graham in the 1950s, even though he himself lives in North Carolina. The Minneapolis building is the center for the evangelistic organization's efforts in film making, radio broadcasting, magazine publishing, and, of course, answering mail.

PTL in MN

Ex-evangelist Jim Bakker is serving 18 years for fraud. The former TV preacher is an inmate at the Federal Medical Center, Rochester. Found guilty of fraud in connection with his PTL (Praise the Lord) theme park in North Carolina, he hasn't given up his preaching. He teaches classes in quitting smoking and tries to convert inmates including porn king Ferris Alexander, a Catholic. "He doesn't talk much about getting out. I've never heard him complain. He's not whining. He's not saying, 'I didn't deserve this,'" a friend said.

A DUET OF DUELS

An unbridled tongue

Colonel Samuel McPhail is known in the annals of Minnesota history for his famous "unbridled" remarks, often made under the influence of alcohol. He was once sent out to find a flour mill that was "misplaced." He reported that he had located "a dam by a mill site, but no mill by a dam site." While looking over his recruits for the Sioux Indian War of 1862, he remarked that they were "too old for milk and too young for whiskey."

The most celebrated story about Colonel McPhail is known as the "walking duel at Redwood Falls." In 1874, Colonel McPhail—60 years old with a flowing white beard—was the most notable resident of Redwood Falls since he had built the stockade and settled the town. His only competition in town was businessman William Gates. Meeting in a saloon one day, the two drank a little too much and began arguing. They each rushed home and got a weapon—McPhail a sword and Gates a muzzle-loader. The famous "walking duel" began when Gates took off down the road to Beaver Falls with the colonel some distance behind. The pace continued for two miles, the colonel gaining not an inch on Gates, when McPhail stopped for refreshments at a brewery, thus ending the duel. Gates continued his walk to Beaver Falls and came home a few days later, the combat over and the argument forgotten. McPhail moved to Lincoln County where he died in 1902 after trying to grow coffee and orange trees in balmy Minnesota.

Pet pig duel

It's recorded in history as the famous duel of 1839 near Seven Corners in St. Paul. It was fought over a pig, owned by a freed slave named James Thompson, who loved his pig more than anything. He had trained it to follow him through the streets of St. Paul. He became extremely upset one morning on finding the pig gone—stolen during the night by Edward Phalen, a man suspected of murdering his own business partner, though it was never proved. When Thompson found his pig penned up at Phalen's, he quickly tore down the pen and the obedient pet followed Thompson home. Phalen, furious, challenged Thompson to a duel, the winner to claim the pig. Thompson licked Phelan, who acknowledged the pig was Thompson's, and the watchers adjourned to Thompson's place to drink wine.

THE ARTS

The world of the arts in Minnesota is as much a result of corporations as it is of individuals. The Dayton-Hudson Company, for example, began in the 1940s to donate 5 percent of its pretax earnings to community and state projects, especially projects involving the arts. By 1990, well over 100 firms were following suit or giving nearly as much. This kind of giving has resulted in such premier arts sites as the Walker Art Center and the Minneapolis Institute of Arts.

The individual artists who were born and/or have worked in Minnesota are known worldwide. One of them, Sinclair Lewis, was the first American to win a Nobel Prize for Literature. Unfortunately, his literature tended to satirize what he knew of Minnesota as he was growing up. Garrison Keillor also writes of growing up in Minnesota, but with humor, not bitterness. Many artists have drawn their inspiration from their love of the Land of Sky-Blue Waters.

- Humor with Pen and Ink
- Preserving Life in Pictures
- Music and Dance
- Shaping Materials
- Poetry in the North
- Awards, Words & Pictures
- Tales to Tell
- An Audience of Children

HUMOR WITH PEN AND INK

"Good grief!"

❆ St. Paul native Charles Schulz, better known to his friends as "Sparky," describes himself as the "epitome of unachievement." Learning to draw by correspondence must have worked, because his comic strip "Li'l Folks" appeared in the *St. Paul Pioneer Press* in 1947. The strip told the adventures of a group of preschoolers with Charlie Brown as the main character. Schulz had named him after a friend from his Minneapolis art school. The strip was purchased by United Features Syndicate in 1950 and renamed "Peanuts" because "Li'l Folks" sounded too much like "Li'l Abner." Schulz was upset—"No one ever referred to small children as 'peanuts.'" But seven newspapers carried the first "Peanuts" strip on October 2, 1950, and the numbers have grown . . . and grown . . . and grown.

In 1965, when Schulz's St. Paul Central High class was planning its 25th class reunion, his name appeared on a list of graduates whose whereabouts were unknown. This was after Schulz had already won an Emmy for his TV special, "A Charlie Brown Christmas," and two awards from the National Cartoonists Society. "Peanuts" is now read by over 200 million readers in 68 countries who speak 26 different languages. Charlie Brown is *Carolius Niger* and Snoopy is *Snupius* in the Latin version. In the October 1, 1990, issue of *Forbes* magazine, Schulz was listed in the top 10 highest-paid entertainers in the United States. He earned $26 million in 1989 but said "I would be drawing the comic strip if I only made $50 a week."

Taking humor seriously

❆ "Before, if you wanted to be a cartoonist, you had to go off to New York or Los Angeles . . . Today with modems and fax machines . . . you can work wherever you want. . . . We feel like we're in a leading center for cartoon art." So says Dave Mruz, president of the Minnesota Cartoonists League. The 150-member group consists of working artists of all kinds—comic-book writers and artists, comic-strip artists, editorial cartoonists, advertising artists, and illustrators. The group meets at O'Gara's piano bar in St. Paul under an original portrait of Snoopy drawn and signed by Charles Schulz. The building that houses O'Gara's itself was, from 1942 to 1952, Charles Schulz's father's barbershop.

Among the members are Peter Kohlsaat, an ex-Duluth dentist, who quit his practice in 1982 and came to Minneapolis to draw and market his own editorial cartoon, "The Nooz." Jerry Van Amerongen creates "The Neighborhood." Wacky Dean Vietor of Minnetonka has a panel in the vein of "The Far Side" that appeared in *The New Yorker* and *USA Today* for many years. "Sally Forth" is created by ex-lawyer Greg Howard.

Comic book artists in the league include Edina artist Dan Jurgens whose specialties are "Justice League of America" characters, Superman, Flash, and Batman. Minneapolis-born artist Curt Swan was one of the early Superman artists. Gordon Purcell draws "Star Trek" comics.

PRESERVING LIFE IN PICTURES

George Catlin's paintings of North American Indians are among the best sources we have of the lives and cultures of the tribes and individuals that existed in the mid-1800s. The Philadelphia artist traveled far and wide to study his subject, which he recognized as a vanishing race. On two journeys—1835 and 1836—he spent time in Minnesota studying the Sioux Indians. At some point during his travels, he painted his name in red on some rocks near Richmond. The area has since become known as Catlin's Rocks. Catlin was the guest of honor at ceremonial Indian dancing at Fort Snelling in 1836. He was also the first traveler to acquaint the public with the fact of the Pipestone quarries.

An artist's rocks

St. Paul-born artist LeRoy Neiman has placed his wildly colored and almost stream-of-consciousness paintings on large walls in office buildings, hotels, and even ships that travel the world. But even greater numbers of people got to see his work during the 1972 and 1976 Olympic Games when he was the official Olympics artist and his quickly done renditions of scenes from the sporting activity appeared on television. Neiman was educated in Illinois and has taught for many years at the Chicago Art Institute.

Sports and art

Dr. William Watts Folwell, first president of the University of Minneapolis, was eager to turn Minnesota into a center for arts, as well as for education. In 1883, he helped found the Minneapolis Society of Fine Arts and was elected its first president. The organization brought paintings from New York for its first exhibit. Within three years, the society had founded the Minneapolis School of Art, and in 1915, its own building was opened as the Art Institute on land donated by Clinton Morrison.

Educating for art

The painter from the Sky-Blue Waters

A Chippewa (Ojibway) born and raised on the Red Lake Reservation, Patrick Des Jarlait grew up observing all the activities of the tribe, and storing the visual memories of them in his mind. Although he got little encouragement to sketch at his early schools, he was later sent to Pipestone Boarding School and then Red Lake Senior High, where his artistic talent was given free rein. While serving in the military during World War II, he held a one-man show of his Indian-theme paintings, every one of which sold. Continuing to paint on the side, he also did commercial work. One of his most famous tasks was the creation of the bear for Hamm's Brewery that appeared for many years in the "land of sky-blue waters" commercials.

Fine arts from trees

The Walker Art Center in Minneapolis was named for a millionaire lumberman, Thomas B. Walker. Originally a surveyor for the railway, he purchased lots of land, keeping the right to log its trees. Log it he did, and, using the huge income, he collected everything he could over the years, gradually adding room after room to his mansion.

Eventually he invited the public in to see the fine collection, and in 1940, the Walker Art Center was started. His paintings, jade, and early ceramics are still housed by the center, which is famous for its twentieth-century collections. In addition to serving as a museum, it has a major art education program. The Minnesota Opera got its start at the center in 1963. And attached to it is the Minneapolis Sculpture Garden (shown in the photo), the largest urban sculpture garden in the United States. Its giant "Spoonbridge and Cherry" has come to symbolize Minneapolis.

MUSIC AND DANCE

The singing gophers

Much of the music of early Minnesota stemmed from the songs sung by the voyageurs, traders, and then seamen. Theodore C. Blegen, writing in *Minnesota: A History of the State*, quotes a ballad of the territorial days that has a newcomer to the area finding just what he wants:

The Gopher girls are cunning,
The Gopher girls are shy,
I'll marry me a Gopher girl
Or a bachelor I'll die.
I'll wear a stand-up collar,
Support a handsome wife,
And live in Minnesota
The balance of my life.

Minnesota's gift to the Confederacy

The most famous song of the South was probably composed in the North. Ohio-born musician and composer Daniel Emmett was the brother of Lafayette Emmett, chief justice of the Minnesota Supreme Court in the 1850s. While on a visit to St. Paul, Daniel apparently spent considerable time working with the tune and the words and even having some St. Paul musicians try them out. The final result, "Dixie," wasn't published until 1859 when Daniel Emmett introduced the song through his traveling minstrel show. It soon became the theme song of the Confederacy during the Civil War.

Mother of folk music

Folk music was her life. Born in Minneapolis, Dawn Greening later moved to Chicago where she developed the Old Town School of Folk Music. The school has featured Mahalia Jackson, Arlo Guthrie and Pete Seeger. She moved to Ft. Collins, Colorado, in 1979 where Greening hosted a folk music show on public radio for 12 years.

Music off the cuff

While visiting Minnehaha Falls, composer Anton Dvorak was unable to find any paper so he wrote some notes (musical ones, that is) on his shirt cuff. His wife apparently sent the shirt to the laundry without realizing what Anton had done, but she was able to rescue the notes from the suds. The shirt cuff music became "Opus 100, The Indian Maiden," a.k.a. "Indian Lament." Dvorak was in the area spending a summer at a Bohemian settlement in Iowa and had come to Minnesota specifically to see Minnehaha Falls.

AWESOME

Greatness began with a stranding

The renowned Minneapolis Symphony Orchestra owes its formation to the enthusiasm and unflagging pushiness of German immigrant Emil Oberhoffer. An accomplished musician, conductor, and composer, he and his wife were traveling with a company of Gilbert & Sullivan players when the money ran out and they were left stranded in Minnesota. Playing anywhere he could, including restaurants and churches, he finally was named conductor of the new Apollo Club men's chorus. Soon moving on to the Philharmonic Club, he began to push for an orchestra to support the large, mixed chorus. Gradually, he got citizens of Minneapolis interested in supporting the idea, and on November 5, 1903, the new symphony orchestra held its first concert—ragged but real. Two years later it moved into the Minneapolis Auditorium, where it remained until 1930 when it moved onto the campus of the university. From 1936 to 1949, the conductor of the the Minneapolis Symphony was Greek-born immigrant Dimitri Mitropoulos, who turned the orchestra into a major recording group.

Supplier to brass bands everywhere

Brass bands are part of most people's lives at some time, if only the sight of one in a parade. But Chatfield's Jim Perkins made them even more important. In 1969, the attorney decided to reconstruct the town's long-defunct brass band. In doing so, he accumulated so much band music that he began the world's only lending library specifically for hard-to-locate music. It is utilized by bands all over the world. (P.S. The band is still functioning.)

On her toes

New York City ballerina Merrill Ashley was born Linda Ashley in St. Paul and raised in Rutland, Vermont. By age 14, she was a scholarship student at the School of American Ballet. George Balanchine, not long before his death, developed a ballet that would especially show off the incredible speed of Ashley's movements, and then another to show her gentle control. Since 1984, she has taught at the same school where she learned in New York.

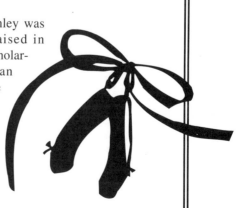

SHAPING MATERIALS

Father of the skyscraper

A system for building skyscrapers was patented by a Minneapolis architect on May 22, 1888. Leroy S. Buffington, known as the "Father of the Skyscraper," devised the method of using a braced steel skeleton with masonry veneer, carried on shelves fastened to the frame at each floor. Using his system, buildings could finally be built to any height, since the need for heavy masonry at the base to carry the load was eliminated. His plans were used in building the Pillsbury A Mill and helped turn Chicago into a city of skyscrapers. He built the West Hotel in Minneapolis several years earlier, putting in it a very unusual sight: a lobby 95 feet high with no support pillars.

The immigrant sculptor

Some of the most memorable statues related to Minnesota were created by a Norwegian, Jacob Henrik Gerhard Fjelde, who arrived in the state in 1888. Although he lived only another eight years, he produced the famed statues of Hiawatha and Minnehaha that are displayed at the Falls of Minnehaha (see pages 26 and 94). They were created for the Columbian Exposition of 1893 in Chicago, then purchased with pennies saved by Minnesota's boys and girls. Fjelde's monument to the First Minnesota regiment, which fought at Gettysburg, is located at that Pennsylvania battlefield.

Browerville's sculptor

Browerville-born sculptor Joseph Kieselewski studied art in the Twin Cities and New York, and won a scholarship in 1925 to study in Europe. He was later awarded the Prix de Rome, the youngest artist ever to receive the prize. Two of his sculptures, the *Gethsemane Group and Our Lady of Lourdes*, are in Browerville's St. Joseph's Roman Catholic Church.

The classical sculptor

St. Paul-born sculptor Paul Manship described himself as jumping "straight from Minnesota to Rome, and then with all possible speed to Greece." After studying under Solon Borglum (the brother of Gutzon Borglum, the sculptor of Mount Rushmore), Manship studied in Europe and then began his life's work of classically styled statues. The first American to have work displayed in London's Tate Gallery, he is probably best known for his Prometheus Fountain (photo at right) at Rockefeller Center and his bronze gates at Bronx Zoo, both in New York City.

Art in the garden

When General Mills built a new but rather stark headquarters building in Golden Valley in 1958, the company began a major program of art acquisition and exhibition, turning the entire building into an art gallery. Ten years later, the gallery was extended into the landscaped grounds surrounding the building when the first outdoor sculpture was commissioned. Today the company has had the grounds landscaped specifically for the display of outdoor sculptures. The inside and outside collections total more than 1,200 items including *The Man with Briefcase* shown at right.

The man who remade his vision

Duane Hanson of Alexandria was the first art major to graduate from Macalester College. He took higher degrees from Michigan's Cranbrook Academy of Art. But in 1967, at age 42, Hanson suddenly destroyed everything he had done that he still possessed and began to specialize in new images made from new materials. He creates plastic human figures set in realistic situations. The first work of his new age—and still one of his most controversial— was called *Abortion*. It showed a dead woman lying under a sheet.

The Man with Briefcase at General Mills

❧ The *Peace Memorial*, located in St. Paul's City Hall and Ramsey County Courthouse, is one of the largest carved onyx figures in the world. Created by Swedish sculptor Carl Milles, it weighs 55 tons. It depicts the figure of an Indian god, one hand raised in greeting, the other holding a peace pipe. On the back are carved tiny figures showing hunting, camping, and fishing, representing a dream of peace. It was dedicated on May 30, 1936, amid controversy because many people found it hard to justify spending $75,000 for a statue during the midst of the Depression. Still, the *Peace Memorial* is considered by many to be Milles's finest work.

The Peace Memorial

POETRY IN THE NORTH

❧ Oklahoma-born poet John Berryman, who became famous for his *Homage to Mistress Bradstreet*, was a professor of poetry at the University of Minnesota from 1954 until his death. He won a 1964 Pulitzer Prize for *77 Dream Songs*. Recognized as one of the great contemporary American poets, Berryman struggled most with alcoholism. On January 7, 1972, he jumped from a bridge in Minneapolis onto the ice below, killing himself. The following year, his own account of his struggle was published in *Recovery*.

A contemporary poet wins Pulitzer Prize

Pulitzer poet ❧ Richard Eberhart was born in Austin in 1904 with poetry in his soul. It began to come out during his education at Dartmouth and Harvard. His first book of poems was published in 1930, before he went to Siam to serve as tutor to the king (though, unlike Anna Leonowens, he didn't get a musical written about his experiences). On his return, he taught, primarily at Dartmouth, until 1959, when he was named Consultant in Poetry to the Library of Congress, a position which has since been renamed Poet Laureate. In 1965, his *Selected Poems, 1930-1965*, won the 1965 Pulitzer Prize for poetry.

A picture worth a thousand words

Alex Hesler, a daguerreotype artist from Chicago, made some views of Minnehaha Falls on August 15, 1852. These primitive photographs later provided inspiration for a permanent part of our culture. Hesler gave one picture to a friend who happened to be a neighbor of poet Henry Wadsworth Longfellow. The Minnesota poet who never visited Minnesota was inspired, or so the legend goes, by the picture of Minnehaha Falls to create what became one of the most famous American poems, *The Song of Hiawatha*, which was published on November 10, 1855. He tells us—

Fjelde's sculpture of Hiawatha and Minnehaha

Ye who love the haunts of Nature,
Love the sunshine of the meadow,
Love the shadow of the forest,
Love the wind among the branches,
And the rain-shower and the snow-storm,
And the rushing of great rivers
Through their palisades of pine-trees, . . .
Listen to these wild traditions,
To this Song of Hiawatha!

AWARDS, WORDS & PICTURES

The Renaissance man ❧ The NAACP's Spingarn Medal was given to Minnesotan Gordon Parks in 1972. Parks was born in Kansas but raised in St. Paul. He became a photographer for *Life* magazine, wrote a number of novels and nonfiction books, composed classical music, and directed films. In 1977, he and some partners took over *Essence*, the magazine for African-American women. Called by many a "Renaissance man," Parks was awarded the National Medal of Arts by President Reagan in 1988.

The writer who saw it all ❧ As life went on in the small Minnesota town of Sauk Centre, the residents couldn't have known that the penetrating eye of young Sinclair Lewis was absorbing everything, and that what he saw would show up in his books. Born Harry Sinclair Lewis in 1885, he attended Yale University and then worked as a reporter and as a writer of short magazine fiction while he planned to work on "serious" novels. His version of serious was satire, first seen in his popular novel, *Main Street*, in which an Eastern-raised woman views the provincialism of life in Gopher Prairie, which he based on Sauk Centre. His fellow Sauk Centerians were not pleased with him, because they all too easily saw themselves in the book. Two years later he published *Babbit*—a name that has entered our language—about a man who has become more and more self-satisfied as he increasingly conforms to the small-town life of which he is a part.

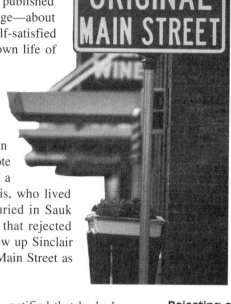

Lewis's other major novels include *Arrowsmith* (see below), *Elmer Gantry*, and *Dodsworth*, all of them acute social criticism that in 1930 won him the first Nobel Prize for Literature given to an American. Not long before his death, he wrote *The God-Seeker,* which tells the story of a missionary in early Minnesota. When Lewis, who lived his later years in Europe, died, he was buried in Sauk Centre's Greenwood Cemetery. The town that rejected him has now named the street where he grew up Sinclair Lewis Avenue and it proudly identifies its Main Street as the "original" one.

Novelist Sinclair Lewis of Sauk Centre, notified that he had won the 1925 Pulitzer Prize for his novel *Arrowsmith*, refused to accept it because, he said, the usually coveted prize tended to make writers "safe, polite, obedient, and sterile." He probably wouldn't attend Sinclair Lewis Days held each July in Sauk Centre either. The celebration is just the kind of thing Lewis would have satirized.

Rejecting an honor

The taller they come

Minnesotans are known for their ability to make up stories, but Oliver Williams takes the medal as the "Champion Liar of Minnesota." Williams operated a hotel in Elbow Lake for 30 years, a hotel known for its lousy service, bad food, and extraordinary stories—Williams was the evening entertainment at no extra charge. He was regarded as a nuisance by most of the townspeople, but even they listened to his stories, which he told mighty tall. Williams lived until he was probably 120 years old and never missed a chance to tell his true-to-the-last-detail stories to anyone who would listen.

Like the reason why Spirit Lake went dry. He said that when he was looking around the dry lake bed, he'd discovered an old rattlesnake skin and knew right away that the snake had fastened itself to one end of a rock while shedding its outer skin. It had then rolled down a hill toward the Mississippi—skin still fastened to the Spirit Lake rock—and with its last roll fell into the river, leaving the hose-like skin behind. All the water from Spirit Lake was siphoned through that natural snakeskin hose into the Mississippi, leaving Spirit Lake dry.

A knight in shining theater

The Minneapolis Theatre Company, better known as the Tyrone Guthrie Theater, was founded in Minneapolis in 1963 as a short-term theater festival. Founded by Sir Tyrone Guthrie, Peter Ziesler, and Oliver Rea, it was intended from the start to be an important showcase for serious drama. Sir Tyrone (husband of actress Katherine Cornell) wrote in his book *In Various Directions* that same year: "Indications are that for such a theater, making no attempt to be popular in the sense of condescending to a public which is presumed incapable of serious effort, there will always be a solid and loyal following." He was right. The Tyrone Guthrie Theater has become a mainstay for serious theatergoers. It is one of the few theaters outside New York City to regularly win Tony awards.

TALES TO TELL

The earliest writer

✣ A young man who grew up at Fort Snelling, which bore his name and where his father was the commander, was William Joseph Snelling. After returning east with his family, he became a writer and published in 1830 a book entitled *Tales of the Northwest*. He drew on his own experiences of Indians, voyageurs, and fur traders to create the novel.

A column from a would-be senator

✣ Some people think Ignatius Donnelly was crazy, others think he was a genius. He himself thought he was going to be the savior of Minnesota. Whatever Donnelly was, it was colorful—a colorful author, statesman, businessman, politician, and colonizer. Having moved to Minnesota to found a town, Nininger, that never got off the ground (see p. 72), Donnelly settled in Hastings and turned to politics, serving first as lieutenant governor and then as a congressman. In 1899, Donnelly ran for the Senate against William D. Washburn, who had beaten him before. Donnelly campaigned tirelessly, convinced that Minnesota would be destroyed if he weren't elected. On election night, awaiting results, he wrote the first chapter of what would become his most famous book, *Caesar's Column*, which sold 700,000 copies.

Set in 1988, the book consists of letters from Gabriel Weltstein, a Ugandan visiting New York, to his brother back home. Gabriel described a New York City—population 10 million—ruled by a group of bankers who used a huge police force and a fleet of demonic balloons to control the city. A huge underworld organization flourished in the city under the leadership of Caesar Lomellini, who was determined to get rid of the bankers. In a massive battle to gain control, 250,000 people were killed as the rulers, police, and demon balloons fought. Lomellini told his followers to build a column, stuffing the dead in wooden boxes cemented together until it reached the sky. Anarchy reigned. Gabriel wisely left town for Uganda and devised a utopian community on a high plateau where his people lived happily ever after untouched by the rest of the world's madness. (Note: Minnesota didn't fall apart after Donnelly lost the election.)

Donnelly also wrote the best-selling *Great Cryptogram*, in which he tried to prove that Francis Bacon wrote William Shakepeare's plays.

The Cannon City minister

Indiana writer Edward Eggleston is best known for his early novel of frontier life, *The Hoosier Schoolmaster*, which he wrote in 1871. However, during the late 1850s before he turned writer, he had served as a Methodist minister in a pulpit in St. Peter. What he observed in that position was some of the hot, heavy, and not always ethical land speculation that was driving Minnesota's population growth. He explored the subject in a novel, the *Mystery of Metropolisville*, which was based on Cannon City.

A Norwegian in Minnesota

Ole Edvart Rölvaag came to Minnesota from Norway as a young man. Educated at St. Olaf College, he later became a professor of all things Norwegian at the same college. When he began to write, he wrote in Norwegian and so, although he was an teacher in America, his novels, which were first published in Norway, had to be translated. His classic novel, *Giants in the Earth*, shows the difficulties of life for Norwegian farmers on the prairie and the problems arising when two different cultures meet. He wrote the book, first in a trilogy, while living in a cabin near Marcell, on Big Island Lake.

The southern novelist from the North

Born in cold, northern Minneapolis, Anne Tyler has become a novelist of the American South. After living in several different Quaker communities, she grew up in North Carolina and has lived in Baltimore since 1967. That city has been the setting for most of her later novels. The first novel was *If Morning Ever Comes*, published in 1964. Since then her popularity has increased at a fast rate. She has had a novel out and selling almost continuously.

The father of Maynard G. Krebs

It may seem hard to believe, but Dobie Gillis and his friend Maynard got their start in St. Paul, in the words of novelist and playwright Max Shulman. The Minnesota writer's first novel was *Barefoot Boy with Cheek*, published in 1943. A satire on college life, it became a musical that ran for more than two years on Broadway. Shulman first created the girl-crazy Dobie in his novel *I Was a Teen-Age Dwarf*, which became the TV show "The Many Loves of Dobie Gillis." Dobie has been on TV continuously since 1959, mainly as a syndicated rerun. Shulman also wrote *Rally Round the Flag* and *The Tender Trap*, both of which became movies.

Voice of an era

Weighing in at 10 pounds, 6 ounces, F. Scott Fitzgerald was a "heavyweight" from his birth in St. Paul. Christened Francis Scott Key Fitzgerald after a star-spangled relative, he grew up on the fringe of the wealthy community, never quite making it. "The rich are different from you and me," he later wrote. However, his mother, Mollie, the daughter of an Irish immigrant, was determined to make him one of the "right" people. He didn't find them at St. Paul Academy where the other boys disliked him enough to run a school-magazine ad for someone who could "poison Scotty or find some means to shut his mouth." A top-notch debater, he also played hard at all sports but wasn't any good—he weighed a mere 138 pounds. But he had a romantic vision of himself as a football hero. Fitzgerald's first published story, "The Mystery of the Raymond Mortgage," was written in 1909 for the academy's magazine.

Many of Fitzgerald's novels were made into films including *Tender is the Night*

As a teenager, Fitzgerald acted in plays at the White Bear Yacht Club on White Bear Lake. While traveling after attending from Princeton, he met Zelda Sayre of Alabama. When Zelda broke off their engagement because he had no way to make good money, he quit his job in New York and returned to St. Paul to prove himself to her. Working 24 hours a day, he quickly rewrote an unsold novel, which Scribner's accepted and published as *This Side of Paradise*. Zelda accepted his proposal and the pair left for New York in 1922 and never came back. He later wrote: "I no longer regard St. Paul as my home . . . I never did quite adjust myself to those damn Minnesota winters . . . though many events there will always fill me with a tremendous nostalgia." However, he became known as "St. Paul's first successful novelist." His fiction centered around St. Paul's fashionable Summit Avenue.

With the publication of *Tales of the Jazz Age* in 1922, Fitzgerald's term, "Jazz Age," became synonymous with the life-style of the 1920s. Fitzgerald captured the empty excess of the wealthy during the Roaring Twenties in his most famous book, *The Great Gatsby*, published in 1924. Not only did Fitzgerald write about these excesses, he lived them. The couple's life-style drove them into poverty by 1931, with Scott an alcoholic and Zelda suffering mental breakdowns. He worked in Hollywood as a scriptwriter for a while but continued to write novels. He died at age 44 from a heart attack before finishing *The Last Tycoon*—never knowing how widely accepted his work would be after his death.

❄ Edina's Judith Guest surprised everyone when a story she had a compulsion to tell became a best-selling novel in the late 1970s. *Ordinary People* explores the communication problems in family relationships. After the death of their oldest son in a boating accident, no one in the family of a successful Chicago attorney talks about it. On the surface, love and family harmony in a beautiful, well-to-do suburb is taken for granted, but underneath, all is not well. Guest's novel was made into a 1980 Oscar-winning film, directed by Robert Redford and starring Donald Sutherland and Mary Tyler Moore.

Ordinary people

❄ Minnesota has produced two biographers who have won two Pulitzer Prizes for their books. William Andrew Swanberg, born in St. Paul in 1907, was a book editor turned biographer. His *Citizen Hearst* won the 1961 Pulitzer for biography, and he won again in 1972 for *Luce and His Empire*. Only the awards judges know whether his earlier book, *Pulitzer*, was prevented from winning the award because of its subject.

Revealing the lives of others

The second biographer is Walter Jackson Bate, who was born in Mankato in 1918 and became a Harvard University professor. He won Pulitzers in 1963 for *John Keats* and in 1977 for *Samuel Johnson*.

❄ One of the most famous Minnesota towns doesn't even exist except in the gently humorous mind of Garrison Keillor, who was born in Anoka. Named Gary at birth, he changed his name to have a stronger-sounding one for writing poetry. But his strength wasn't poetry, it was story-telling. Raised in a Plymouth Brethren community, he grew up with little awareness of most entertainment forms, but the Brethren were great story-tellers. He absorbed the twin joys of stories and radio as he grew. Becoming a short-story writer, he contributed regularly to *The New Yorker* magazine.

Don't bother looking for the town

In 1968 Keillor began a public radio program called "A Prairie Home Companion," which was a weekly collection of the stories, songs, and ads that made up the kind of radio programming that flourished in the 1930s, even before Keillor was born. Very early in the program, he started telling tales of the people in the fictional Minnesota town of Lake Wobegon, "the little town that time forgot and the decades cannot improve." By 1974, the local program was going into the homes of the entire upper Midwest, and in 1979 it became a regular feature on National Public Radio. Keillor's 1985 book, *Lake Wobegon Days*, brought his nonexistent but oh-so-real town to life on the printed page. On June 13, 1987, "A Prairie Home Companion" went off the air. Keillor announced, "I want to be a writer again. I'm tired and it is time to stop." However, he soon began broadcasting again from New York, as well as writing novels. In 1992 he returned to live near the Twin Cities.

AN AUDIENCE OF CHILDREN

Little books on the prairie

Young girls had known and loved the Laura Ingalls Wilder books for years, but then in 1974, Michael Landon's TV program, "Little House on the Prairie," became immensely popular and sales of the Wilder novels took off into outer space and opened up curiosity about life in old Minnesota, especially Walnut Grove, where the TV program supposedly took place.

Laura Ingalls was born in Wisconsin, near Lake Pepin, in 1867. When, as a widow, she began writing stories about her childhood at the urging of her daughter, she started there, with *Little House in the Big Woods*, which was published in 1932. Her family then moved to Walnut Grove, with the story continuing in *On the Banks of Plum Creek*. There she was able to go to school for the first time and the family suffered the grasshopper plague of the 1870s (see p. 23). It was also in Minnesota that Laura's sister, Mary, was blinded by scarlet fever. Soon after, the family moved to South Dakota. Her story continued through her marriage to Almonzo Wilder and the birth of her children. The writer died in 1957 in Missouri. Walnut Creek has a Laura Ingalls Wilder Museum.

Supporting a family with art

Before he died, Wanda Gag's father, Anton, told his daughter one last thing: "What Papa has left undone, Wanda will have to finish." Anton was an artist in New Ulm, but, without a patron, he hadn't made much money. He wanted his daughter, Wanda, to carry on his legacy. However, as the oldest daughter, though only 15, in a family of seven children and with an ill mother, Wanda had to support the family after his death. She made postcards to sell at the drugstore. She painted Easter eggs and valentines, made hand-painted birthday books and bookmarks, and gave children drawing lessons. She later earned money by contributing to the "Junior Section" of the *Minneapolis Journal*. She won a scholarship to the Minneapolis School of Art and later to a New York art school. As an adult, Wanda moved her brothers and sisters to a farm in New Jersey, which she called All Creation. One of her books, *Millions of Cats*, continues to be a favorite children's story. Her 1940 autobiography is called *Growing Pains*.

She turned Mankato into "Deep Valley"

Children's book critic Irene L. Cooper said of Mankato-born Maud Hart Lovelace, "Lovelace broke no new ground, reached no dazzling heights. She did something almost as difficult, she endured." And endure she has. Maud Hart, who was married to another writer, Delos Lovelace, lived all her life in Minnesota. When she began to write in the late 1930s, she called upon her own childhood in Mankato to create the town of Deep Valley, the home of Betsy, Tacy, and—in later books—Tib. In a series of 10 books that have continued to grip young readers, the three girls grow up, go to college, and marry. Maud Hart Lovelace patterned the girls after herself and her sisters.

THE ENTERTAINERS

A St. Paul newspaper ran the following advertisement in 1874: "FOR SALE CHEAP! a new panorama of Minnesota 7 feet high and 375 feet long, with views of the leading cities, rivers, waterfalls, prairies, and public buildings." Panoramas were what passed for motion pictures before motion pictures were invented.

Since then, entertainment, both for Minnesotans and involving Minnesotans, has grown and evolved, but the audiences can't be much more enthusiastic than they were a century ago. One of the greatest names in show business ever, Judy Garland, was a product of the state.

- Hometown Entertainment
- The Business of Beauty
- North Stars and Starlets
- Music in Motion
- TV Time

HOMETOWN ENTERTAINMENT

A living panorama

Panoramas were unrolled like "movies" while the presenter provided accompanying music and entertaining stories. One early panorama artist, Henry Lewis, decided to paint the entire Mississippi River and got a group of investors to underwrite his adventure, which he was sure would "make a fortune for us all." He arrived at Fort Snelling in June 1848 ready to paint his journey down the river. His first problem was mosquitoes. "We hardly landed (at Little Crow's Village) when we were attacked by hundreds. Our fire attracted thousands. And we ate our supper attended by millions . . ." All along the way, Lewis made sketches—Red Wing's Village, Lake Pepin, Wabasha Prairie (Winona). He sketched through Wisconsin, Iowa, and Illinois and finished his panorama one year after making his boat trip. The whopping great 3,975-foot-long result opened on September 1, 1849, in St. Louis. The artist later sold the panorama to a Dutchman who took it to India. It was never seen again.

The night out

It used to be that every small town in Minnesota had a dance floor or ballroom with a name such as the Blue Moon, the Hollyhock, the Golden Rule, the Prom, or the Swan Lake. It was the polka and the waltz that got them built. "There were ballrooms within arm's length of each other all over Minnesota," according to Dodie Wendinger, executive director of the Minnesota Music Hall of Fame. For many girls in small towns the ballrooms were like palaces, and they looked forward to being old enough to go. "On a Saturday night, you turned on the radio, rolled up the carpet, and Dad danced with you, he taught you the rules. He had you step on his feet and he danced, and you got the feeling of dancing, of the music." Almost 50 ballrooms still survive in Minnesota, more than in any other state.

THE BUSINESS OF BEAUTY

Here she comes!

Minnesota has contributed three Miss Americas to the roster of beauties:

Sorry, Miss USA
In 1988, Sue Bolich of Edina was scheduled to represent Minnesota in the Miss USA contest, hoping to go on and become Miss World, when she was arrested for shoplifting. Thus ended her quest.

BeBe Shopp (real name: Beatrice Bella), Miss America 1948, came from the farm community at Hopkins. She played the glockenspiel in her high-school band and performed on the vibraharp for her talent performance. The newspapers turned her statement about not believing in wearing falsies into a one-woman crusade against them. Shopp was the first Miss America to go abroad during her reign.

1977's beauty was **Dorothy Kathleen Benham**, a resident of Edina, and the stepdaughter of a choir director. She called herself "an old-fashioned girl."

Gretchen Elizabeth Carlson of Anoka, Miss America 1989, was described by one Miss America groupie as a "brainchild with a really sexy smile."

"Let's Be Beautiful"

That was definitely the slogan (as well as the column title) of actress and beauty writer Arlene Dahl, who was born in Minneapolis in 1928. Seen modeling in New York, the beautiful woman got onto Broadway and then into movies, starring first in *My Wild Irish Rose*, apparently because of her memorable red hair. Appearing mostly in light-hearted comedies, she spent her off-screen time preparing a newspaper column that encouraged women to do the best they can with their appearance. That blossomed into several books, starting with *Always Ask a Man*, and a major international beauty-consulting business. Dahl was married for a time to Tarzan Lex Barker and for another time to actor Fernando Lamas, when she became next-generation actor Lorenzo Lamas's mother.

The cover girl

Apparently Minnesota-born Cheryl Tiegs doesn't want people to know where in the state she was born, but born she was, in 1947. She grew into a California-style beauty and became a widely sought model and cover girl for the Ford Agency. She was on "Good Morning, America" for a while as a beauty commentator, before writing a book, *The Natural Way to Beauty*. She is a partner in a sportswear company that manufactures clothing under her name for Sears, Roebuck & Co.

NORTH STARS AND STARLETS

No time to object

Actor Lew Ayres (born Lewis Ayer in Minneapolis in 1908) was trained as a musician and had his own orchestra in his late teens. But then he was discovered by Hollywood and made his first movie in 1921. Mild and handsome, he became best known for playing young "Dr. Kildare" in a long sequence of movies well past the time he was as young as the character he played. He had a thriving screen career until World War II, when he declared himself a conscientious objector and lost his popularity, even though he worked as a medic. His most famous role was *All Quiet on the Western Front* in 1930.

The actress, the flyboy, and the bra

When wealthy flyboy, inventor, and entrepreneur Howard Hughes saw Jane Russell's picture, she was on her way to stardom and sex-goddess status. *The Outlaw*, Hughes's first major picture starring the girl who was born in Bemidji, wasn't released for three years because Russell's extremely low-cut dress went against the motion-picture standards of the time. After its release in 1947, Russell went on to make numerous films including *Gentlemen Prefer Blondes* (1953) with Marilyn Monroe.

Legend holds that Hughes designed a special cantilevered bra for well-endowed Jane Russell—maybe even that he invented the brassiere just for her. However, she confessed in her autobiography years later that while Hughes did design one for her to wear in *The Outlaw*, she only wore it briefly in her dressing room. Finding it very uncomfortable, she removed it before going back on the set . . . and that was the end of that bra.

A star is born

"It's a swell state, Minnesota." That's what Frances Ethel Gumm, better known as Baby to her family and Judy Garland to the world, had to say about her home state. Born on June 10, 1922, in Grand Rapids, where her father owned a theater, she and her two sisters did a song-and-dance act under the unfortunate name of "The Glum Sisters." The family remained based in Grand Rapids until Frances was 12, when her name was changed to Judy Garland and the family moved to California. The following year she made a short musical with Deanna Durbin, her first appearance on film. After being wasted on several Andy Hardy films, she won the part of Dorothy in *The Wizard of Oz* over Shirley Temple. The role brought her a special Oscar in 1939 (children weren't given regular Oscars until years later).

One of the early singing reviews Garland received said, "Possessing a voice that, without a P.A. system, is audible throughout a house as large as the Chinese [Grauman's Chinese Theatre], she handles ballads like a veteran, and gets every note and word over with a personality that hits audiences." *Celebrity Register* worded Garland's quality another way: They said she had the "single indispensable attribute of a top performer . . . when the performer is 'on,' the audience, hot or cold, senses the presence of a star."

In 1961, the mother of singers Liza Minnelli and Lorna Luft (plus a son) won a Grammy for her album *Judy at Carnegie Hall*. She was nominated for Oscars for her roles in *A Star is Born* and a non-singing role in *Judgment at Nuremberg*.

Judy in Grand Rapids

A Yellow Brick Road in Grand Rapids leads to the Itasca County Historical Society Museum in the historic Central School, not far from the house where Frances Gumm lived. Within the museum is a special Judy Garland museum, which sponsors a Judy Garland Festival every June.

Winner of a new category
☆ The first actress to win an Oscar for a supporting role was Litchfield-born Gale Sondergaard, in 1936, for *Anthony Adverse*. Born Edith Holm Sondergaard, she was exotic looking and often played villainesses. Her final film was *Echoes* in 1980.

The grumpy odd couple
☆ Actors Jack Lemmon and Walter Matthau, best known as a twosome for their 1968 film *The Odd Couple*, found themselves being an odd couple again in March 1993, when they were staying at Minneapolis's Whitney Hotel while filming a new movie called *Grumpy Old Men*.

⭐ St. Cloud's Byron Ellsworth Barr changed his name to Gig Young when he became an actor working at the Pasadena Playhouse. Good-looking and relaxed, he frequently played appealing cads. He was one of a family of swindlers on the 1964-65 TV series "The Rogues." In 1969, he won a Best Supporting Actor Oscar for his role in *They Shoot Horses, Don't They?* After divorcing actress Elizabeth Montgomery, he married actress Kim Schmidt in 1978 but only three weeks later he apparently shot her and then took his own life.

The End

⭐ Her family moved continuously, so it was pure chance that actress Jessica Lange was born in Cloquet in 1949, but she still returns to Minnesota frequently. After working in Paris for several years, she moved to New York to become an actress. Her first film role failed to overcome the memory of Fay Wray in the first version of *King Kong*, but then she got better and so did her films. She won an Oscar for Best Supporting Actress in 1982 for *Tootsie*. Lange has a daughter from her relationship with ballet guru Mikhail Baryshnikov as well as two children with playwright Sam Shepard.

After the gorilla bit

⭐ Movie producer Mike Todd was probably more famous for being the only one of Elizabeth Taylor's husbands to die while married to her than for his Academy Award-winning film *Around the World in Eighty Days*. Born Avrom Hirsch Goldbogen in Minneapolis in 1909, he began working in show business in 1933, producing stage numbers for the Century of Progress Exposition in Chicago. He spent many years on Broadway, producing musical revues and other extravaganzas à la Florenz Ziegfeld. He ultimately developed a special three-dimensional filming technique called Todd-AO, which he used for the 1956 Oscar winner. He died in 1958 in a plane crash in New Mexico.

A life on wide screen

⭐ It says at the beginning of the 1971 film *Billy Jack* that it was directed by T.C. Frank, but he's really Minneapolis-born Tom Laughlin, who also starred as Billy Jack. The character, who also appears in *The Trial of Billy Jack* and *Billy Jack Goes to Washington*, is a part-Vietnam hero, part-karate master half-Indian, and a mythic do-gooder who takes on the violent and corrupt in society. Roger Ebert says, "The movie has as many causes in it as a year's run of the *New Republic*. There's not a single contemporary issue, from ecology to gun control, that's not covered."

A cult favorite

Director Hill

Minneapolis-born George Roy Hill began acting in Ireland after World War II, but when he returned to the United States, it was to direct, back when TV dramas were live and the opportunities for things to go wrong were infinite. He won a number of early Emmys for his dramatic productions and then moved on to Broadway with such memorable shows as *Look Homeward, Angel* and *Period of Adjustment*. It wasn't until 1962 that he went to Hollywood, where he certainly made up for lost time. He created the fabulous partnership of Paul Newman and Robert Redford in *Butch Cassidy and the Sundance Kid* in 1969, and then won an Oscar for their partnership reprise in 1973's *The Sting*.

Theatrical movies filmed in Minnesota since 1970

Airport
. . . and the earth did not swallow him
The Baboon Heart
Beyond Bob
Blood Hook
Catch Me If you Can
Crossing the Bridge
Drop Dead Fred
The Emigrants/ New Land
Equinox
Far North
Foolin' Around
Graffiti Bridge
Grumpy Old Men

The Heartbreak Kid
Ice Castles
Iron Will
Loose Ends
Meantime
The Mighty Ducks
Now I Lay Me
Old Explorers
Patti Rocks
The Personals
Purple Haze
Purple Rain
Rachel River
Resident Alien
Sign O' the Times
Slaughterhouse Five
Take This Job and Shove It
That was Then, This is Now
Trauma
Twenty Bucks
The Usual
Wildrose
You'll Like My Mother
Youngblood

Movie music

Just as early Hollywood musicals meant the choreography of Busby Berkeley, so the musical scores of such movies meant Minneapolis-born George Stoll. His first score was *Broadway Melody of 1938*. *For Me and My Gal, Meet Me In St. Louis, Babes in Arms,* and *Ziegfeld Girl* were among Stoll's other shows. He won an Oscar in 1945 for the score of *Anchors Aweigh.*

The making of 2001

Stanley Kubrick asked for the Minneapolis firm of Honeywell's help when he planned the film *2001: A Space Odyssey.* Four engineers from the Systems and Research departments spent four months on the project. They developed an inch-thick notebook of ideas with drawings and details from how to design an antigravity suit, a radiation monitoring gun, and HAL 9000, the artificial intelligence that ran the spaceship. Many of the aspects of the 1968 movie—such as artificial intelligence—are no longer science fiction.

MUSIC IN MOTION

Minneapolis playwright and musician John Olive created a 1992 play that is regarded as the world's first polka musical. Called *Evelyn and the Polka King*, it is a "caper" comedy featuring a five-piece polka band, a missing daughter, and stolen money.

The polka playwright

The three Andrews sisters, Patti, Laverne, and Maxine, became known outside Minnesota in 1937 with their recording of a Yiddish song, "Bei Mir Bist Du Schön," an unusual circumstance for the Norwegian family. They became immensely popular during the 1940s, especially as entertainers traveling to visit the troops abroad during the war. Among the biggest hits of the Andrews Sisters was "I Can Dream, Can't I?" and the very different "Beer Barrel Polka."

Sister act

First of the "Tonight Show" bands

Bandleader and composer Skitch Henderson was born in England, where he acquired his real name of Lyle Russell Cedric Henderson. He has never told the full story of how he acquired the name "Skitch," but it probably involved some black eyes in the western Minnesota town of Halstad where he grew up. That was also where his aunt taught him to play the piano. Playing with dance bands through the '30s and World War II, he became musical director for Frank Sinatra and Bing Crosby. When Steve Allen started the "Tonight Show" in 1954, Skitch Henderson's became the first name band in TV.

Funky music came from Lipps, Inc.—pronounced *lip-sync*—a twosome formed in Minneapolis by multi-instrumented Steven Greenberg and vocalist Cynthia Johnson, who had been the 1976 Miss Black Minnesota USA. Their No. 1 hit was "Funkytown" in 1980. The song's title, unfortunately, referred to Greenberg's boredom with his hometown.

Do their lips move?

Oscar Pettiford was a reservation-born Native American who, when he was home, was in Minneapolis. But growing up, he was rarely home, because his family band, consisting of his father and 11 brothers and sisters, was usually on the road. Called "the most technically capable and melodically inventive bassist" in the jazz world of the late 1940s, he played with every major jazz group and also had his own band for many years.

The bottom beat

Musician Marty Balin of the Jefferson Airplane was arrested in 1970 in Bloomington for possession of marijuana and contributing to the delinquency of minors. He was holding a raucous party in his hotel room at 5:30 in the morning when police entered and found several underage girls at the party. Balin's sentence was dropped on appeal from a year's hard labor to a $100 fine.

MJ and Marty

Rocky horror rock group ★ Among the wilder groups of the highly drugged era of rock was the Tubes, formed in 1972. Two of the members were from Minnesota: bass player Rich Anderson, born in St. Paul, and guitarist Roger Steen, born in Pipestone. The group was formed in San Francisco in 1972 and had an early hit album in Britain called *White Punks on Dope*. Straightening up their act a little (and dressing their girls somewhat more fully) so that they could merge into the mainstream, they began to record for Capitol Records but never had a major hit.

Eagles take off ★ Bernie Leadon, a native of Minneapolis, played guitar for Linda Ronstadt but had left her group when she formed a new backup group consisting of Glenn Frey, Don Henley, and Randy Meisner. Leadon, drunk and swinging one night, wandered on stage and joined the group, which made such a good sound that Ronstadt kept the new quartet together—at least, briefly. They set off on their own, becoming the Eagles. They won a Grammy in 1972 for "Lyin' Eyes" from the album *One of These Nights*. Leadon, who played banjo, mandolin, and guitar, left the band in '75 and started his own group, Natural Progressions.

Purple Prince ★ Yes, his name really is Prince—Prince Rogers Nelson, born in Minneapolis in 1958. His father was a jazz pianist with the Prince Rogers Trio, which he honored when his son was born. Young Prince moved back and forth between divorced parents and other relatives, finally ending up living in the basement of his best friend, who joined him in forming a band called Champagne. Three different recording companies offered him contracts, but he wanted control. He recorded his first album, *For You*, at a local studio in 1978, recording all the instruments himself and writing most of the music. He's been described as "fusing the 69 flavors of soul, gospel, rock, funk and punk into one sweet cone." His 1984 film *Purple Rain* is a thinly veiled autobiography filmed in Minneapolis. Since that year, he has recorded under his own label, Paisley Park, and in 1987 he built Paisley Park Studios, in Chanhassen. Among his No. 1 hits are "When Doves Cry" (1984), "Let's Go Crazy" (1984), "Kiss" (1986), and "Batdance" (1989).

The Jets

Eight Minneapolis kids, all from one family named Wolfgramm, made up a band called the Jets. The children of immigrants from Tonga, they started recording in 1986 and had several songs that reached the Top 40, including "Crush on You" and "You Got It All."

Songwriter a.k.a. Bob Dylan

Robert Allen Zimmerman was born in Duluth on May 24, 1941, and grew up in Hibbing. He didn't start using the name Bob Dylan (for the poet Dylan Thomas) until he began performing in high school. Dylan ran away from home several times before he left permanently to travel the country, often hopping freight trains. These travels inspired many of his social "protest" songs in the 1960s. He gained his initial fame for the song "Blowin' in the Wind." Other songs of his include "Like a Rolling Stone," "Mr. Tambourine Man," and "The Times They Are A-Changin'."

TV TIME

Two Minneapolis brothers made it big on TV. James (born 1918) and Peter (1926) Aurness both changed their names when they became actors. After recovering from Anzio-acquired wounds, James went to California and was spotted doing little theater. He became James Arness, better known as Matt Dillon, before the young actor with that name came along. He played the marshal on "Gunsmoke" for 20 years. His younger brother Peter became Peter Graves after serving as a newscaster in Minneapolis for several years. Graves starred in "Mission Impossible" and the miniseries "Winds of War."

The marshal and the mission

Hey! Coach!

A TV series that takes place in Minnesota is ABC's "Coach," a sitcom starring Craig T. Nelson as the football coach at Minnesota State. It started with a trial run in the spring of 1989 and has been on regularly since November of that year.

Bullwinkle J. Moose, who first found fame on the cartoon show "Rocky and His Friends," lives in Frostbite Falls, Minnesota. The not-ter-ribly-bright moose acquired his own show, "The Bullwinkle Show," in September 1961, and appeared on TV regularly until 1973. Like "Rocky and His Friends," "The Bullwinkle Show" was created by Jay Ward.

"Why don't you pull a rabbit out of the hat, Bullwinkle?"

The beauty from St. Paul

Blonde (though not originally) and voluptuous Loni Anderson, who first became famous on "WKRP in Cincinnati" and then became even more famous for marrying Burt Reynolds, was born in 1945, in St. Paul. She has a daughter by a very short-lived marriage when she was a teenager, and she and Reynolds have adopted a child.

Showing off Minneapolis

"The Mary Tyler Moore Show," one of the best-loved comedies in TV history, began in September 1970 with Mary Richards (actress Mary Tyler Moore) arriving in Minneapolis to hunt for a big-city job. The small-town Minnesotan went to work for a TV station, the nonexistent WJM-TV. The show, which lasted seven years, made a showcase of Minneapolis and helped turn it into a popular place to move to. The main characters in two spin-offs from the show, Rhoda and Phyllis, moved out of Minneapolis when their turn came.

Marshall for the defense

An actor for all media, E.G. (for Edda Gunnar) Marshall was born in Owatonna in 1910. He played on Broadway and in numerous movies. His face was already familiar to TV viewers in 1961 when he began his first (and one of TV's best) series, "The Defenders," in which he played the father of a father-and-son team of courtroom lawyers. Robert Reed, later of "The Brady Bunch," played his son. Marshall won two Emmy awards—in 1962 and 1963— for his role.

Emmy-winning Ed

Minneapolis-born actor Ed Flanders became known to the widest public for his Emmy-winning role of Dr. Westphal on "St. Elsewhere" in 1982. He had previously won a Tony and an Emmy for *A Moon for the Misbegotten* and an Emmy as Harry Truman in "Plain Speaking."

The athletic Mr. Anderson

Richard Dean Anderson, the star of the adventure series "MacGyver," was born in Minneapolis in 1950. The son of musicians, he hoped to become a hockey player, but two broken arms convinced him there was another way to go. In the years before he made it onto "General Hospital" as Dr. Jeff Webber, he combined acting and job hunting with lots of athletics. Anderson even made a 5,600-mile bicycle trip by himself from Minneapolis to Alaska and back.

From soaps to sitcoms

Julia Duffy, a St. Paul native, was out of a job as Dr. Althea Davis's daughter, Penny, in 1982 after the daytime soap, "The Doctors," folded. Duffy didn't stay unemployed for long. She next played an empty-headed princess in a short-lived medieval fantasy, "Wizards and Warriors." Success was found in Vermont on "Newhart" as the funny, sometimes self-infatuated maid, Stephanie Vanderkellen. She played the role from 1983 until 1990. From there she moved on to fill in the spot Delta Burke left on "Designing Women." Her stay was short—Delta's shoes were too big to fill.

MILLING, MINING, MANUFACTURING

First there were the furs, then the farmers. Next came the mines, and then the mills. Minnesota has always been a state that grew as business grew, starting in 1821 when five Swiss families settled near Fort St. Anthony, becoming the first strictly agricultural settlers.

And they never stopped coming. For 30 years during the last century, men came from northern Europe to look for work. They crowded together in Bridge Square, Minneapolis, sitting on the curbs by day and spending their nights in nearby dingy flophouses as they waited to be called for jobs cutting timber or laboring in the wheat fields, the railroad camps, or the mines. The square was considered to be the greatest labor center in the Northwest.

Today it's done differently, but Minnesota has continued to be a great place for turning ideas into products and businesses.

- Farming the Land
- Jolly Giants and Dinty Moores
- Computer Control
- The Money Men
- Building on Inventions
- Communicating with the World
- Flour Miller to America
- Timber Tales
- Minnesota Shows Its Metals
- The Merchandisers
- Travel by Water
- Travel by Land

FARMING THE LAND

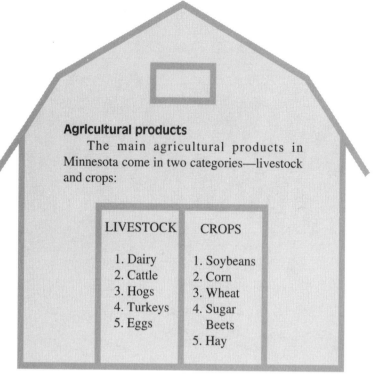

Agricultural products

The main agricultural products in Minnesota come in two categories—livestock and crops:

LIVESTOCK	CROPS
1. Dairy	1. Soybeans
2. Cattle	2. Corn
3. Hogs	3. Wheat
4. Turkeys	4. Sugar Beets
5. Eggs	5. Hay

The wild rice supply

($) Do it the old way and it will stay. Minnesotans are allowed to harvest wild rice only in the Indian way to protect the state's supply. They must manually shake the ripe grains off the plants, preferably into a canoe. Cultivated "wild" rice was first planted near Bemidji in 1950 when two farmers flooded a field and planted wild rice. A big industry centered in Clearwater, Polk, Beltrami, Aitkin, and Itasca counties has developed in recent years. Question: When is wild rice no longer wild?

Feeding cattle was Grimm

($) His neighbors thought immigrant farmer Wendelin Grimm was crazy. After all, you're supposed to feed cows corn during the winter, right? But Grimm thought otherwise. He had arrived in Carver County in 1858 with a 20-pound sack of alfalfa seed and planted some each year. Most of it was destroyed by the tough winters, but some survived and the neighbors began to notice that his cattle looked mighty good, even after a winter when food supplies were low. His answer was his "everlasting clover," which he had developed year by year into a hardy variety that could withstand the worst that Minnesota threw at it. Grimm alfalfa is among Minnesota's prime contributions to agriculture.

That's a cheese!

In 1914, a 6,000-pound cheese was made on a railroad flat car and shipped to the State Fair in St. Paul. It was probably the biggest cheese ever produced in one day.

$ A new $30-million ethanol plant will be operational in Winnebago by December of 1993. Five hundred farmers will sell 5 million bushels of corn a year to the plant, which will provide 40 new jobs and 15 million gallons of ethanol annually. Although ethanol doesn't do much to improve the atmosphere, it cuts down on the amount of oil imported for gasoline and gives farmers a new market for their crops.

Making ethanol

The murdering farmer

The nation as a whole didn't quite understand the depth of the farming recession in the early 1980s until news came that farmer James Lee Jenkins had lured the president and chief loan officer of the Buffalo Ridge State Bank into an ambush at a farm the bankers had foreclosed on several years earlier. The two bankers, Rudy Bluthe and Toby Thulin, were found shot to death, and Jenkins and his 18-year-old son Steven had disappeared. Some weeks later Jenkins was found in Paducah, Texas, having committed suicide. Steven turned himself in. His trial was held in Ivanhoe, Minnesota, in April 1984. He was found guilty of first-degree murder.

Oh Tannenbaum!

Christmas trees are big business in Minnesota. Approximately 400 Christmas tree growers provide over 800,000 trees each year valued at $25 million. The state ranks eighth nationally in the $1-billion business.

JOLLY GIANTS AND DINTY MOORE'S

$ George A. Hormel & Company, the largest independent meat and food processor in the United States and a Fortune 500 company, located in Austin, has the dubious honor of being the creator of one of the world's least respected foods, Spam. The maligned "mystery meat" made its debut in 1937 when Hormel executives needed to find a way to use surplus pork shoulder. George's creative son, Jay C., developed a product of chopped ham and pork shoulder called spiced ham (a.k.a. Spam) that needed no refrigeration. U.S. servicemen in World War II jokingly called it "meat that failed its physical." But Soviet leader Nikita Khrushchev couldn't understand the American attitude and remarked in his biography, "There were many jokes going around in the army, some of them off-color, about American Spam; it tasted good nonetheless. Without Spam, we wouldn't have been able to feed our army." Even Edward R. Murrow commented on Spam during a London report in 1942: "This is London. Although the Christmas table won't be lavish, there will be Spam for everyone." Even though the product is still derided, more than 3 million pounds of it are sold each year.

450 cans of Spam each minute!

Did "ja" know?
Jeno Francisco Paulucci is a Duluth man who has brought ethnic foods to America. In his Chinese guise he started ChunKing Chinese foods in 1954. Thirteen years later he sold the company to R.J. Reynolds and turned to pizza, creating Jeno's, Inc.

$ During the Depression, the Hormel meat-packing company canned a huge quantity of meat and potatoes in round tins for distribution to the hungry. But the program ended before Hormel used up its supply of tins. To get rid of them, they filled the tins with a stew that they called Dinty Moore's. It became the backbone of many people's diets and a handy way of carrying food for campers and hikers.

Another canned goodie

The cream of the crop

$ Minnesota Cooperative Creameries Association became the central shipping agent for a group of dairy cooperatives in 1921. Located in Arden Hills, the association's main product was butter, which it decided to package under a single label in 1924. Ideas for brand names were solicited from the member farmers and, by the end of the year, the name "Land O'Lakes" was chosen. The runner-up was "Maid O' the West." Land O'Lakes has grown to become the biggest food-marketing cooperative in the United States, with over 350,000 member farmers.

Exploding to success

$ Alexander Anderson, a scientist from Red Wing, discovered puffed rice in 1901. Anderson worked for the New York Botanical Garden,

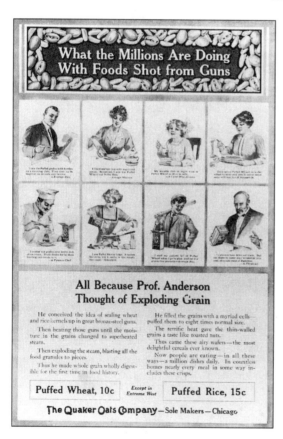

trying to find a way to produce starchy foods that would be easier for the body to digest. One day he tried cooking rice by putting some in a test tube, sealing the tube airtight, and putting it in an oven. When he took the tube out of the oven and broke it open, the rice exploded eight times bigger than normal, puffy and easy to eat. Anderson patented his process and wrote to friends in Minnesota's grain business. They brought Anderson to Minneapolis and set him up in a lab to continue work on refining his "invention." An assistant said of Anderson's many narrow escapes from explosions, "It's a wonder he doesn't blow himself up with the rice!"

A Chicago cereal company, Quaker Oats, heard about Anderson's work. They bought Anderson's patents and hired him to build a "puffing" machine that would be safe. He invented a "puffing cannon" that loaded and fired both rice and wheat automatically. The food was introduced at the St. Louis World's Fair in 1904, where people had to be shown what to do with it.

Here comes the Schwan's man!

$ In 1952 the owner of a family dairy in Marshall was looking for a way to increase income when he put one truck on the road to deliver ice cream to families at a time when other delivery businesses were selling their trucks. Since then Schwan's business has grown into a huge service that takes food products to people's homes at the time they say they want it, and at reasonable prices. The squarish yellow trucks of Schwan's Ice Cream and Finer Foods are recognized coast to coast.

Building a giant

Ward Cosgrove of the Minnesota Valley Canning Company brought a new kind of pea from England that was long, wrinkled, and large. It was unlike anything available at the time and Cosgrove bragged about its size, calling it the "green giant." The company applied for a new patent for "green giant," but since the words were descriptive they weren't patentable. After adding a giant as the company's symbol, they received their patent in 1925. The giant was colored green to "express the green of growing things in the rich earth of the Minnesota Valley . . ." The word *jolly* was added in 1935, along with a nice leaf outfit and a big grin.

Pillsbury (see p. 122) bought Green Giant in 1979 (and moved its headquarters to Chaska). However, the company and the city of Blue Earth, at the heart of the LeSueur Valley, erected the biggest giant in the world that year.

Green Giant

Statue at Blue Earth
Height: 55.5 ft including base
Weight: 8,000 pounds
Smile: 48 inches
Shoe Size: 78
Cost: $43,000

COMPUTER CONTROL

From gliders to computers

($) Northwestern Aeronautical Corp. of St. Paul built 1,500 wooden gliders during World War II. They were used to carry soldiers during airborne assaults, and many of NAC's craft were used in 1944 in the Normandy landings that started freeing Europe from the Nazi yoke. When the war ended and NAC had nothing to make, John E. Parker, the president, and Nebraskan William C. Norris, started making the earliest versions of computers. The company became Engineering Researching Associates (ERA) and produced the Atlas computer for the National Security Agency by 1950. The company was then purchased by Remington Rand, which was later bought by Sperry Gyroscope and became Sperry Rand, which produced Univac, the first major commercial computer.

Computers and supercomputers

($) When Sperry Rand, which had been the leader in computers, was being trounced by IBM, several men, including the original founder, William Norris, who had designed the Atlas, left and formed Control Data Corporation in Minneapolis to build large scientific computers. Its chief designer in later years was Seymour Cray who was capable of designing supercomputers that could handle the biggest problems imaginable. In 1972 Cray left to form his own company, Cray Research. He developed the world's most powerful computer, the liquid-cooled CRAY-2. It has a capacity of 32 million bytes of main memory and can carry out 250 million operations per second. Now they're getting even faster and more powerful.

Controlling the heat

$ Swiss-born Albert Butz came to Minnesota as a child. Although he later worked as a subscription book salesman in St. Paul, his real love was inventing and tinkering at his workbench. In 1884, he organized Butz and Mendenhall Hand Grenade Fire Extinguisher Company to market one of his inventions. His fire extinguishers were glass balls filled with water suspended from ceilings. These balls were supposed to drop from the ceiling in case of fire and extinguish it. At this same time Butz also invented a "damper flapper" that automatically adjusted the dampers in a furnace so that room temperatures could be constant without continual manual adjustment of dampers. But it didn't sell well because few furnaces and boilers were equipped with dampers that could be hooked to the device. He sold his damper flapper patent to his lawyers in the Twin Cities and moved to Chicago.

Through a failure and a reorganization, Minnesota businessman W.A. Sweatt became the owner of the Butz patent by 1902. Bit by bit, people began to see the value of the apparatus. But they found a major competitor in Honeywell Heating Specialties Co. of Wabash, Indiana. Also, neither company could grow because their patents blocked each other's development. Though the owners of the two firms disliked each other intensely, they merged their companies in 1927 into Minneapolis-Honeywell. Honeywell, Inc., is now the fourth largest publicly held company in Minnesota, with over 58,000 employees.

THE MONEY MEN

The big lender

$ In 1878, Frank Mackey of Minneapolis opened a finance company in the back of his jewelry store to lend money to employees between paychecks. In 1930, his was one of more than 30 such companies that were consolidated into Household Finance Corporation. During the Depression, the company set up a consumer education department to teach consumers how to deal with credit. One pamphlet showed that a family of five could live on $150 a month. In 1981, the firm's name was changed to Household International.

The big embezzler

$ Austin's Geo. A. Hormel & Co. firm was doing splendidly in the early 1920s: it had been a major supplier of meat to the armed forces in World War I, and had 1,000 Austin people on its payroll. Then Ransome J. Thomson became the company's assistant controller. Informing friends that he had inherited money from an aunt, he bought a farm on the Minnesota-Iowa border and began to develop it. Gradually it became a large chicken farm, a commercial dance pavilion, and even a resort catering to families. But at the same time, Hormel's accounts were showing a curious decline. Jay, the founder's son, located a "transfer of funds" check that showed funds going to Thomson and soon discovered that the man had stolen well over $1 million by continually moving funds among the company's many accounts. Now the company did not have the cash to make a payment on its own loans. The banks were ready to foreclose on the firm and shut it down when Hormel pledged everything he owned to guarantee the loans. The company was saved, and Thomson was sent to prison for 15 years.

💲 The infamous Northfield bank robbery wasn't even scheduled for Northfield. It was meant to take place in Mankato on September 7, 1876, but when the James and Younger gang rode into town and found Main Street crowded (with a convention, but they didn't know that), they abandoned their plans and set their sights on Northfield's First National Bank. The gang included the two James boys, three Younger boys, Clel Miller, William Stiles, and Charles Pitts.

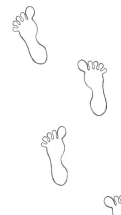

The gang members quietly spread themselves around the downtown area, while three of them entered the bank. During the robbery, they gunned down cashier Joseph Lee Heywood. An alert merchant sounded the alarm and rushed back to his hardware store and began handing out guns to anyone who wanted one, setting up a gunfight as the robbers emerged from the bank. Bob Younger was wounded, Clel Miller killed, and Stiles and Miller were left behind as the others escaped. A posse of 1,000 men took off after the robbers on a manhunt that lasted for weeks before they found Cole and Bob Younger and Charles Pitts near Madelia. Pitts was killed, but the Youngers surrendered, were taken to jail at Faribault, and eventually sentenced to life in prison. The James brothers, never captured, made their way to Missouri on stolen horses under cover of night. All this trouble for a mere $290!

The Younger brothers were paroled on July 14, 1901. Cole went to Missouri and joined the Frank James Wild West Show, but James killed himself in St. Paul. Northfield holds a "Defeat of Jesse James Celebration" each year. The main attraction is a large supply of foot-shaped "De Feet of Jesse James" cookies. Now that's taking a bite out of crime.

💲 In the early 1930s, when St. Paul was wide open to crooks, especially of the Chicago variety (see p. 62), kidnapping became an accepted way for a gang to make money. Harry Sawyer, St. Paul's crime boss, offered the gang made up of Ma Barker's sons and Alvin Karpis an idea—the kidnapping of William A. Hamm, the wealthy owner of Hamm's Brewery. On June 15, 1933, Hamm was nabbed while walking to his home. He was driven to Bensenville, Illinois. His family—against orders—promptly told the police. However, they managed to pay the $100,000 ransom demanded. Hamm was driven back to Minnesota and was released near the town of Wyoming. Roger "The Terrible" Touhy in Chicago was accused of the kidnapping but was acquitted. Al Capone, who was trying to get rid of Touhy's competition, then set up a fake kidnapping of Jake Factor. Touhy was found guilty of that deed and sent to prison. The Barkers and Al Karpis remained free.

Karpis and the Barkers, convinced that they had found the easiest way to get money, proceeded, on January 17, 1934, to kidnap Minneapolis banker Edward G. Bremer. They doubled the ransom, which was paid, though with difficulty. They had made a hash of several money-delivery attempts, making the process take three weeks, while Bremer was hidden in the same Illinois hideaway. Those screwups ultimately got Alvin Karpis convicted of kidnapping and sent to Alcatraz Prison for life. That "life" was short—he was shot while attempting to escape in 1939.

The home-grown kidnapper

💲 Perhaps taking the idea from newspaper headlines, Ironton loafer John Henry Seadlund and friend, James Atwood Gray, decided to kidnap someone famous. They prepared two box-like dugouts to hold the victim. The first was at Emily, Minnesota, and the second (a just-in-case box) was constructed at Spooner, Wisconsin. On September 25, 1934, they were driving through Franklin Park, Illinois, when they stopped an expensive Lincoln and forced the wealthy-looking driver, Charles S. Ross, a greeting-card manufacturer, from the car. They sped to Minnesota and parked their victim in the Emily dugout. They collected $50,000 in ransom from Ross's wife. Seadlund was captured when he paid in marked ransom money at the Santa Anita racetrack in California. He led the G-men to the graves of both Ross, his victim, and Gray, his partner, hidden in the Spooner dugout. Ironton's John Henry Seadlund was executed in Illinois on July 14, 1935.

The billionaire

💲 J. Paul Getty was born in Minneapolis in 1892, definitely not in poverty, because his father was already a millionaire oil dealer. J. Paul learned young how to wheel and deal in oil leases and made his own first million by the time he was 24, at which time he left Minnesota forever. It's estimated that he was worth at least $4 billion when he died in 1976.

BUILDING ON INVENTIONS

The miraculous mistake

💲 3M should probably be 2M today. The name of the huge 3M company stands for Minnesota Mining and Manufacturing, but it does no mining today. Maybe the third M is for "mistake!"

Five men—two railroad workers, a lawyer, a doctor, and a butcher—started the company to mine an abrasive mineral called corundum in Two Harbors. There wasn't much of the mineral and it didn't work anyway. They made only one sale of the material in two years and were going bankrupt when they switched to making sandpaper in the more traditional fashion and found themselves at least managing to stay in business. One stockholder, Lucius Pond Ordway of St. Paul, and a plumbing store owner who settled the company's indebtedness to him by taking stock, kept 3M going. Gradually, failures began to give way to successes. When William McKnight was appointed national sales director, he investigated customer complaints, developed a better product, and sales increased. With the developing auto industry, new abrasives were needed and the company developed a paper with aluminum oxide that could be used with metal. In 1921, 3M introduced wet-or-dry sandpaper and became the leader in the field.

The auto industry again propelled 3M toward new products because painting two-tone cars required a tape that could be applied and removed without damaging the surface. In 1925, 3M invented masking tape that could be pulled off without causing damage. An early customer told a salesman to "take this tape back to your stingy Scotch bosses and tell them to put more adhesive on it." That complaint inspired 3M's brandname of

"Scotch." A laboratory technician, Richard G. Drew of Minneapolis, developed the see-through cellophane tape now called Scotch tape in 1930. Today, tapes of all kinds—from recording to video to industrial—are important products of the company. In the summer of 1992 the 3M/Dwan Museum opened in Two Harbors to celebrate the history of sandpaper. 3M no longer mines corundum—only profits!

Those can't-do-without-'em notes

3M encourages new ideas from its employees, both for products and ways to help the environment. Art Fry of St. Paul used scraps of paper to keep his place in his choir hymnal, but the paper always fell out and he had to hurriedly scramble to the right page. During one of his exasperating choir practices, he remembered a little-known adhesive invented years before by 3M scientist Dr. Spencer Silver. The forgotten adhesive held but could be removed easily. Fry worked for a year and a half before taking his "sticky" notes to the marketing department. Their response was lukewarm until the results from a free city-wide giveaway in Boise, Idaho, revealed that 90 percent of those trying "Post-It Notes" would buy them again. That was 1978. The rest is history. They are now one of the top five office products in the nation and are sold in over 50 countries.

3M prides itself on being environmentally sound. *Landfill* **is not a popular word. The company uses materials once destined for the landfill in other products. These women are packaging a liquid absorbent for industrial use. It is made from the trim material from 3M face masks.**

$ Wool underwear wasn't very comfortable before George Munsing of Minneapolis patented a method of covering wool thread with silk in 1888. The silk took the itch out and launched Munsing and two partners into business under the name Northwestern Knitting Company. Later known as Munsingwear, the company specialized in underwear. In 1891, the company took out another patent for the "union suit," one-piece underwear that became popular overnight. Union suits were made until 1969 and brought back again in 1978 when the energy crisis forced people to wear one-piece "long johns" to keep warm.

Getting the itch out of underwear

$ Fred Jones invented truck air conditioning for a friend who had a trucking business because the ice used for cooling fresh foods often melted in hot weather. Jones and a friend formed the Thermo King Company, which adapted air conditioning for ships, autos, railroad cars, and airplanes. These innovations helped spur the development of the frozen food industry. In his lifetime, Jones took out over 50 patents, which included movie-ticket dispensers, portable X-ray machines, and a motor for ice-cream makers.

The cool inventor

Hey, Culligan Man!

$ Emmett Culligan of Porter was a young man who knew the value of prairie when no one else did. After college, he earned several hundred thousand dollars by buying cheap prairieland, clearing it, and sowing flax. It was there, so he used it. He did the same with a machine that used natural minerals to filter other, unwanted minerals from water. In 1924 in St. Paul, he started a company that manufactured and sold water softeners. However, having had to fight a long legal battle about patents, he was in no shape to withstand the Depression, and he went broke. Several years later, working in Illinois, he devised a scheme by which people wouldn't have to buy the softeners, they could just lease them. In 1936, in Northbrook, Illinois, Culligan was at it again. And this time his business succeeded. Franchises opened all over the country and housewives began calling for their Culligan man.

COMMUNICATING WITH THE WORLD

First newspaper

$ The first newspaper published in Minnesota territory was the product of New Hampshire-born journalist James Madison Goodhue. The *Minnesota Pioneer* was published in 1849 at St. Paul. Originally he was going to call it the *Epistle of St. Paul*, but he was talked out of that punning name. Goodhue used the paper to spread word of the joys of life in Minnesota, hoping to attract more people to the territory. Although the paper's name and ownership changed, today's *St. Paul Pioneer Press* is a direct descendant of Goodhue's paper.

The biter bit

$ James M. Goodhue was known for the strong language he used in attacking wrongs and people who didn't measure up—in his opinion. On January 16, 1851, Goodhue printed an especially pointed attack against Judge Cooper—seems the judge wasn't around enough to defend himself and that was Goodhue's complaint. He also called him a "miserable drunkard," and "an ass." The paper hadn't been out long when Joseph Cooper, the judge's brother, met Goodhue on the steps of the capitol. Instead of a friendly greeting, Cooper yelled, "I'll blow your *@^%* brains out," and both gentlemen drew pistols. The sheriff arrived immediately and took away their guns, but Cooper pulled out a knife and Goodhue drew another pistol. In the scuffle that followed, Goodhue was stabbed and Cooper was wounded. No one was arrested, and both men survived. Goodhue contended that Cooper's attack was part of a long-standing murder conspiracy against him. When Goodhue died of natural causes in 1853, most of St. Paul's citizens were surprised he had lasted so long without being murdered by an angry reader!

Turning on radio and TV

$ The first radio station in Minnesota was WLB, the University of Minnesota station, in 1921. It later became KUOM. The first TV broadcast in Minneapolis took place in 1931, carried out by George W. Young of radio station WDGY. It was a brief and fuzzy picture of Mayor Kurze. KSTP in Minneapolis began to experiment with television about that same time, but it wasn't until April 27, 1948, that the station began to operate as the state's first commercial TV station, broadcasting to an estimated 2,500 sets in the Twin Cities area.

$ St. John's University at Collegeville started a small radio station, KSJR, in 1967, to carry classical music and other features that were missing from regular radio. By 1971 it had become Minnesota Educational Radio, and three years later Minnesota Public Radio. It soon became known throughout the nation for its star performer, Garrison Keillor, originally of Anoka (see p. 99). In 1982, MPR was one of the founders of American Public Radio.

Talking to the public

Off with the gag

In 1925, Minnesota passed a law restricting news-papers from publishing obscene or malicious items, as a way of fighting the anti-Semitic papers that were multiply-ing in the area. The newly organized American Civil Liberties Union decided to help the little *Saturday Press* fight the law on the basis of the First Amendment. The U.S. Supreme Court ruled in 1931 that Minnesota's "gag law" was unconstitutional, the first time it had ruled in such a case.

$ St. Paul native DeWitt Wallace, the son of the Macalester College president, was recuperating from a wound acquired at Verdun, France, during World War I, when he became frustrated at the length of many magazine articles and began to look for a solution. He spent many long hours practicing condensing articles so that no information was lost and they were smooth and readable. After the war, he moved to New York, where he ran into Lila Bell Acheson, whom he had previously met in Tacoma, Washington. They married and began to solicit start-up funds by mailing out promotion circulars. They soon accumulated $5,000, with which they sought subscriptions to a totally new kind of magazine, the *Reader's Digest*, in 1922. During World War II, Wallace was at times accused of trying to direct opinion instead of just condensing, but the controversy made the magazine continue to grow. By 1980 it had a circulation of 30 million, making it the biggest magazine in the world. In 1972, the Wallaces received the Medal of Freedom for their philan-thropic works.

Little articles, big magazine

$ He may have been born on April Fool's Day, but William Benton was no fool. Vice president of the University of Chicago, the Minneapolis-born advertising executive discovered in 1943 that Sears Roebuck & Company owned the *Encyclopaedia Britannica*, which had originally been British, and wasn't doing very much with it. He persuaded Sears to donate it to the university, and the board accepted on condition that Benton invest some of his own money in it. He agreed, and gradual-ly came to own the encyclopedia, paying royal-ties to the university. He brought the encyclope-dia back to the respect it had previously had, and by the time of his death in 1973, it had earned almost $50 million for the university.

The inadvertent encyclopedia owner

MINNESOTA AND ITS NEWSPAPER PULITZERS

Westbrook Pegler was a reporter who won a 1941 Pulitzer Prize for reporting on racketeering in labor unions. Usually, however, there was not enough agreement on the controversial writer for any group to give him a prize. Growing up in Chicago, Minneapolis-born Pegler became a stringer for the United Press by age 16 and soon after was sent to Europe to cover World War I. Starting a column in 1925, he rarely thereafter did straight reporting. Instead, he became known for his acerbic wit, outrageous opinions, and great readability.

Minneapolis-born journalist **Harrison Salisbury** graduated from the University of Minnesota and went right to work for United Press. In 1944, he was sent to the Soviet Union, from which he sent dispatches describing the end of World War II. In the years following the war he was a one-man bureau in Moscow for *The New York Times*. He watched the worst of the Stalin years and purges, unable to report much of it because his dispatches were censored. When he returned to the United States after Stalin's death, he was able to describe what had been kept secret before and in 1955 he won a Pulitzer Prize for international reporting. He published two large volumes on Russian history, which are regarded as standards in the field. During the Vietnam War, Salisbury wrote against America's actions and some government leaders tried to discredit him. Many people believe that he was denied a second Pulitzer because of his opinions. Salisbury had a 1978 best seller with *Black Nights, White Snow*.

A Minnesota newspaper has won the Pulitzer Prize only one time—in 1948, when **Nat S. Finney** won for national reporting on the *Minneapolis Tribune*.

FLOUR MILLER TO AMERICA

The Pillsbury plus

$ Charles A. Pillsbury, a native of New Hampshire, gave up his retail shop in Montreal and went to Minnesota, where his uncle, John S., was already running a hardware store in St. Anthony. John loaned Charles the money to purchase a third share in the Frazee and Murphy flour mill on June 4, 1869, turning it into the impressive-sounding Pillsbury Flour Mills Company. His trademark, Pillsbury's Best XXXX, was adopted in 1872. The symbol XXX had long been used by bakers to denote quality. Pillsbury added an extra X and the word "Best" to make sure consumers understood that his flour was of premium quality. In 1883, his Pillsbury A Mill, the largest in the world, opened, using the all-new roller technology. Only a few years later, Charles sold out to an English group, but remained on the job with the highest salary ever given to an American executive. Starting in 1907, Pillsbury began to buy back his old company from the English combine.

Charles's uncle, John S. Pillsbury, didn't remain just a retailer. He became the governor of the state in 1876, and one of the main problems he had to deal with was the economic losses of farmers from the five-year plague of grasshoppers (see p. 23). Having served on the board of regents of the University of Minnesota from 1863 to 1895, John S. Pillsbury is called the "father of the university."

Among the companies that Pillsbury owns are Burger King, Green Giant, Baker's Square, Totino's Pizza, and Häagen-Dazs ice cream.

The biggest explosion

On the morning of May 2, 1878, at about 7 A.M., the Washburn A Mill in Minneapolis—largest flour mill in the United States—blew up. Two other explosions, in the Humbolt and Diamond mills, followed. Eye witnesses told of seeing the whole roof of the mill lifted 500 feet in the air by the force of the explosion. Eighteen men were killed and all of surrounding Minneapolis caught on fire. Nothing like this had ever occurred anywhere in the world and the story made international headlines. For a while, people feared Minneapolis would burn to the ground.

An investigation into the cause of the disaster began immediately, but, since all the men in the Washburn factory had died, the results were inconclusive. There was never a real explanation of the explosion, but Dr. R.J. Taylor of Galesburg, Illinois, deduced that the flour-laden air had formed "nitroglycerin" and had been ignited by a spark from a cigar, a whip, or some sort of friction. His estimate of the force of the explosion—equal to 30,323 25-pound kegs of gunpowder—has never been disputed.

Something good did grow from the tragedy—a greater understanding of dust explosions. Researchers learned that mill dust suspended in the air would explode like gunpowder when ignited. Cadwallader C. Washburn rebuilt with dust catchers in the mill. He also began to use porcelain or steel rolls, devices that not only lessened the hazard of fire, but also revolutionized the milling industry by increasing the amount of flour produced from the grains of wheat.

The Olympics of flour

Gold medals were awarded to the Washburn, Crosby Company of Minneapolis on June 8, 1880, for showing the best flour at the Miller's International Exhibition in Cincinnati. From these awards, the "Gold Medal" brand of flour came to be. The Washburn, Crosby Company merged with other mills in 1928 and became General Mills. Two years later, the company introduced Bisquick, a ready-to-use, pre-mixed flour developed from the idea of a young executive named Carl Smith.

Some brands General Mills now owns include Red Lobster, Parker Brothers, Eddie Bauer, Ship 'n Shore, Lionel, and Kenner.

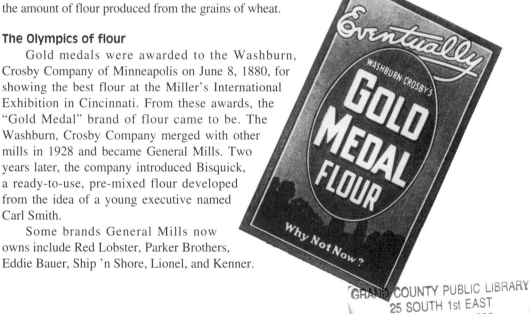

A woman for all seasons

1936

1986

$ The Washburn Crosby Company (later General Mills, Inc.) created an imaginary woman named Betty Crocker in 1921 to handle inquiries from homemakers about cooking and baking. "Crocker" was the last name of a retiring executive and "Betty" just seemed like an all-American name. By 1940, a company survey revealed that 90 percent of the country's housewives "knew" Betty Crocker—some even believed she was a real person. Only Eleanor Roosevelt was more popular.

To stay contemporary, Betty Crocker's look has changed seven times since 1936. The 1965 Betty Crocker was drawn to look like Jackie Kennedy; the 1968 version was more like Mary Tyler Moore; and the 1972 version was more businesslike as feminism took root in the country. The current Betty Crocker appeared in 1986 amidst a debate about whether to change her racial background. Company officials decided that "consumers see Betty Crocker as white." Over the years, the popular Ms. Crocker has received fan mail, including numerous marriage proposals. And then there are fans like syndicated columnist Bob Greene, who organizes Betty Crocker look-alike contests as a way of showing his love for her.

TIMBER TALES

Lincoln logs

$ One of the most famous logging raftsmen on the upper Mississippi was Abraham Lincoln's cousin, Captain Stephen B. Hanks. In 1843, he piloted the first raft of logs to St. Louis from St. Croix. In 1857 he won a $1,000 prize by reaching St. Paul first in a field of twenty boats and opening up the navigation season.

Paul, Babe, and Minnesota

$ Paul Bunyan grew to dimensions far beyond those of a questionable local logging legend (see p. 58) because of an advertising man named W.B. Laughead. He had heard all about Paul Bunyan, his exploits, and his Blue Ox, Babe, when he worked in Minnesota's logging camps as a young man. When Laughead was given the job of developing an advertising campaign for Red River Lumber Company in 1914, his knowledge of Paul Bunyan came in handy. The whole campaign was developed around the bigger-than-life lumberjack. It was so popular the company had to publish a promotional booklet with additional adventures.

Paul Bunyan and Babe the Blue Ox at Bemidji.

MINNESOTA SHOWS ITS METALS

$ Seven brothers by the name of Merritt acquired from their pioneer father the belief that there was iron in the Mesabi. They spent two decades looking for it, but never finding the ore . . . until November 16, 1890, when the leader of one crew working near Virginia found red soft hematite, which contained 64 percent iron. They began to bring out the ore, even organizing the Mountain Iron Company to manage it and a railroad to carry it. But the brothers, called the Seven Iron Men, lost control of the range to others with more fiscal smarts.

The Merritt way

Minnesota has three iron ranges—the Vermilion, the Cuyuna, and the Mesabi. The demand for Minnesota iron ore reached its peak during World War II when nearly 85 percent of all iron ore smelted into steel came from Minnesota mines. Minnesotans can proudly say that "modern America was built on the rocks of Minnesota." Still a leader in iron ore production, the state provides about 70 percent of the iron mined in the country today.

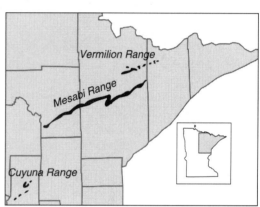

The Vermilion Range

The Vermilion is 100 miles long and 5 to 10 miles wide. The ore deposits run vertically, so shafts had to be dug and mined conventionally. The ore was first mined by prospector George Stuntz, who opened the Breitung mine in 1875 and began shipping ore in August 1884. Stuntz established the little town of Tower, which was a three-day, two-night trip from Duluth. Life was very hard, with the winters making it even harder. A shopkeeper in Tower wanted a 6-foot thermometer that wouldn't freeze at minus 40° F.

Stuntz established the Soudan mine, the deepest and oldest mine in Minnesota. The first iron shipped out of it was the first ore carried by train in Minnesota, on July 30, 1884. It soon became known as the "Cadillac of mines" because its hard rock made it almost impossible for cave-ins to occur, the ventilation was good, and the tunnels were dry with no poisonous gas.

The mine still contains some of the richest ore in the world, but new technology and economics forced its closing in 1963, when the mine was at 2,400 feet. The Tower-Soudan mine, donated by U.S. Steel to the state, is now a 1,000-acre state park. Visitors can take a small train deep into the lowest level of the mine.

$ Cuyler Adams was a well-known mining engineer who discovered and developed the last great mineral range in Minnesota, the Cuyuna Range, in Crow Wing County, starting in the 1890s. The range was named after his dog, Una—he took the first three letters of his name and added his dog's name to get Cuyuna. The first mine in the range, the Kennedy Mine, opened in 1911. The range was found to contain ore with a high percentage of manganese, which is scarce in the United States. Ninety percent of the manganese the United States needed during World War II came from this range.

The Cuyuna Range

The giant Mesabi

The Mesabi Range, locally known just as "the range," is located some 75 miles northwest of Duluth near Hibbing, Chisholm, Virginia, and Eveleth. Nicollet called the area "Missabay Heights," though *mesabi* is the name given to a legendary Ojibway giant. The Mesabi is 110 miles long and 2 to 120 miles wide. By October 1892, the first ore shipment left the town of Mountain Iron, the starting point of the range.

Such financial giants as John D. Rockefeller, Andrew Carnegie, Henry W. Oliver, and James J. Hill of the Great Northern Railroad provided the money to develop the Mesabi Range. In 1901, J. Pierpont Morgan, the New York financial magnate, consolidated the Carnegie, Rockefeller, and Oliver interests into the powerful U.S. Steel Corporation. In nearly a century of operation, billions of tons of ore have been shipped from the Mesabi. Over 30 percent of the world's iron ore was mined in the Mesabi during the 1940s. Its wealth promises to last another 200 years.

The first mining strike in the Mesabi

(S) Mine workers in the Mesabi Range went on strike in 1916, with the support of the International Workers of the World, the IWW or "Wobblies." The strike was planned by the Metal Mine Workers' Industrial Union, trying to get a hold on the workers. The IWW sent in its top organizers to help, including Elizabeth Gurley Flynn, the "Rebel Girl." The state American Federation of Labor opposed the strike because the strikers were unskilled immigrants rather than skilled workers. Women and their children did much of the picketing. However, the strike was called off after only three months when funds had run out and it became clear that there would be no support coming from outside. Within weeks, the sawmill workers of the area began a union movement, also organized by the IWW.

The biggest pit

(S) Hull Rust Mahoning Mine at Hibbing is the world's largest open-pit mine. Visible from outer space as a "man-made Grand Canyon," it was made by the removal of 1.4 billion tons of earth. Part of it is still being mined by the Hibbing Taconite Company. When the mine was being expanded in 1918, the original town of Hibbing had to be moved to make way for the enlarged hole. The bottom of the open pit is now flooded.

$ Henry Eames, state geologist, started the Minnesota "Gold Rush" when he prospected in the Vermilion Lake area in 1865. He had discovered iron ore, but that wasn't what he wanted. He told an associate, "To hell with iron . . . its gold we're after." The specimen of quartz he took back to St. Paul was more exciting to him because he was sure it contained gold. The sample was delivered to Governor Stephen Miller who sent it off to the mint in Philadelphia to be examined. The U.S. Mint reported that the 3-pound piece of quartz was estimated to contain $25.63 in gold and $4.42 in silver to the ton. The governor made the report public in September and Minnesota had visions of replacing California as the Gold Rush state. Speculators pointed out that gold mining was profitable at only $6-$8 per ton and this was almost $30 to the ton. By 1866 about 300 people were prospecting at Vermilion Lake. The gold rush died down as fast as it began—not a trace was found.

Fools' gold rush

THE MERCHANDISERS

$ Richard Warren Sears, a native of Stewartville, was working as a railway station agent in North Redwood in 1886 when a misdirected shipment of watches arrived on his platform. He sold them to other railway agents up and down the line. Taking his profit, he moved to Minneapolis and opened a watch store. Succeeding further, he moved his business to Chicago, where he hired a young watch repairman named Alvah C. Roebuck. Their first catalog, distributed in 1887, still went to station agents, but the following year they began to sell to the general public, always offering a money-back guarantee. Selling the watch company, Sears and Roebuck moved to Minnesota and started a mail-order company. On moving back to Chicago, the first Sears, Roebuck & Co. catalog revolutionized merchandising. In 1895, Roebuck sold his part of the business to Julius Rosenwald. In 1993, Sears went out of the catalog business.

Pocket watches and catalogs

$ George Draper Dayton, a native New Yorker who became a Minnesota banker-turned-realtor, found himself in 1895 the owner of a piece of corner property in downtown Minneapolis. He built an office building, where two young men named Mosher and Loudon wanted to open a dry-goods store, but lacked sufficient capital. Dayton agreed to provide the capital. He wasn't silent for long, however, because it quickly became clear that Mosher and Loudon didn't have the smarts to compete. Dayton bought them out and began to run the store with his son, Draper Dayton.

The grand retailer

At approximately the same time, the J.L. Hudson Company of Detroit was developing along similar lines. Although Hudson's purchased Dayton's, the two chains of stores developed separately for many years. Dayton's started the Target chain of discount stores in 1961, with the first store in Roseville. In 1966, it created B. Dalton Bookseller. It also owns the Mervyn's chain and Marshall Field & Company. In 1984, Hudson's and Dayton's combined to become Dayton Hudson Department Store Company, the largest individual department store company in the country, employing 168,000 people.

Serious quality

Bemidji Woolen Mills has produced its red "buffalo plaid" lumberjackets since 1920. The jackets are made individually and are advertised as "seriously long-wearing." A customer returned her jacket in 1988 with a minor complaint, a button had fallen off and she didn't have a replacement. The jacket had been purchased in 1930, but the company was happy to replace it.

Minnesota malls

The nation's first enclosed mall, called Southdale, was built at Edina in 1956. It is a two-story mall built by Dayton's. In 1992, the world's largest enclosed mall (a record that will probably not stand very long) was opened with the Mall of America, in Bloomington. The mall is a 4.2-million-square-foot complex with a 7-acre theme park. It was built at a cost of $625 million. LEGO Imagination Center (at left) is among the retailers.

TRAVEL BY WATER

Navigating the river

$ The *Virginia*, first steamboat to navigate as far north as Fort Snelling, set off from St. Louis on April 21, 1823. Major Lawrence Taliaferro, Indian agent at the fort, as well as Great Eagle, a Sauk chief, and an Italian refugee named Beltrami were among the passengers. Since the river wasn't well known, the boat traveled only by day except once when a huge forest fire made night travel possible. Beltrami later wrote that the fire looked like "the undulating lava of Vesuvius or Aetna. This fire accompanied us with some variations for fifteen miles." After 20 days and 729 miles, the *Virginia* reached Fort Snelling, becoming the first steamboat to travel that far up the Mississippi. That same year, however, the famous ship hit a snag near the mouth of the Ohio and sank where its hull remains today.

It was another 27 years before a steamboat succeeded in reaching the Falls of St. Anthony, and it took a reward to make it happen. On May 7, 1850, the steamboat *Anthony Wayne* reached the falls, earning $200 for the captain.

The whaleback

Alexander McDougall was an immigrant from Scotland who was raised in Canada and then settled in Duluth. Starting at age 16 as a deckhand, within 10 years he was playing a major role in the design of passenger ships for the Anchor Line. Fascinated with the task of moving freight on the Great Lakes, he designed and patented a special kind of freighter used for moving iron ore, coal, and grain.

$ The government chartered the *Fanny Harris* to take troops from Fort Ridgely to St. Paul in April 1861, a journey of 300 miles. The Minnesota River was flooded, and the boat's captain decided to leave the dangerous river channel at Belle Plaine rather than fight the raging water, uprooted trees, and floating houses. The flooded fields looked like a safer route than the raging river. The boat "jumped" the bank as the throttle was thrown open while passengers hung on to anything attached. After going 10 miles across flooded land, the *Fanny Harris* made its way back to the river channel and got to Fort Ridgley in the record time of four days—a speed record that was never broken! Who said you can't travel as the crow flies?

Overland boat trip sets record

TRAVEL BY LAND

$ When the enlargement of the area being strip-mined at Hibbing forced the mining company to announce that the entire town would have to be moved, two men, Carl E. Wickman and Andrew G. Anderson, hired a large open car to transport people from the old town to the new. They owned a Hupmobile, which they had purchased hoping to start a dealership, but it was too much car for the people in the area. Liking the ease with which they made money, they merged with an in-town taxi service to form the Mesaba Transportation Company. Wickman, who remained in charge, soon ordered a vehicle especially made to carry lots of people at once. It was probably the world's first bus.

Leave the driving to them

In the 1920s, an Oakland, California, company came out with the Safety Coach, which had seven rows of seats each holding four people. This bus became known as a Greyhound. Wickham's company became Northland Transportation and acquired smaller bus lines. During one six-week period, he bought out 60 small bus lines. In 1930, he reorganized all his holdings as The Greyhound Corporation. The Chicago-based company guarantees you can "Leave the driving to us."

$ In 1954 three Roseau entrepreneurs, Edgar and Allan Heteen and David Johnson, formed Polaris Industries, Inc. (named after the North Star) to make corn cribs, farm elevators, straw choppers, and various other equipment. Dave and Allan, tired of using skis to reach their favorite winter spots, scrounged parts from the new company and built a machine that moved across snow. Edgar, angry at their dreaming and scheming, sold the contraption to a wealthy local businessman to pay their bills. Allan, undaunted by Edgar's anger, started on "Number 2," which, once again, Edgar sold to meet the payroll. That first year, Edgar sold six "iron dogs," as the early snowmobiles were affectionately called. By 1990, Polaris employed 1,100 people in Roseau and made payroll easily on sales of $300 million annually.

Winter fun

In-line wheels

💲 In 1980, two former high-school hockey players from Minneapolis, Brennan and Scott Olson, had an idea for a way to train for winter hockey all summer long. They made a pair of roller skates with the four wheels in a line instead of at four corners of a rectangle. Calling their company Rollerblade, Inc., they started producing their products from a garage and selling them to hockey players. By 1987 the company started marketing Rollerblades as a fitness product and quickly captured 70 percent of the market. Over 700,000 people now glide to fitness on ultramodern polyurethane wheels. The company has more than 400 employees at their plant in Minnetonka.

PAN
The Queen of the Highway

His follow-through was the problem

Samuel Conner Pandolfo was a con man or a genius—or both. His Pan Motor Company of St. Cloud had 23,000 stockholders before it had a car (the stock was sold on the basis of sample cars built by someone else). He even built Pan Town, a subdivision of nice houses for his workers. Pan eventually manufactured over 750 cars but was forced—many people say, by dirty Detroit competitors—to shut down, and his company became a widely cited example of illegal stock promotions. Others say Pandolfo was a crook and deserved his stay in prison on a 1919 conviction for mail fraud in the Chicago courtroom of Judge Kenesaw Mountain Landis.

NORTH COUNTRY SPORTS

Minnesota has always been a sports arena, since the Native Americans played a lacrosse-type game in the open areas of the woodlands. The voyageurs and lumberjacks challenged each other in contests of skill. And, though the state may not have been represented in the major leagues and associations for many years, things have since changed greatly. In fact, for 11 months in 1991 and 1992, the Minneapolis area became the focus of all sporting eyes in the nation. In that one brief period, four major events were held at the Metrodome: the Stanley Cup finals, in which the North Stars unexpectedly appeared, the college basketball Final Four, the Super Bowl, and the World Series, which was won by the Minnesota Twins. In addition, the U.S. Open golf tournament was held at nearby Chaska. There's certainly nothing mediocre about the Minnesota sporting life.

- In the Air—Fun and Science
- Those Arenas
- Minnesota's Own in Baseball
- The Cities' Twins
- Slam Dunk
- The College Pigskin Game
- The Pro Pigskin Game
- The Pro Football Hall of Famers
- In the Ring
- Stars on the Ice
- Snow Time
- Odds and Ends
- Angling for Pleasure

IN THE AIR—FUN AND SCIENCE

The Great Northwest what?

The first known balloon ascension to take place in Minnesota was by William Markoe in 1857. Balloons were still pretty hot stuff (air-wise, and they still are) in 1881 when Samuel A. King launched his *Great Northwest* at Minneapolis on September 12. King's intention was to carry seven reporters and a military observer from Minnesota to the East Coast. His huge balloon was capable of the feat—after all, it was 95 feet high and 185 feet around the bag. But some plans just go awry, and this was one of them. The *Great Northwest* landed in a farmer's field just east of Minneapolis.

First woman in space   Minnesota-born Jeannette Ridlong became the wife of Swiss-born scientist Jean Felix Piccard, which opened up many fascinating opportunities for her, one of which gave her the privilege of being the first woman in space. Her husband, along with his twin brother Auguste, was one of the prime researchers into the upper atmosphere. In fact, he started flights of people in sealed gondolas, being carried to altitudes far beyond the point where breathing is possible. On October 23, 1934, at Ford Airport in Dearborn, Michigan, the husband and wife ascended in a hydrogen-filled balloon, with Jeannette piloting the balloon while Jean worked with the instruments that were measuring cosmic radiation. They reached an altitude of 57,579 feet, 11 miles, becoming the first balloonists to reach the stratosphere and allowing Jeannette to legitimately be referred to as the first woman in space. Thereafter, she piloted five other craft into the stratosphere. After Jean's death, Jeannette Piccard became a consultant to NASA.

On July 29, 1974, at age 82, Jeannette Piccard achieved another of her lifelong dreams. In a church service in Philadelphia, she and 10 other women who had long been deacons in the Episcopal church were ordained into the priesthood by four bishops who felt that women should not be kept out of the priesthood. Three years later, she and another of the 11, Dr. Alla Bozarth Campbell, were recognized by the bishop of Minnesota as priests "in good standing."

Ah youth!

AWESOME

Donna Wiederkehr achieved a record of setting the most hot-air balloon records ever by any person on one flight. The fourteen-year-old girl from St. Paul achieved this honor on March 13, 1975, during a flight that lasted 2 hours and 40 minutes, with the balloon reaching an altitude of 1,200 feet.

Balloon into space   As part of the U.S. Air Force's research into the effects of high altitude on humans for future space flight, Major D.G. Simons launched the *Man High II* on August 19, 1957, from the town of Crosby. He had no chance to enjoy the view, however, because he was encased in a metal capsule only 8 feet long and 3 feet in diameter. He was supposed to record what happened to him physically and psychologically during the flight. Meant to last 24 hours, the balloon got caught in severe storms and it was an additional eight hours before Simons's craft landed at Elm Lake, South Dakota. Recording instruments showed that the balloon rose to 105,000 feet (that's almost 21 miles!) during the flight, an altitude record.

The Lone Eagle

Aviation hero Charles A. Lindbergh, Jr., was born in Michigan, but he lived in Little Falls with his parents until he graduated from high school. His father was a prominent attorney who served in the House of Representatives from 1907 to 1917. Charles A. Lindbergh State Park in Little Falls is named for the famed pilot's father, not him (see p. 52). However, the pilot attended the dedication in 1974, just weeks before he died at his home in Hawaii.

The man who became known as the Lone Eagle gave up engineering school to learn to fly in Lincoln, Nebraska. In that era when the sight of an airplane was still awesome, he flew major exhibition shows for a while and then piloted the U.S. mail, until he learned about the $25,000 prize being offered for the first non-stop flight from New York to Paris. Some St. Louis, Missouri, businessmen funded the building of his Ryan monoplane, which he called the *Spirit of St. Louis*. Packing every cubic inch of the aircraft with fuel, he barely got airborne from Roosevelt Field on May 20, 1927, and $33^1/_2$ hours later he arrived in Paris, a hero. Never again was he without public attention, adulation, or anger. He wrote the story of his flight in *We*, making his aircraft a featured character in the book.

Lindbergh married Anne Morrow, the daughter of the U.S. ambassador to Mexico, and after flying around the world, they settled in New Jersey. In March 1932, their son was kidnapped from his second-floor nursery and murdered. Bruno Hauptmann was convicted of the crime and executed. The "Lindbergh Act" passed as a result makes taking a victim across state lines a federal capital crime.

On the grounds of the Minnesota State Capitol, a statue created by Paul Grandlund in 1985 depicts Charles Lindbergh, Jr., as a boy and a man.

At the beginning of World War II, Lindbergh became a fierce isolationist, causing many people to accuse him of being a Nazi. However, once the United States became involved, he served both in the United States and in the Pacific as a civilian technician. Lindbergh's 1953 book, *The Spirit of St. Louis*, won a Pulitzer Prize for biography.

THOSE ARENAS

The mighty Metrodome

The Hubert H. Humphrey Metrodome is the home of the Minnesota Twins, the Minnesota Vikings, and the University of Minnesota Golden Gophers football team. The first air-supported dome in major league baseball, the structure was begun in December 1979 and opened in 1982. Twin Cities' fans weren't so sure the Dome was going to be a good thing because it appeared to represent the end of tailgate parties and the nostalgia of macho football viewing in the bitter cold. There was even a "Dump the Dome" movement, though it came to naught once the Dome opened. The Dome seats about 63,000 people for baseball and football. Karal Ann Marling, professor of American Studies at the U. of M., describes the Metrodome as having "an uncanny resemblance to a cuddly sugar bowl."

The Metrodome must be lucky because by 1993 the Twins had lost only one post-season game in the Dome since it opened in 1982, losing to Toronto in 1991 during game two of the World Series.

The Target Center

When Harvey Ratner and Marv Wolfenson were arranging the Timberwolves' franchise (see p. 140), they also planned a new downtown stadium for Minneapolis. Dayton Hudson's Target Stores came in on the plan and the new arena was called the Target Center. It officially opened on October 13, 1990, with a "Jump Ball." The building includes a 160,000-square-foot health club, the 13th in Ratner and Wolfenson's chain. The arena holds more than 20,000 people and boasts more restrooms than any other sports arena in the nation (and more than half of them are for women—a real breakthrough for reality!).

MINNESOTA'S OWN IN BASEBALL

Millers and Saints

Minneapolis and St. Paul had professional baseball teams by the mid-1880s and belonged to the same league. For 70 years, the games played between the two teams were more than games—they became battles for civic pride and honor. The Minneapolis Millers played at Nicollet Park and the St. Paul Saints played at Lexington Park. By 1920, the teams were featuring doubleheaders in double places—a morning game in one park, followed by an afternoon game in the other.

St. Paul White Sox?

In 1900, Ban Johnson, head of the Western League, took Comiskey's St. Paul team and moved it to Chicago. He renamed his league the American League and renamed the team the White Sox in commemoration of the old Chicago White Stockings. When the American Baseball League was organized in Philadelphia that year, it included teams from Minneapolis, Chicago, Indianapolis, Detroit, Buffalo, Cleveland, Kansas City, and Milwaukee.

Charles Albert Bender was a Chippewa Indian born in Brainerd in 1884. He attended the Carlisle (Pennsylvania) Indian School where Jim Thorpe was later a student. Bender, known as "Chief," joined the Philadelphia Athletics in 1903 and became one of Connie Mack's favorite starters. Mack said, "If everything depended on one game, I just used Albert." Bender took the A's to five World Series, including their first one, in 1910. After leaving the Athletics, Bender was a baseball coach with the U.S. Naval Academy and the Chicago White Sox. Minnesota's only Baseball Hall of Famer up to 1993, Bender was inducted in 1953.

Minnesota's one and only

The Sting

In the summer of 1887, the community team at Dassel won the first game of a season-ending doubleheader much too easily, the town of Hutchinson thought. When it was discovered that Dassel had hired a professional team, Hutchinson wasn't to be outdone. They secretly hired professional players along with an umpire, Jack Bennett from Minneapolis. On the day of the second game, all of Hutchinson went to Dassel, confident of a win. Bennett arrived in Dassel, supposedly to advertise a Minneapolis exposition. Dassel's pros recognized Bennett, and persuaded him to ump the game.

Wagers were placed—odds of 4 to 1 against Hutchinson. The score was 6-3 in the bottom of the ninth in favor of Dassel when Bennett started to earn his pay. He didn't call a single strike when Hutchinson was at bat and the final score was 9 to 6. No one suspected Bennett—after all—he had been hired by the Dassel people, right?! Hutchinson spectators cleaned up, winning the game, their wagers, and bragging rights, too. Double-crossing Dassel had been double-crossed.

Chick Gandil, a native of St. Paul, was a first baseman who played for the Chicago White Sox for four of his 10 years in baseball. Fans forget now that he had a good record prior to 1919, but that year he was apparently the instigator of the infamous Black Sox Scandal. Apparently he told some gamblers that he was certain several members of the team could be bribed to fix the World Series, and he was right. The great Sox team made a miserable hash of the series, letting the Cincinnati Red Sox win. When Comiskey asked Ban Johnson, the head of the American League, to investigate, Johnson called the team owner a crybaby. But by the summer of 1920 rumors had grown until Eddie Cicotte, one of the guilty ones, went to the grand jury and confessed. Gandil and seven other players were tried and acquitted because the confessions they had made to the grand jury went "missing" and could not be entered in evidence. However, no one ever took the possibility of their innocence seriously, and none of them ever played in pro ball again.

The dirty Sock

A lousy spot in the record book

Roger Maris was born in Hibbing and grew up and started his baseball career in Fargo, North Dakota. He was heading toward football at the University of Oklahoma when a Cleveland Indians scout saw him and he began to play for the farm team. In 1959 he became a right fielder for the New York Yankees—and he hit his stride as well as the ball. In 1960, he hit 39 home runs and was named American League Most Valuable Player. Then, in 1961, he and teammate Mickey Mantle went on a spree of matching homers hit for hit. Mantle was injured but Maris just kept on hitting homers until he broke Babe Ruth's long-standing record of 60 in a season in the last game of the fall.

But the baseball world wasn't ready for someone to top the Babe, so Maris went into all the record books with an asterisk next to his name pointing out that he had accomplished the deed in a season that was two games longer than Babe Ruth's season, as if that made him a fraud. Sadly, much of the public and press turned on him, apparently resenting that a "nobody" from the Midwest—even one who won a second MVP award—would dare challenge the great Babe's record. Maris's batting record went downhill from there, though his downhill was better than most batters' uphill. He was traded to the St. Louis Cardinals, helping to take them to the World Series two years in a row. Maris died of cancer at age 51. In the 1990s, he was declared as ineligible for the Baseball Hall of Fame.

When the girls played

The All American Girls Professional Baseball League, started by Philip K. Wrigley during World War II, consisted primarily of teams from Illinois, Wisconsin, Michigan, and Indiana, but Minneapolis fielded a team for one year—1944—called the Minneapolis Millerites. However, before the next season they moved to Grand Rapids, Michigan, as the Chicks.

Not-so-hot records

Pitcher Jerry Koosman was born in Appleton in 1943. He spent 12 years with the New York Mets before joining the Minnesota Twins for five years. While he was with the Mets, however, he managed two records of painful memory. In 1962, he struck out 62 times! And he pitched the ball that gave Pete Rose his 4,000th major league hit.

Winning Winfield

Drafted in all three major sports (in baseball by the Padres, in football by the Vikings, and in basketball by Atlanta and Utah), Dave Winfield chose baseball after graduating from the University of Minnesota. Born and educated in St. Paul, he went right to the San Diego Padres in 1973 and batted .277 his first year. In 1979 he became the first Padre voted to the All-Star Game starting lineup. The next year he signed with the New York Yankees where he stayed until being traded to the California Angels in 1990. He signed with the Toronto Blue Jays in 1991 and won a World Series with the club in 1992.

THE CITIES' TWINS

The Minnesota Twins was the new team that appeared when the old Washington Senators left the District of Columbia in 1961, purchased by Calvin Griffith. The current owner is Carl R. Pohlad, a Twin Cities banker. He purchased the team from Griffith in 1984.

The new kid on the mound

When the team started, the player to be given number 1 was shortstop Zoilo Versalles (who was named American League MVP in 1965). The manager was Cookie Lavagetto. The team played their season opener in 1961 at New York on April 11, and they finished the season in ninth place.

The Minnesota Twins have played in the World Series three times and won twice.

The Champs

> 1965, lost to Los Angeles Dodgers, 3-4.
> 1987, beat the St. Louis Cardinals, 4-3
> 1991, beat the Atlanta Braves, 4-3

Twice the bases were loaded for the Minnesota Twins during one inning of a game against the Cleveland Indians on July 18, 1962. And each time a spectacular batter came to the plate. Bob Allison and Harmon Killebrew both drove home all the runners—all in one inning!

Wow!

Retiring the greats

The Minnesota Twins have retired three numbers because of the greatness of the player who wore them:

No. 3 - Harmon Killebrew - Number retired August 11, 1974. He was one of the best home-run hitters in baseball history with 573 career home-runs, placing him fifth on the all-time home-run list. During his 14 seasons with the Twins, he hit 475 homers. In 1969, he was named American League Most Valuable Player. Nicknamed "Killer," Killebrew was elected to the Baseball Hall of Fame on January 10, 1984, the first Minnesota Twins player to be so honored.

No. 19 - Rod Carew - Number retired July 19, 1987. Known as a finesse player, Rod Carew averaged .329 during his 19 major league seasons. He won seven American League batting titles during his 12 years with the Twins. The 1977 American League MVP ended his career with 3,053 hits, placing him 12th on the all-time hit list. He was elected to the Baseball Hall of Fame in 1991.

No. 6 - Tony Oliva - Number retired July 14, 1991. Nicknamed Tony-O, Tony Oliva won three American League batting titles during his 15-year playing career with the Twins. When knee injuries cut his career short, he became a coach with the Twins.

That 1991 year

The 1991 Minnesota Twins became the first team in baseball history to go from last place one season to first place the next, when they clinched the American League West title. It happened on September 29, 1991, when Chicago lost to Seattle. The Twins went on to win the American League Championship series four games to one on October 13, 1991, when they beat the Toronto Blue Jays 8-5.

Kirby Puckett gets a hi-five from the bat boy during the 1991 World Series championship.

The 1991 World Series, won on October 27 by the Minnesota Twins, is considered one of the most exciting series in baseball history by many sports followers. For starters, both the Twins and their opponents, the Atlanta Braves, were in last place in their leagues the year before, and they became the first two teams in major league history to totally reverse their fortunes the following year. Also, four of the seven games of the series were decided on the final swing of the bat, though no previous Series had more than two such exciting games.

After the series, Minnesota Twins' Manager Tom Kelly was named 1991 American League Manager of the Year.

Some Twins' records:

First American League team to draw three million fans in a season, in 1988.

Team record for fewest errors in a season—84 in 1988.

Spring training attendance record of 112, 355 at Lee County Sports Complex, Fort Myers, Florida, 1991.

Kent Hrbek, first baseman, has hit more indoor home-runs than any other player in history, 139. One of them—480 feet on September 9, 1984—was the longest ball ever hit in the Metrodome.

SLAM DUNK

Finally a champ!

Although no Minnesota college basketball team has ever won the NCAA championship, the University of Minnesota team was finally victorious in the 1993 National Invitational Tournament.

Janet on the court

The small Finnish community of New York Mills made it onto the big-time maps in the 1970s when they had local girl Janet Karvonen leading the school to three consecutive state championships in basketball. She scored more points than any other girl or boy in state history. After sifting through more than 150 college offers, Janet went to Old Dominion, taking the team to the NCAA women's finals, and then moved on to Louisiana Tech where she repeated the trip.

Before the Los Angeles Lakers, there were the Minneapolis Lakers. During its years in Minneapolis, the team won six professional championships, five in the NBA and one in an earlier league that merged with the NBA. The Minneapolis Lakers won their first NBA Basketball Championship in 1950 when they beat the Syracuse Nationals four games to two. Jim Pollard (who was wanted by teams all over the country before he went to the Lakers), Slater Martin, and George Mikan (see below), all early team members, are in the Basketball Hall of Fame.

The Laker Years

The Laker franchise, purchased for $15,000, was that of a defunct Detroit team of the National Basketball League. Ben Berger, local theater owner, and Morris Chalfen, founder of the "Holiday on Ice" skating show, were only vaguely interested in buying it. But a reporter for the *Minneapolis Tribune*, Sid Hartman, played a major role in their decision. He persuaded the two to put on an exhibition game in town and 5,000 people turned out to see teams from Sheboygan and Oshkosh play ball. That convinced Chalfen and Berger that basketball could succeed in Minneapolis.

The great Laker

Minnesota's greatest basketball player was from Illinois. George Mikan went into professional basketball after playing for DePaul University all the way through college and law school. He joined the Chicago American Gears just briefly before heading to Minneapolis and the Lakers. Unlike most players of the time he played with his glasses strapped onto his head. He was the first player in history to score 10,000 points, and he led the Lakers to six world championships in seven seasons. In 1950 he was named by the Associated Press as the greatest basketball player of the first half of the century. When the American Basketball Association was formed in 1967, Mikan, then a lawyer in Minneapolis, became the first commissioner. He resigned in 1969 when the office of the ABA was moved to New York City.

With George Mikan on the Lakers, there wasn't much another team could do but try to keep the ball away from him. In a game against the Fort Wayne Pistons in 1950, the ball was dawdled with so often and for so long that the final score was 19 to 18, in favor of the Pistons. And it broke all records for being boring—fewest points scored in a quarter, half, and game, as well as fewest shots. NBA president Maurice Podoloff resolved that wouldn't happen again, and the rule forcing a team to shoot within 24 seconds or give up the ball was passed.

The slo-o-o-ow game

The turn-around kid

"If he had turned me down then, I'd have gone out of business," said Lakers president Bob Short in reviewing the effect that Elgin Baylor had on the Minneapolis team in 1958. The African-American from Seattle accepted Short's offer and, from a team that had been failing, went on to become Rookie of the Year and All-Star Most Valuable Player. On November 8, 1959, Baylor achieved a single-game record of 64 against the Celtics and about a year later upped it to 71, against the Knicks. Virtually single-handed, Baylor was responsible for making the Lakers a team that someone would want to buy, so that it moved on to Los Angeles in 1960.

The Hall of Famers

Minnesota has no natives in the players' roster of the Basketball Hall of Fame. However, it does have a coach and a contributor.

The coach is Detroit Lakes native **George E. Keogan**, born in 1890, one of the early coaches who made college basketball important. He was head coach at Notre Dame University for 20 years, during which his teams won 77 percent of their games. Keogan died in action in 1943 and was elected to the Basketball Hall of Fame in 1961.

The man named as a contributor is **Clifford B. Fagan**, born in Mankato in 1911. He was responsible for spreading the National Federation of High School Athletic Associations and co-founded the Basketball Federation. The president of the Hall of Fame from 1963 to 1969, he was elected to the Hall in 1983.

After 29 years!

The NBA came back to Minnesota in 1989, 29 years after the Lakers left, in the form of an NBA expansion team, the Minnesota Timberwolves, owned by Harvey Ratner and Marv Wolfenson. The two are owners of a major chain of health clubs, the Northwest Racquet, Swim and Health Clubs. A far cry from the Lakers' franchise price, the Timberwolves cost $32.5 million. On June 15, 1989, the team acquired 11 players in an NBA expansion draft, and in October, they began playing a six-game preseason schedule at the Humphrey Arena. Their major point maker has been Tony Campbell, who had a 1989-90 season record of 1,903. Campbell, from New Jersey, came to the Timberwolves as a free agent after being with Detroit and Los Angeles.

Picking a Timberwolf
In 1986, a contest was held to choose the name of the new team, and 1,284 different nicknames were suggested. The two that were finally submitted to Minnesota city councils to choose between were the Polars and the Timberwolves.
The Timberwolves won, 2-1.

The Minnesota Timberwolves' first-round draft pick in 1992 was Christian Laettner, the star center at Duke University and the only non-professional to play on the U.S. "Dream Team" in the 1992 Olympics. Not everyone was happy about the team as a whole, especially after decades of only amateurs being allowed to play. LeRoy Walker of the United States Olympic Committee said, "The USA basketball federation . . . didn't so much choose a team as anoint one." He added that Laettner was "a kind of token." The player who had been called the "student prince of college basketball" had taken Duke to two consecutive NCAA titles. The Timberwolves, as an expansion team in need of building, was given third choice in the 1992 draft pick. The 6-foot, 11-inch Laettner got a first-year salary of more than $2 million.

The Timberwolves also had two other players on 1992 Olympic teams. Luc Longley, who is from Australia, played with the Australian team in both the 1988 and 1992 games. Gundars Vetra of Lithuania played for the Unified Team (the old Soviet team).

Better Laettner than never

THE COLLEGE PIGSKIN GAME

National Football Championships at Minnesota:

The University of Minnesota has taken several national championships in football:

1934, under Bernie Bierman
1935 (shared with Southern Methodist), under Bernie Bierman
1940 and 1941, under Bernie Bierman
1960, under Murray Warmath.

The Classic

Minnesota took on Maryland in the first Hall of Fame Classic football game, at Legion Field in Birmingham, Alabama, in 1977. Minnesota, lost 17 to 7.

The Gopher who became a movie

Bruce P. (a.k.a. "Boo") Smith was a Faribault child who got an early start at power football by playing on the high-school team when he was only in eighth grade. At the University of Minnesota he was the star halfback and captain of the Golden Gophers in 1941, chosen All-American and the winner of that year's Heisman Trophy. So popular was he that the following year Columbia Pictures made a less-than-memorable (though that was probably not intentional) movie called *Smith of Minnesota*, starring—you guessed it!—Boo Smith himself. He joined the Great Lakes team in 1942 and was sixth in the nation in rushing. After serving in World War II, he joined the Green Bay Packers, then the Los Angeles Rams, though his promise didn't hold up. Smith, Minnesota's only Heisman Trophy winner, died of cancer at only 47 years old. He was named to the College Football Hall of Fame in 1972.

College Football Hall of Famers
from the University of Minnesota

Players and starring year
Edward L. Rogers, 1903
Robert Marshall, 1906
John Francis McGovern, 1910
Albert Baston, 1916
Herbert W. Joesting, 1927
Bronislaw Nagurski, 1929
Francis L. Lund, 1934
Ed Widseth, 1936
Bruce Smith, 1941
Richard Kay Wildung, 1942
Leo Nomellini, 1949
F. Clayton Tonnemaker, 1949
Paul Robert Giel, 1953

Coaches and induction year
Henry L. Williams, 1951
Herbert O. Crisler, 1954

The Stanford miracle   Clark Shaughnessy, Minnesota All-American-turned-college football coach, surprised everyone by turning the so-so Stanford team into national champions in 1940. He attributed the success on bringing back the almost forgotten T formation to college ball, based on the talents of Frankie Albert. In 1945, he left college ball and became coach to the Los Angeles Rams and then moved to Chicago as assistant to George Halas. He was named to both the National Football Foundation Hall of Fame and the Helms Hall of Fame.

Gloomy Gil   College football coach Gilmour Dobie wasn't called "Gloomy Gil" for nothing. The Hastings native was continually convinced that whatever team he was working with was going to go down in defeat. He never gave compliments for good playing because he was certain that it would never happen again. But somehow, Gloomy Gil managed to produce 14 unbeaten teams in 31 years of coaching North Dakota State, Washington, Navy, Cornell, and Boston College. Despite his pessimism, he was named to the College Football Hall of Fame.

Little Brown Jug   Michigan was a football superpower even in 1903, but on October 31 they met their match at Northrup Field in front of 20,000 Minnesota fans. Michigan came on the field first led by their great, unstoppable halfback, Willie Heston. Minnesota played inspired football that day and held Heston. Back in 1903 there were no pass plays or fancy formations—it was just brute line strength pounding away at brute line strength until somebody dropped.

When Minnesota kindly sent some cooling water to the Michigan team, the student manager, eyeing it suspiciously, sent out for something to pour it into. The result was a 30-cent putty-colored five-gallon jug. Thanks to incredibly good luck and a happy crowd that rushed onto the field before the clock ran out, the game ended in a tie. The Michiganders headed home, leaving the water jug behind. The next day, Minnesota's equipment manager, Oscar Munson, found the jug. He sent a message to Coach Yost in Ann Arbor: "We have your Little Brown Jug. Come and win it!" The two teams have fought to reclaim the Little Brown Jug each year since.

THE PRO PIGSKIN GAME

The first pro   Pudge Heffelfinger, born in Minneapolis, played college football at Yale, making a record that cause many to call him the greatest college player of the era. A member of the first All-American team, he was a lineman who had a tendency to pick up other players and toss them at the oncoming team. On November 12, 1892, he was paid to play for the Allegheny Athletic Association, making him the first professional football player. In 1916, he offered to help the Yale team prepare for a game against its rival Ivy League colleges. Leaping into the fray, he accidentally knocked out five college men and was ordered off the field.

From uniform to robes

Alan Page, a native of Ohio, began work on his law degree at the University of Minnesota while playing defensive tackle for the Minnesota Vikings. He was part of a defensive line that came to be known as the "Purple People Eaters." One of the rare players who was never injured, he played 218 straight games plus 16 post-season and 4 Super Bowls. In 1978, he moved on to the Chicago Bears.

Just as persistent at his legal education, he earned his law degree from the University of Minnesota in 1979. He became a full-time lawyer after retiring from football and then moved into the attorney general's office. There aren't many contested elections for Supreme Court justice in Minnesota, because usually new judges are appointed temporarily and then elected without competition. When Page's opportunity to run kept being taken away from him, he sued Governor Arne Carlson. A substitute Supreme Court found in Page's favor, and he ran successfully, with opposition, in 1992. He became the first African-American and the first Pro Football Hall of Famer (he was inducted in 1988) to serve on the state's highest court.

A player for all reasons

He moved like a tank through a football field, usually just closing his eyes and charging—a technique that often had Bronko Nagurski crashing into walls. However, it worked for this football hero. Having played high-school ball in International Falls and Bemidji, the Canadian-born tank moved on to the University of Minnesota, where he was an All-American tackle and fullback. George Halas's Bears wanted him and the Bears got him. He was known for playing equally well as an end, a tackle, and a fullback. Called by many the greatest football player of the first half of the twentieth century, Nagurski was the first person inducted into both the College Football Hall of Fame and the Professional Football Hall of Fame. In 1941, the high school in International Falls paid him tribute by choosing the nickname "Broncos" for their sports teams.

"Hey, I wrote a book!"

Austin's John Madden was raised in California with hopes of being a pro football player and even got drafted onto the Philadelphia Eagles, but when an injury sidelined him he went back to school and studied coaching. In 1969 he became the head coach for the Oakland Raiders. During his time with the Raiders, they took seven division championships, one AFC cup, and a Super Bowl, which he snatched from his native Vikings in 1977 with a 32 to 14 win. He became an instantly recognizable public figure when he made his first TV commercial for Miller Lite beer. In 1984, he surprised everyone by writing a book, called *Hey, Wait a Minute! I Wrote a Book!*

**Even before
the Vikings**

Pro football in Minnesota hasn't been limited to the Vikings. They've just been around since 1961. Duluth had its own teams:
>Kelleys, 1923-25 (NFL)
>Eskimos, 1926-27 (NFL).

Then in the Twin Cities there was:
>Minneapolis Marines, 1922-24 (NFL)
>Minneapolis Redjackets, 1929-30 (NFL).

Tsk tsk!

The Vikings share with the Denver Broncos the dubious title of most trips to the Super Bowl without a win—four. The Vikings went to the granddaddy of all games in 1970, when they lost 23-7 to Kansas City. Then:
>in 1974 they lost 24-7 to Miami
>in 1975 they lost 16-6 to Pittsburgh
>in 1977 they lost 32-14 to Oakland.

The only way the Vikings have gotten to the Super Bowl since then has been to buy tickets when it was held at the Metrodome in 1992.

The scrambling quarterback

Not only was he able to hit a target, Fran Tarkenton was himself a moving target. Sacking this Minnesota Viking quarterback wasn't a simple task. If a designated play went wrong, he would simply break out of the pocket. His quick scrambling didn't always go his way. Tarkenton often received criticism for throwing interceptions. His rookie year, he threw four touchdown passes, beating the Chicago Bears 37-13. After five years (1961-66), he was traded to the New York Giants. Tarkenton didn't move mountains or skyscrapers in the Big Apple. By 1972, he was back in Viking country leading the team to a 62-22-2 record from 1973 to 1978. During his playing career, Tarkenton was a quarterback who escaped serious injury even with all his scrambling. In 16 years he suffered only bruised ribs. He was inducted into the Pro Football Hall of Fame in 1986.

Viking benefit

Dennis Green, head coach of the Minnesota Vikings, is one of two African-American football coaches in the NFL. Before coming to the Vikings, he was head football coach at Northwestern and Stanford and assistant for the San Francisco 49ers. He was named Big Ten coach of the year in 1982 when Northwestern won three games ending a victory drought.

THE PRO FOOTBALL HALL OF FAMERS

Born in Willow River in 1903, **Ernie Nevers** attended high school near Superior, Wisconsin, and then moved to California. In 1924, as a member of the Stanford University team, he played all 60 minutes of a game while he was recovering from two broken ankles. Many years later *Sports Illustrated* called Nevers the best college player of all time. The following year he turned pro, and in 1926 he was pro-just-about-everything. In that one year he played pro basketball and football in Chicago and pro baseball for the St. Louis Browns. On November 28, 1929, he carried off a feat that has never been equaled. He scored all 40 points for the Chicago Cardinals against the Chicago Bears—6 touchdowns and 4 extra points, for a final score of 40-7. Nevers was elected to the Pro Football Hall of Fame in 1963.

Nevers and more

"Big Kies," otherwise known as **Walt Kiesling**, born in St. Paul in 1903 was Ernie Nevers's dependable blocker. In 1938 Kiesling turned to coaching and worked with the Pittsburgh Steelers until 1945. He was named to the Pro Football Hall of Fame in 1966.

A man who was ahead of his time in devising plays, coach **Sid Gillman**, a native of Minneapolis born in 1911, took the Los Angeles Rams to the Western Division title in his first year as head coach, 1955. Four years later he moved to the Chargers. He was named to the Hall of Fame in 1983.

Thorpe's shadow

Halfback Joe Guyon was a full-blooded Native American, usually overshadowed by Jim Thorpe. Born at Mahnomen at the White Earth Indian Reservation, he went to Carlisle Indian School where he met Thorpe, and then took Georgia Tech to the national college championship. He played professionally with the Canton Bulldogs, Cleveland Indians, Oorang Indians, Rock Island Independents, Kansas City Cowboys, and New York Giants, the first four with teammate Jim Thorpe. He was inducted into the Hall of Fame in 1966.

Little Falls takes pride in another "L" in addition to Lindbergh. Jim Langer, born 1948, was a little-noticed player at Royalton High School before going on to South Dakota State, hoping to play pro baseball. But his arm failed and he turned to football. As a free agent, he made a quick move from the Cleveland Browns to the Miami Dolphins, where he spent the next ten years, gradually becoming recognized as one of the best centers ever. His first year he played on the Super Bowl VII team, which had a perfect 17-0-0 season in 1972. For five years straight he was named All-Pro and played in the Pro-Bowl, and played on two more Super Bowl teams. Choosing to head north again, he was traded to the Vikings in 1980 and put in two more years. Langer was named to the Pro Football Hall of Fame in 1987.

Little Falls' Langer

IN THE RING

Moving the ring ◄ Hibbing's reputation was almost ruined in August of 1901 when the annual firefighters' convention came to town. Three days of sporting events had been planned, including wrestling, horse racing, and boxing, with a final bout scheduled between local favorite Jim Arnold and Jack Beauscholte. It was said that Jim Arnold trained on beer—you could tell by the size of his gut—and Jack Beauscholte was known as the "battling demon from St. Paul." It didn't really matter to Mayor Twitchell that prize fighting was illegal in Minnesota until a deputy, alerted to the immoral event by a local pastor, arrived in Hibbing ready to shut down the fight. The organizers had rented a tent to hold 1,200 and had invested $1,500—they would be ruined! When Itasca County officials offered to shift the event to the open woods of their jurisdiction, the offer was immediately accepted and a logging train was loaded with everything and everyone. The fight took place in a clearing in the woods where Arnold and Beauscholte fought to a 10-round draw.

St. Paul in the ring

St. Paul boxer Mike O'Dowd won the middleweight title from Al McCoy on November 14, 1917, by a knockout. An immensely popular boxer, his fans were furious when he lost the title in 1920 to Johnny Wilson in a 12-round decision. He tried to regain the title the following year but lost again.

The Gibbons family ◄ The name Gibbons was big stuff in boxing in the 1920s, and it belonged to two St. Paul men, brothers Tom and Mike. Tom, the elder, was a middleweight who turned heavyweight. He took on champ Jack Dempsey in a title fight on July 4, 1923, and held on for all fifteen rounds before the decision went against him. He quit the ring after being knocked out (the only time) by Gene Tunney. His younger brother, Mike, made no bones about being a middleweight and he never did have a title fight. Between them, the Gibbons boys had 119 wins, 7 losses, 5 draws, and 101 no decisions.

STARS ON THE ICE

Minnesota ice hockey ◄ As ice hockey moved south from Canada, it took hold in Minnesota. The first organized game of ice hockey in the state was played between two Minneapolis city teams in January 1895. By 1906 ice hockey had spread across the state. Most youngsters played road hockey all day on outdoor rinks or on frozen rivers. Magazines served as shin pads and fathers made the hockey sticks. Skates were often shared with one player using them for several hours before giving them up to someone else. In 1912 St. Paul opened its Hippodrome and Duluth had its Curling Club for hockey and ice skating. After World War I, the sport mushroomed on the Iron Range with the construction of numerous indoor arenas.

The small town of Eveleth didn't get left behind in the big world of competitive hockey. Its first Hippodrome was built in 1921, which enabled the town to compete against much larger rivals from Pittsburgh, Cleveland, Duluth, and St. Paul. The young boys of Eveleth, used to seeing some of the best players in North America, played street hockey all day long. As a hockey hotbed, Eveleth thrived. In 1927-28 the junior college team was invited to represent the United States at the Olympic Winter Games. Unable to raise the funds, the United States had no hockey representative in 1928, but Eveleth claimed to be the "Hockey Capital of the United States" from that time forward. Its high school team won the first Minnesota State High School Championship in 1945.

In 1967 a group of Eveleth citizens known as the Project H Committee conducted an intensive ice hockey research program and discovered that no other town of Eveleth's size in the country had contributed so much to the sport of ice hockey, and no other state had contributed more than Minnesota. It only seemed right that the United States Hockey Hall of Fame be built in Eveleth, where it opened in 1971 on Hat Trick Avenue. Of the seventy-five inductees prior to 1993, twenty-nine are native Minnesotans.

The "Hockey Capital"

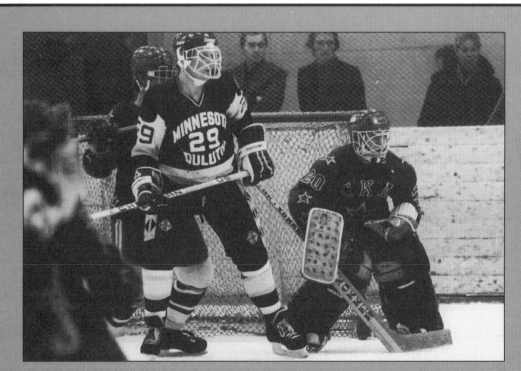

December 1984 was a historic occasion for the University of Minnesota-Duluth Bulldogs and the United States. It was the first time a U.S. collegiate hockey team toured the Soviet Union. The team played the Junior Red Army in Leningrad and in Moscow, splitting a two-game series. The Bulldogs' star number 29, Brett Hull (son of Bobby Hull), stands ready for the Junior Red Army's onslaught.

The Edina wonder

Edina High School's hockey coach from 1958 through 1991 was Willard Ikola, formerly a goaltender on the University of Michigan and 1956 Olympic teams. During those years the Edina Hornets had an incredible record of 600-140-38. The Eveleth-born coach was inducted into the U.S. Hockey Hall of Fame in 1990.

Sticking up for America

The son of Italian immigrants, John Mariucci forsook his southern heritage and became one of the first American powerhouses in ice hockey. Born in Eveleth in 1916, he went to the University of Minnesota and turned pro in 1940, joining the Chicago Blackhawks. When he became captain in the 1947-48 season, he was the first American-developed player ever to captain an NHL team. In 1953 he returned to the U. of M. as the coach, finally going to the Minnesota North Stars in 1966. In both those positions he got to follow his inclinations and use more American-trained players than was customary. He was named to the U.S. Hockey Hall of Fame in 1973.

Coach of the icy "Dream Team"

Herbert P. Brooke, born August 5, 1937, in St. Paul was a U. of M. player under John Mariucci and went on to coach the 1980 U.S. Olympic team. The chant "Herbee, Herbee" was familiar during his tenure at the U. of M. where he guided the Gophers to three NCAA titles in the 1970s. Herbee coached the New York Rangers from 1981 to 1985 and came home to the Minnesota North Stars in 1987. Herb Brooke was coach of the 1980 "Miracle on Ice" Olympic team at Lake Placid that unexpectedly won the gold medal by beating Finland 4-2. Twelve members of that fantasy team were from Minnesota.

Father North Star

Walter Bush, Jr., born in Minneapolis in 1929, brought professional hockey to Minnesota through the Minneapolis Bruins and used all his clout to see that a National Hockey League franchise came to Minnesota. On October 21, 1967, the Minnesota North Stars played their first game at the Metropolitan Sports Center and Bush's dream was realized, although he couldn't have suspected that the northern team would move to the southern climes of Fort Worth, Texas, in 1993 to become the Dallas Stars. Bush was named to the U.S. Hockey Hall of Fame in 1980.

Minnesota marvels

"The Riverboat Gambler," a.k.a. Minneapolis-born Reed Larson, is a defensive hockey player on the Detroit Red Wings. On February 18, 1984, he passed the all-time points list, achieving 430 points in ten seasons. In 1981 he achieved only the second hat trick in American hockey. Eveleth-born hockey player Mark Pavelich became the first American-born hockey player to score five goals in a National Hockey League game, on February 23, 1983.

Lucky LoPresti

Chicago Blackhawks goalie, Elcor-born Sam LoPresti, played a record-breaking game on March 4, 1941, against Boston. LoPresti made 27 saves in the first period, 31 in the second, and 22 in the last, and Chicago lost by one, 3-2. "Lucky" LoPresti's merchant ship was torpedoed in February 1943 and he spent 42 days in a lifeboat before being rescued. He was inducted into the Hockey Hall of Fame in 1973.

Other Minnesotans in Hockey Halls of Fame

More Minnesota natives who have been inducted into the U.S. Hockey Hall of Fame are listed below. Those with an asterisk (*) and a date after the name were enshrined in the Hockey Hall of Fame in Toronto.

Administrators

Founder of the Minneapolis Millers, Frank W. "Nick" Kahler, enshrined in 1980, born Dollar Bay 1891

Founder of the top amateur team, the Warroad Lakers, Calvin C. Marvin, enshrined in 1982, born Warroad 1924

Head of the Amateur Hockey Association Harold Trumble, enshrined in 1985, born August Minneapolis 1926

Coaches

38-year Eveleth High School coach Clifford R. Thompson, enshrined in 1973, born Minneapolis 1893

High-school coach Oscar J. Almquist, enshrined in 1983, born Eveleth 1908

Pittsburgh Penguins head coach Bob Johnson, enshrined in 1991, born Minneapolis

U.S. Olympic team and National Team coach John E. "Connie" Pleban, enshrined in 1990, born Eveleth 1914

Players

Frank J. (Coddy) Winters, enshrined in 1973, born Duluth 1884

Edwin N. "Doc" Romnes, enshrined in 1973, born White Bear Lake 1907

Francis F.X. (Moose) Goheen, enshrined in 1973, born White Bear Lake 1894 (*1952)

Cully Dahlstrom, enshrined in 1973, born Minneapolis 1913

Frank C. Brimsek, enshrined in 1973, born Eveleth 1915 (*1966)

Michael G. Karakas, enshrined in 1973, born Aurora 1911

Virgil Johnson, enshrined in 1974, born Minneapolis 1912

Tony Conroy, enshrined in 1975, born St. Paul 1895

John Mayasich, enshrined in 1976, born Eveleth 1933

Hub Nelson, enshrined in 1978, born Minneapolis 1907

Bob Dill, enshrined in 1979, born St. Paul 1920

Tommy Williams, enshrined in 1981, born Duluth 1940

Jack McCartan, enshrined in 1983, born St. Paul 1935

Billy Christian, enshrined in 1984 born Warroad 1938

Louis Robert "Bob" Blake, enshrined in 1985, raised in Hibbing, born Ashland, Wisconsin, 1916

Kenneth J. Yackel, enshrined in 1986, born St. Paul 1932

Larry Ross, enshrined in 1988, born Duluth 1922

Robert H. Paradise, enshrined in 1989, born St. Paul 1944

Roger A. Christian (Billy's brother), enshrined in 1989, born Warroad 1935

Willard Ikola, enshrined in 1990, born Eveleth 1932

John Matchefts, enshrined in 1991, born Eveleth 1932

SNOW TIME

Getting started   The St. Paul ski club challenged the Red Wing club to a ski tournament held in St. Paul on February 8, 1887. Actually planned for the previous year but shut out by bad weather, it was the first tournament held in the Midwest.

Minnesota has more than 12,000 groomed snowmobile trails. It is also where the snowmobile was invented (see p. 129).

Injuries plagued the "Old American"

Called the "Old American" by European skiers, Lutsen-born Cindy Nelson was 28 at the time she was meant to ski in the downhill in the 1984 Olympics. She had been on the U.S. World Cup team every year since she was 15 and was only 17 when she was chosen for the 1972 Olympic team. However, she dislocated her hip and was unable to ski in time. She went on to win a bronze medal in Innsbruck in 1976. She skied in '80 at Lake Placid though she did not place. Finally, in 1984, she had an injured right knee that kept her out of the downhill. Retirement called.

National Ski Hall of Fame

Minnesotans remembered in the National Ski Hall of Fame and Ski Museum at Ishpeming, Michigan, include:

Ole R. Mangseth, born in Norway, lived in Coleraine, pioneering ski jumper

Col. George Emerson Leach, mayor of Minneapolis and manager of the 1924 U.S. Olympic Ski Team (America's first)

Grace Carter Lindley of Minneapolis and Wayzata, Women's National Slalom champ in 1938

George Stanley Kotlarek of Duluth, ski jumping competitor and promoter

Carl Holmstrom, born in Sweden but resident of Duluth, competitor, official, and promoter for 50 years

Lars Haugen of Minneapolis (born in Norway), who spent years in the West building up skiing there

Harold A. Grinden of Duluth, National Ski Association (now U.S.S.A.) and Olympic Games official, and originator of the National Ski Hall of Fame and Ski Museum

Sverre Fredheim, Norwegian-born St. Paul-resident, ski jump champion from 1930 to 1955.

Sigurd Overbye, born in Norway, resident of St. Paul, member of the first U.S. Olympic Ski Team in 1924, and winner of three national cross-country ski championships

Eugene A. Wilson of Coleraine (born in Remer), who won first, second, or third place in 69 of 80 major jump meets.

John Beargrease

The John Beargrease Sled Dog Marathon is the main long-distance dogsled race in the lower 48 states. Its path covers 470 miles from Duluth to Grand Portage. Held in January each year since 1984, it is named for a Chippewa mail carrier who traveled his route a hundred years ago by dogsled.The mushers vie for a $10,000 first prize, traveling through 13 checkpoints in the four days the race lasts. Two shorter races go from Grand Marais to Beaver Bay (100 miles) and Two Harbors (130 miles).

Curling is coming

Curling, a game played by sliding a heavy, round stone across the ice toward a target, has long been a popular game in the Bemidji area, where the curling season is from November to April with competitions called bonspiels. The northern town has been the home of several junior curling champions. In July 1992, the International Olympic Committee approved curling as an Olympic medal sport by 2002. It had been a demonstration sport in 1922, 1932, 1988, and 1992. The famed Bemidji Curling Club may be the training area for future Olympic champions.

John Beargrease Sled Dog Marathon

ODDS AND ENDS

Pshaw!

The dean of women was shocked when a group of female students tried to start a track club at the University of Minnesota in 1910. "I should hate to have anyone think we have a girls' track team. I am willing to have the girls run for exercise. But I do not want anything done in a competitive way." It wouldn't have been "ladylike," so the team wasn't organized.

You know you have it made as an athlete if your face is on the Wheaties cereal box. But it wasn't until 1933 that Wheaties began its association with sports. General Mills agreed to sponsor Minneapolis Millers games on WCCO radio. A billboard at the ballpark was painted with the phrase, "Wheaties, The Breakfast of Champions," after it had been coined by a Minneapolis ad agency. Some people say if it weren't for these Wheaties baseball broadcasts Ronald Reagan wouldn't have been president. He was a baseball announcer for the Cubs when he was voted most popular Wheaties radio announcer. He won a free trip to the Cubs' training camp in California and a Warners Brothers screen test. The rest is history.

Breakfast of Champions

Thanks, Ralph   On a summer day in 1922, 20-year-old Ralph Samuelson of Lake City was bored with aquaplaning on a single flat board tied fairly tightly behind a boat. Purchasing two pine boards on credit for $1 each, he held the ends over his mother's tea kettle, then put them in a vise for two days so that they curved upward. Fastening them to his feet, and adding a long rope to the back of his brother's 24-foot clamming boat, he tried out his new invention on Lake Pepin. By 1925, Samuelson was waterskiing around Lake Pepin at 80 mph, with a huge audience on shore wondering what he was trying to prove. In those years, he experimented with most of the tricks that future waterskiers would take for granted. However, injuries forced him to lead a more quiet life as a turkey farmer.

In 1963, Samuelson sent documentation from the Minnesota Historical Society about his "invention" to the American Water Ski Association in Florida. Forty-four years after his first "ride," Samuelson was given credit by the American Water Ski Association as the "Father of Water Skiing." More glamorous places such as Cypress Gardens, Florida, and the French Riviera had previously claimed to have originated the sport. A statue of Samuelson was erected in 1976 in Lake City to honor him. He died the following year.

The great Patty Berg   When you say "golf" in Minnesota, you say Patty Berg, the first of the really great women golfers. As a child, the Minneapolis native was

a natural athlete. She played baseball and track, was a speed skater, and was quarterback on a local boys' team. She became a force in women's golf when she won the National Amateur title in 1938. By 1940, she had won all the big American women's golf titles, and then became the first winner of the new U.S. Women's Open. She won 83 golf tournaments between 1935 and 1964. Becoming golf's goodwill ambassador, sponsored by the Wilson Athletic Company, she said, "Too many people have the wish to win, when what they really need is the will to win." She helped found the Ladies Professional Golf Association, and served as its first president, starting in 1948. She was the leading money winner of the tour three times during the 1950s. In her 40s, in 1959, she drove a hole-in-one during the U.S. Women's Open, the only person ever to do so. Berg was elected to the World Golf Hall of Fame in 1974. The LPGA named their top award the Patty Berg Award. Patty Berg has been joined by only seven other women golfers in the PGA Hall of Fame.

Setting a record   Charles "Chick" Evans shot a record low total score of 286 in the U.S. Open Golf tournament in Minneapolis in 1916. By winning the Open, he became the first golfer to win both the U.S. Open and the U.S. Amateur in the same year.

The Great Dan Patch

Dan Patch, an extraordinary harness-racing horse, paced a mile at 1 min. $55^{1}/_{4}$ seconds on September 8, 1906, at the Minnesota State Fairgrounds, to break the world's record. The horse was so fast that he never had any real competitors . . . he just raced the clock. During his career he ran the mile 73 times under a minute and broke the world record 14 times. The famous horse was owned by M.W. Savage

of Minneapolis who had purchased him for $60,000. When Dan Patch died on July 11, 1916, Mr. Savage was so distraught that many people believe he died of a broken heart the next day. Dan Patch's record held for 33 years before it was broken by that $^{1}/_{4}$ second. A movie was made about the horse in the 1950s.

Playing gently

Kittenball was invented in Minneapolis's Engine House No. 19. Lt. Louis Rober and his fellow firefighters worked 24-hour shifts and had to do something to pass the time. Rober invented a game somewhat like baseball (except it had a large ball, a smaller diamond, and underhand pitching) that could be played on the vacant lot next to the firehouse. Rober's fellow workers named the game "kittenball" after the name of their team, the Kittens. By 1900 there were enough fire-station teams to form a league and the sport spread across the United States. By 1933 a national organization formed uniform rules and called the game "softball."

Even better than Johnny Weissmuller

Tracy Caulkins of Winona started winning gold medals at age 15 when the young swimmer took five gold medals in the 1978 world championships. She was at her height in 1980 when the U.S. boycotted the Olympic Games being held in the Soviet Union. Somehow she managed to survive some bad times in the following years and reached a new peak at the Los Angeles Olympics in 1984, where she won three gold medals. By the time she retired, she had 48 national titles and set 61 American and 5 world records.

ANGLING FOR PLEASURE

Some fishing facts

• One study revealed that 97 percent of all children in the state go fishing.

• Minnesota has 5,483 fishing lakes and 15,000 miles of fishable streams.

• The waters generate $1.3 billion in revenue each year and support 28,000 jobs.

• One-third of all tourists who visit Minnesota go fishing and 35 million pounds of fish (northern pike, bass, panfish, walleyes) are caught each year.

• A fishing tournament in midwinter at Gull Lake has attracted more than 5,000 fisherman where 9,000 holes were drilled in a half-mile square of ice.

• The Minnesota record walleye was caught at Saganaga Lake in 1979 and weighed in at 17 pounds 8 ounces. Each year over a million anglers spend $500 million catching four million pounds of Minnesota walleye. Maybe that's because the state has 1,700 walleye lakes, more than any other state.

Catch 'em young
Minnesota has 2.3 million "anglers." On "Take a Kid Fishing" weekend the state suspends license requirements for adults if they have fishing partners under 16 years of age.

Fishing's Living Legend

Tom Zenanko is so good at angling that he is the youngest fisherman to be inducted into the Freshwater Fishing Hall of Fame as a "Living Legend of American Sportfishing." He's been a pro for about 15 years so he knows the waters all over the North American continent and he still ranks Minnesota as No. 1 for freshwater fishing. "It might be walleyes in downtown St. Paul, lake trout in Duluth, trophy panfish around Alexandria, or muskies in Lake Calhoun. In the Twin Cities area alone, I have over 60 good fishing lakes within an hour of my home, plus the Mississippi and St. Croix rivers. There's always something that will bite. . . ."

CALENDAR OF EVENTS DAY BY DAY

If there is an asterisk (*) after an item, check the index for where more information can be found in this AWESOME ALMANAC.

JANUARY

1 African-Americans in Minnesota held a political convention in 1869

Soap opera actor Walter N. Greaza born in St. Paul 1897

U.S. Hockey Hall of Famer Edwin N. "Doc" Romnes born in White Bear Lake 1907

Sawmill workers went on strike, supported by the International Workers of the World, but failed, 1917

3 St. Paul Circle of Industry, a sewing circle, began to raise money for a school 1848

The state legislature convened for the first time in the new capitol, 1905

Writer Beatrice Joy Chute born in Minneapolis 1913

Andrews Sisters' Maxine Andrews born in Minneapolis 1918 *

4 Former CIA Director William Colby born in St. Paul 1920

5 First woman in space Jeannette Piccard born 1895*

Vice president and presidential candidate Walter "Fritz" Mondale born in Ceylon 1928 *

6 Physician and educator John C. Lilly born in St. Paul 1915

7 Devastating "Blizzard of '73" struck the state in 1873 *

Olympic gold medal hockey player Steven Janaszak born in St. Paul 1957

Poet John Berryman committed suicide from a Minneapolis bridge 1972 *

8 U.S. Supreme Court upheld Minnesota law banning foreclosure on mortgages 1934

9 Olympic gold medal hockey center Rob McClanahan born in St. Paul 1958

10 Starting this day, northeastern Minnesota was given the name Arrowhead country 1925

11 The International Joint Commission to settle boundary matters between the U.S. and Canada signed 1909

Swimmer Tracy Caulkins, winner of three gold medals in the 1984 Olympics, born in Winona 1963 *

The "Super Bowl Blizzard," a.k.a. "Blizzard of the Century," hit Minnesota 1975

12 A blizzard across western Minnesota claimed 109 lives 1888

Minneapolis got its first glimpse of an airplane, flown by Alex Heine, 1913

Duluth Amphitheater collapsed under weight of snow during a hockey game; everyone escaped 1939

13 Cruiser *Duluth* launched by the wife of Duluth's mayor at Newport News, Virginia, 1944

Senator and presidential candidate Hubert H. Humphrey died at Waverly 1978 *

15 The Goodhue-Cooper duel was fought, 1851*

17 College and pro football coach Joseph Bach born in Tower 1901

Sculptor Duane Elwood Hanson born in Alexandria 1925 *

Millionaire Edward G. Bremer kidnapped by the Barker-Karpis gang 1934 *

18 John L. Sullivan fought Patsey Cardiff in 6-round match at Washington Rink 1887

A 36-day record cold snap of temperatures below zero began, 1936

19 Aurora Ski Club in Red Wing founded 1886

Charles A. "Chick" Gandil, ringleader of Chicago Black Sox scandal, born in St. Paul 1888 *

Actress Tippi (Natalie Kay) Hedren, best known for *The Birds* and being Melanie Griffith's mother, born in 1935 in New Ulm

20 U.S. Hockey Hall of Famer Sam L. LoPresti born in Elcor 1917 *

Iranian hostage L. Bruce Laingen of Minnesota released 1981 *

Strikers at the Hormel succeeded in shutting down the plant at Austin 1986

21 College Football Hall of Fame coach Gilmour Dobie born in Hastings 1879 *

22 Station KSJR of St. John's University made first broadcast, starting what became Minnesota Public Radio, 1967 *

23 First bridge over main Mississippi, a wire suspension bridge at Minneapolis, opened 1855

Astronaut Robert D. Cabana born in Minneapolis 1949 *

Actor Richard Dean Anderson born in Minneapolis 1950 *

25 Musician Heidi Wolfgramm, member of the Jets, born in Minneapolis 1969 *

Muriel Buck Humphrey became Michigan's only female senator 1978, taking her husband's seat after his death

26 Governor of Illinois Frank Lowden born in Sunrise 1861

Psychologist Phyllis Kronhausen born in 1929

27 Famous speech, "The Glories of Duluth," delivered by J. Proctor Knott in Congress 1871 *

28 False fears of an Indian massacre spread across Roseau Valley, 1891

29 U.S. Hockey Hall of Famer Frank J. "Coddy" Winters born in Duluth 1884

American Baseball League founded, including a Minneapolis team, 1900 *

White House Department Store fire imperiled downtown St. Paul 1909

U.S. Hockey Hall of Famer Billy Christian born in Warroad 1938

31 Minneapolis Society of Fine Arts founded 1883

FEBRUARY

1 The first St. Paul Winter Carnival opened 1886*

2 Character actor Frank Albertson born in Fergus Falls 1909

3 Illinois Territory, which included Minnesota east of the Mississippi, created by Congress 1809

4 "Reverse discrimination" fighter Allan Paul Bakke born in Minneapolis in 1940 *

6 Redwood County established 1862

Actor Mike Farrell, who played B.J. Honeycutt on "M*A*S*H" from 1975 to '83, born in St. Paul 1939

7 Sinclair Lewis, first American writer to win the Nobel Prize for literature, born 1885 in Sauk Centre *

Kidnapped millionaire Edward G. Bremer released after $200,000 ransom paid 1934*

8 First ski tournament in Midwest held in St. Paul 1887

Mayo Foundation for Medical Education and Research at Rochester incorporated 1915 *

Statue of Senator Henry M. Rice was placed in U.S. Capitol's Statuary Hall, 1916 *

College Football Hall of Famer and Heisman Trophy winner Bruce P. Smith born in Faribault 1920 *

9 U.S. Hockey Hall of Famer "Moose" Goheen born in White Bear Lake 1894

Leech Lake Dam reached a record low temperature of minus 59° F, 1899

10 Minnesota east of the Mississippi fell into British hands 1763

Zebulon M. Pike raised the Stars and Stripes above Leech Lake 1806 *

11 The Duluth, Mesabi and Northern Railway Company was organized 1891

12 Minnesota became first state to make Abraham Lincoln's Birthday a legal holiday, 1895

13 Isanti County established 1857

William Williams hanged at St. Paul—the last capital punishment in the state, 1906

President Theodore Roosevelt established Superior National Forest 1909 *

Golfing great Patty Berg born in Minneapolis in 1918 *

14 Gov. Comstock started 8-day "bank holiday" to ease the run on bank cash, in 1933; Franklin D. Roosevelt followed suit nationally

15 Oscar-winning actress Gale Sondergaard born in 1899 in Litchfield *

16 Waseca County Horse Thief Detectives organized, 1864

Pokegama Falls matched a record low temperature of minus 59° F, 1903

Singer Patti Andrews of the Andrews Sisters born in Minneapolis 1920 *

17 Norman County established 1881

18 Swift County established 1870

19 Novelist and poet Kay Boyle born in St. Paul 1903

20 Twelve counties established 1855 (see list on p. 12-13)

Democratic mayor of Minneapolis Donald Mackay Fraser born in Minneapolis 1924

21 Pope, Traverse, Stevens, Big Stone, and Chippewa counties established 1862

22 Chippewa Indians ceded the land between the Red and Swan rivers 1855

23 Houston County established 1854

Winona County established 1854

Meeker County established 1856

TV journalist Sylvia Chase born in Northfield 1938

Mark Pavelich became first American-born hockey player to score five goals in one game 1983 *

24 New treaty defined boundary in north 1925 *

25 Charter for the University of Minnesota signed by the governor 1851 *

Morrison and Sherburne counties established 1856

Watonwan County established 1860

Kittson and Marshall counties established 1879

26 Enabling Act for statehood approved by Congress 1857

Nininger City, which would become a famous ghost town, incorporated 1858 *

Hubbard County established 1883

27 St. Peter Company organized in St. Paul 1873 *

Waseca County established 1857

Actor William Demarest, the uncle in "My Three Sons," born in St. Paul 1892

28 St. Anthony and Minneapolis were consolidated under name Minneapolis 1872

Oakland Raiders tightend Roger Hagberg born in Rochester 1939

Record-breaking hockey player Mark Pavelich born in Eveleth 1958 *

MARCH

1 Territory of Illinois established, including present-day eastern Minnesota, 1809 *

The state capitol was destroyed by fire, 1881

Patrick Des Jarlait, Ojibway artist, was born at Red Lake Reservation 1921 *

Musician Rudy Wolfgramm, born in Minneapolis 1970 *

3 Louisiana Territory, including Minnesota, organized 1805 *

Minnesota Territory organized, with Alexander Ramsey as governor 1849 *

Fillmore County was established 1853

St. Louis County, largest in the state, was established 1855

4 St. Paul was incorporated as a city 1854

5 Seven counties established 1853 (see list p. 12)

U.S. Hockey Hall of Famer Kenneth J. Yackel born in St. Paul 1932

6 Hennepin County established 1852

Dred Scott Decision, regarding slave taken to Fort Snelling, rendered 1857 *

Grant and Lyon counties were established, and Wilkin was renamed, 1868

Lac qui Parle and Yellow Medicine counties established 1871

Lincoln County established 1873

Hall of Fame football coach Clark D. Shaughnessy born in St. Cloud 1892 *

7 U.S. Hockey Hall of Fame coach Oscar J. Almquist born in Eveleth 1908

Eisenhower's adviser and speechwriter, Gabriel Hauge, born in Hawley 1914

8 Basketball Hall of Fame coach George E. Keogan born in Detroit Lakes 1890

The U.S. Supreme Court decided a boundary line dispute at Duluth in favor of Wisconsin 1920

9 Cook County established 1874

10 The Louisiana Purchase, which included western Minnesota, was formally transferred to the U.S., 1804 *

Early college football star Harold Erickson born in Maynard 1899

11 Illustrator and children's author Wanda Gag born in New Ulm 1893 *

12 Duluth went out of the city business 1877 *

13 Kanabec County established 1858

Country singer Liz Anderson born in Roseau 1921

Donna Wiederkehr of St. Paul set a record number of hot-air balloon flight records in one flight, in 1975 *

14 U.S. Hockey Hall of Famer Virgil Johnson born in Minneapolis 1912

Humorist/dramatist Max Shulman born in St. Paul 1919 *

15 Arrowhead Bridge connecting Duluth and Superior, Wisconsin, opened 1927

16 Singer Susie Allansto of *Jesus Christ Superstar* born in Minneapolis 1952

18 Becker, Clay, and Otter Tail counties established 1858

Novelist and short-story writer Margaret Culkin Banning born in Buffalo 1891

U.S. Hockey Hall of Fame hockey promotor Frank W. "Nick" Kahler born in Dollar Bay 1891

Actor Peter Graves born in Minneapolis in 1926*

19 White Earth Chippewa Reservation established 1867

20 Kandiyohi County established 1858

21 Children's writer Mary L. Davis born in Worthington 1935

22 Tom Gibbons, boxer who fought Jack Dempsey, born in St. Paul 1891 *

Ex-Secretary of Commerce Maurice Stans born in Shakopee 1908

Movie producer Michael Todd died in plane crash at Grants, New Mexico, 1958 *

23 Mrs. Anne Evards Bilansky is first white person executed in state 1859

Minnesota became first state to ratify amendment allowing 18-year-olds to vote, 1971

24 Editor Jane Grey Swisshelm's printing press was smashed by antiabolitionists 1858 *

General Lauris Norstad, former commander of NATO, born in Minneapolis 1907

26 Louisiana Purchase broken in half, with the northern half, including Minnesota, attached to Indiana 1804 *

Marauding Dakotas attacked settlers at Springfield (now Jackson) 1857

Football player Gino "Duke" Cappeletti, first AFL player to make a field goal, born in Keewatin 1934

27 The Aerial Bridge at Duluth began to carry passengers 1905

28 Minneapolis radio station KSTP began broadcasting 1928

29 Presidential candidate Senator Eugene McCarthy born in Watkins 1916

31 John Dillinger escaped from a St. Paul gun battle with the FBI, 1934 *

APRIL

1 Publisher-politician William Benton born in Minneapolis 1900*

2 Alexander Ramsey became the first governor of Minnesota Territory 1849 *

4 State flag adopted by the legislature, 1893 *

5 A prohibition law, later declared unconstitutional, was adopted, 1852

Middleweight boxing champ Mike O'Dowd born in St. Paul 1895 *

Pulitzer poet-dramatist Richard Eberhart born in Austin 1904 *

Author-journalist Mary Welsh Hemingway (fourth wife of Ernest) born in Walker 1908

6 First baptism was held in the Mississippi River, at St. Paul, 1851 *

8 Nobel Prize chemist Melvin Calvin born in St. Paul 1911 *

Voyageurs National Park established near International Falls 1975 *

9 First Aerial Lift Bridge opened at Duluth 1905

10 Sports announcer John Madden, game-winning coach of the Oakland Raiders, born in Austin 1936 *

11 Father Hennepin and his companions taken prisoner by the Sioux 1860 *

12 Heavyweight boxer Billy Miske born in St. Paul 1894

Political figure Warren Grant Magnuson born in Moorhead 1905

U.S. Hockey Hall of Fame coach Larry Ross born in Duluth 1922

13 Governor and perennial presidential candidate Harold Edward Stassen born in West St. Paul 1907 *

14 Sauk Rapids leveled by a tornado that took 79 lives in the area, 1886

15 Browns Valley was starting point for settler stampede into Lake Traverse Indian Reservation in North and South Dakota 1892

Actress Hilda Simms born in Minneapolis 1920

16 Philip Winston Pillsbury, president & CEO of Pillsbury, born in Minneapolis 1903

17 Pioneer Guard, first volunteer militia in the state, formed in St. Paul 1856

College Football Hall of Famer Herbert W. Joesting born in Minneapolis 1902

U.S. Hockey Hall of Famer Tommy Williams born in Duluth 1940

18 Michigan Territory, including present-day Minnesota, established 1818 *

Minnesota law passed banning farm foreclosures, challenged in court, 1933

Emmy-winning soap opera actress Dorothy Lyman born in Minneapolis 1947

Actor John James born in Minneapolis 1956

19 Pipestone Quarry set aside for Native Americans, 1858 *

The unnecessary ride of Sam Brown 1866 *

State song adopted, 1945 *

20 Wisconsin Territory, including present-day Minnesota, established 1836 *

Itasca State Park, Minnesota's first state park, established 1891

Mayo Foundation announced discovery of cortisone 1949 *

Oscar-winning actress (for *Tootsie*) Jessica Lange born in Cloquet 1949 *

21 First attempt to get to Fort Snelling by steamboat 1823

First home game of the new Minnesota Twins, lost 5-3 to Washington, 1961

22 Wilbur "Little Indian" Moore of the Washington Redskins born in Austin 1916

U.S. Hockey Hall of Famer Robert H. Paradise born in St. Paul 1944

NBA expansion team of the Timberwolves approved 1987 *

23 Bud Wilkinson, head coach of the University of Oklahoma for 17 years, won 3 national championships, born in Minneapolis 1915

George Mikan of the Minneapolis Lakers scored 40 points in one game, over Syracuse, 1950*

24 U.S. Hockey Hall of Famer Connie Pleban born in Eveleth 1914

American Lutheran Church formed by three denominations, at Minneapolis 1960

25 Children's author Maud Hart Lovelace born in Mankato 1892 *

U.S. Hockey Hall of Famer Bob Dill born in St. Paul 1920

26 Official day of prayer for deliverance from the grasshopper scourge 1877 *

27 KSTP began to broadcast as first commercial TV station in Minnesota 1948 *

28 First newspaper, the *Minnesota Pioneer,* started in St. Paul 1849 *

29 Actor Richard Carlson of TV's "I Led Three Lives" born in Albert Lea 1912

U.S. Hockey Hall of Fame amateur promotor Calvin C. Marvin born in Warroad 1924

30 Alvin Karpis was arrested by J. Edgar Hoover personally for kidnapping of William A. Hamm, 1936 *

MAY

2 Tragic flour mill explosion in Minneapolis took 18 lives, 1878 *

3 3-cent Minnesota Territory stamp issued at St. Paul 1949

4 The removal of Dakota Indians from Minnesota began, 1863

5 Baseball Hall of Fame pitcher Charles "Chief" Bender born in Brainerd 1884 *

Novelist Sinclair Lewis rejected his Pulitzer Prize 1926 *

6 Protestant missionaries Samuel W. and Gideon H. Pond began working with Indians 1836

St. Paul founded as Pig's Eye 1840 *

7 Indiana Territory established, including eastern Minnesota 1800 *

Oscar-winning musical director George Stoll born in Minneapolis 1905 *

Writer Anne Powers born in Cloquet 1913

8 Nicolas Perrot claimed Upper Mississippi Valley for France 1689 *

U.S. Hockey Hall of Famer and Minnesota's "Hockey godfather," John Mariucci, born in Eveleth 1916 *

9 Ex-Secretary of Agriculture Orville Lothrop Freeman born in Minneapolis 1918

Political activist-poet-clergyman Daniel J Berrigan born in Virginia 1921 *

11 Minnesota admitted as the 32nd state 1858 *

Publisher Nicolas Herman Charney born in St. Paul 1941

3-cent Minnesota Statehood stamp issued at St. Paul 1958

12 Science fiction writer Philip Wylie born in Beverly 1902

1980 Olympic gold-medal hockey player Dave Christian born in Warroad 1959

16 St. Paul's Pig's Eye sewage disposal plant—now a Superfund site—opened, 1938

Baseball pitcher Jack Morris born in St. Paul 1955

Musician Marty Balin of the Jefferson Airplane, arrested in Bloomington 1970 *

20 Charles A. Lindbergh of Little Falls made first solo transatlantic flight 1927 *

21 Specialist in Native-American music Frances Densmore born in Red Wing 1867

Mark Twain arrived in St. Paul on the journey that he wrote about in *Life on the Mississippi* 1882 *

Main building of the Walker Art Gallery opened 1927

22 The Fourth Minnesota fought at Vicksburg, with heavy casualties, 1863

Leroy Buffington, Minneapolis, received skyscraper construction patent, 1888 *

U.S. Hockey Hall of Famer John Mayasich born in Eveleth 1933 *

Bob Dylan (really Robert Zimmerman) celebrated his bar mitzvah 1954

Anne Bancroft became first woman to reach the North Pole, 1986 *

23 Twelve counties established 1857 (see list on p. 12)

Minnesota National Forest (later called Chippewa) established by Congress 1908*

Pulitzer Prize-winning author/educator Walter Jackson Bate born in Mankato 1918 *

24 Battle of Pokegama, a Sioux raid, 1841

Journalist Hedley Williams Donovan born in Brainerd 1914

Singer/composer Bob Dylan born in Duluth 1941 *

25 The steamboat *Governor Ramsey* made first trip up Mississippi above Falls of St. Anthony 1850

First edition of the *Minneapolis Tribune* was published 1867

26 Naturalist/writer Henry David Thoreau began journey through Minnesota 1861

"Matt Dillon" actor James Arness born in Minneapolis 1923 *

27 Pro Football Hall of Famer Walter Kiesling born in St. Paul 1903 *

Stillwater native Charles Strite obtained a patent for pop-up toaster, 1919

29 Railroad baron James J. Hill, born in St. Paul 1916

5-cent John Ericsson Statue stamp issued at Minneapolis 1926

30 First shipment of grain made from Duluth on the steamer *St. Paul,* 1871

31 Actress Lea Thompson, Lorraine McFly in three *Back to the Future* films, born in Rochester 1961

JUNE

2 Reuben Herbert Mueller, National Council of Churches founder, born in St. Paul 1897

Science fiction writer and editor Lester del Ray born in Clydesdale 1915

Mine workers in the Mesabi Range struck in 1916

3 Burlesque queen Lillian St. Cyr born in Minneapolis 1917

4 Missouri Territory, which included Minnesota, formed 1812 *

Pillsbury Flour Mills Company founded by purchasing an older company 1869 *

6 Actor Walter Abel born in St. Paul 1898

Government official William R. Stratton born in St. Paul 1934

7 First women delegates attended national political convention in Minneapolis 1892 *

The town of Virginia was destroyed by fire 1900*

Entertainer Prince (Prince Rogers Nelson) born in Minneapolis 1958 *

8 Ex-President Fillmore arrived in St. Paul by celebration steamboat 1854

Washburn, Crosby flour won a gold medal at an exhibition in Cincinnati, and became Gold Medal flour 1880 *

C. C. Beck, "Captain Marvel" cartoonist, born in Zumbrota 1910

Artist LeRoy Neiman born in St. Paul 1926 *

10 Nobles Expedition left St. Paul for Canada 1859*

Oscar-winning actress/singer Judy Garland born in Grand Rapids 1922 *

11 Wadena County established 1858

Football player Ernie Nevers born in Willow River 1903 *

12 Iowa Territory, including part of present-day Minnesota, established 1838 *

13 Duluth citizens finished digging the canal by trickery 1871 *

Last "A Prairie Home Companion Show" broadcast from World Theater in St. Paul 1987 *

14 Actor-dancer Gil Lamb born in Minneapolis 1906

15 Minnesota opened to white settlement by cession of land from Dakota and Chippewa 1838

Three African-Americans lynched by a mob of 5,000 in Duluth 1920

William Hamm, Jr., kidnapped by Barker-Karpis gang in St. Paul 1933 *

16 "Minnesota Man" discovered in Otter Tail County 1931 *

17 Jolliet and Marquette discovered the Mississippi from the Wisconsin River 1673

Twin Cities' "Census War" began with arrest of 7 census takers 1890 *

The first "Good Roads Day" was introduced in 1913

Theatrical director David Ross born in St. Paul 1922

18 Government-sponsored Nicollet expedition started 1838 *

The town of Virginia burned down 1893 *

Minnesota Day at the Pan-American Exposition in Buffalo, New York, 1901

Emmy-winning actor E. G. Marshall born in Owatonna 1910 *

10-cent blue airmail stamp issued at Little Falls 1927

An Anoka tornado took 9 lives and demolished 50 homes, 1939

19 U.S. Congress decreed that the St. Peter's River henceforth be called Minnesota River 1852

21 Voluptuous actress Jane Russell born in Bemidji 1921 *

22 Theatrical and movie producer Michael Todd born in Minneapolis 1909 *

59 people were killed by a tornado in Fergus Falls 1919 *

24 Swedish Midsummer festival held each year in Minneapolis-St. Paul, as well as Duluth

25 Real estate mogul Arthur Rubloff born in Duluth 1902

26 The St. Lawrence Seaway officially opened in 1959, connecting Duluth to world trade

27 Former governor of Minnesota Rudy Perpich born in Carson Lake 1928

"Designing Woman" Julia Duffy born in Minneapolis 1951 *

28 Both eastern and western Minnesota placed in Michigan Territory for two years 1834

29 Physician William Mayo, co-founder of Mayo Clinic, born in Le Sueur 1861 *

Comedienne-actress Joan Davis born in St. Paul 1907

30 Chick Evans shot record low total score of 286 in U.S. Open Golf tournament in Minneapolis 1916 *

Toxic chemical cloud from derailed train forced evacuation of 50,000 people in Duluth in 1992

JULY

1 Supreme Court ruled, for first time, that gag law was unconstitutional, 1931 *

2 Sieur Du Luth claimed the region around Mille Lacs for France 1679 *

The 10-mile St. Paul and Pacific began to carry passengers between St. Paul and St. Anthony 1862

Battle of Gettysburg, with First Minnesota fighting, 1863 *

Artist-author Hannes Vajn Bok born in 1914

3 U.S. Hockey Hall of Famer Cully Dahlstrom born in Minneapolis 1913

4 Gunnlaugur Petursson, state's first Icelandic settler, settled on Medicine River, 1875

Half tones used for first time in America in *Minneapolis Journal* 1896

St. Paul-born boxer Tom Gibbons lost decision to Jack Dempsey in heavyweight title fight 1923 *

6 Singer La Verne Andrews of the Andrews Sisters born in Minneapolis 1915 *

Moorhead matched a record high temperature of 114° F. 1936

Author Louise Erdrich born in Little Falls 1954

8 Annual Minnesota Loon Festival began at Brainerd, attended by 3,500 "loonies," 1988

12 Critic Dennis Frawley born in Minneapolis in 1942

Walter Mondale announced from St. Paul Geraldine Ferraro, first woman vice presidential candidate, as running mate 1984 *

Oakland A's Terry Steinbach of New Ulm named All-Star MVP, 1988

13 Henry Rowe Schoolcraft discovered Lake Itasca, source of the Mississippi, 1832 *

Steamer *Seawing* capsized on Lake Pepin, killing 90, 1890

16 State seal adopted 1858 *

17 Henry Schoolcraft camped at the falls of the St. Croix 1832

Minnesota Twins got two triple plays in same inning 1962 *

18 Governor Karl Rolvaag born in Northfield 1913

19 Surgeon Charles Horace Mayo, co-founder of Mayo Clinic, born in Rochester 1865 *

Bernie Leadon, member of singing group the Eagles, born in Minneapolis in 1947 *

Musician Leroy Wolfgramm of the Jets born in Minneapolis 1966 *

Robert Asp's reproduction Viking ship arrived in Bergen, Norway, after sailing from Duluth 1982 *

20 Middleweight boxer Mike Gibbons born in St. Paul 1888 *

"Bloody Friday," Minneapolis police fired on strikers, killing 2, 1934

The first Minneapolis Aquatennial Summer Festival began, 1940

21 Minnesota troops among first casualties at Battle of Bull Run, 1861

Tornado hit Lake Benton area, destroying 2,000 square miles 1883

22 Cabinet member-farmer Bob Bergland born 1928 in Roseau

23 Sioux (Dakota) Indians gave up most of their Minnesota land in Treaty of Traverse des Sioux, 1851

A Brainerd mob lynched two Indians, setting off the "Blueberry War," 1872 *

25 Territorial Republican convention held at St. Paul 1855

Journalist Midge Decter born in St. Paul 1927

27 The cornerstone for the new capitol was laid in St. Paul 1898

Mrs. Virginia Piper kidnapped in Minneapolis 1972; released after husband paid $1 million ransom

28 U.S. Hockey Hall of Fame coach Willard Ikola born in Eveleth 1932 *

Actress Linda Kelsey born in Minneapolis 1946

29 Art historian Sumner McKnight Crosby born in Minneapolis 1909

Beardsley reached a record high temperature of 114° F., 1927

30 Defensive hockey player Reed Larson born in Minneapolis 1956

31 Split Rock Lighthouse opened 1910 *

AUGUST

1 First territorial legislature was elected 1849

Publisher Wilford Hamilton Fawcett, Jr., born in St. Paul 1909

Rich Anderson, bassist for the Tubes, born in St. Paul 1947 *

2 Pulitzer-winning columnist Westbrook Pegler born in Minneapolis 1894 *

4 Congressed approved the rights of Minnesota's land squatters 1854

Children's author Dana Faralla born in Renville 1909

5 8 more Sioux chiefs gave up their lands by the Treaty of Mendota 1851

U.S. Hockey Hall of Famer Jack McCartan born in St. Paul 1935

U.S. Hockey Hall of Fame coach Herbert P. Brooks born in St. Paul 1937 *

Actress Loni Anderson born in St. Paul 1945 *

6 Minnesota separated from Wisconsin when Wisconsin became a state 1846 *

Diplomat and Iranian hostage Bruce Laingen born in Odin Township 1922 *

7 Author/producer Garrison (Gary Edward) Keillor born in Anoka 1942*

8 Composer Arthur Morton born in Duluth 1908

9 Webster-Ashburton Treaty signed, fixing boundary with Canada 1842 *

11 Actress and beauty writer Arlene Dahl born in Minneapolis 1928 *

13 Fire in Minneapolis caused $2 million damage and left 1,500 homeless, 1893

14 U.S. Hockey Hall of Famer Hub Nelson born in Minneapolis 1907

15 The daguerreotypes on which *Song of Hiawatha* was based were made 1852 *

Swift Company payroll robbed of $30,000 by Barker-Karpis gang 1933

Minnesota Twins' manager Tom (T.K.) Kelly born in Graceville 1950

16 Children's writer Marchette Gaylord Chute born in Minneapolis 1909

17 Four young Santee Dakota carried out Acton Massacre, starting Dakota Uprising, 1862 *

18 46 soldiers from Fort Ridgley ambushed at Redwood Ferry by Dakota, half killed, 1962

A large black bear was killed in the lounge of the Hotel Duluth, 1929

Lawyer-author Vincent Bugliosi, prosecutor of Charles Manson and author of *Helter-Skelter,* born in Hibbing 1934

19 Senator David F. Durenberger (R, Minnesota) born in St. Cloud 1934

Ski champion Cindy Nelson born in Lutsen 1955 *

D.G. Simons made first balloon flight going higher than 100,000 feet, at Crosby 1957 *

First State Wildflower Route dedicated 1989 *

20 Dakota attack on Fort Ridgely 1862

Broberg family massacred at Bronson Lake 1862

21 Eliza Winston, slave of a visiting Southern family, was freed, 1860 *

Tornado struck Rochester, killing 35 and leading to founding of Mayo Clinic, 1883*

A tornado wiped out Tyler's business district and killed 37, 1918

22 Publisher Arthur Harrison Motley born in Minneapolis 1900

Baseball player Paul Molitor born in St. Paul 1956

25 Color-TV developer Elmer William Engstrom born in Minneapolis 1901

Pipestone National Monument near Pipestone was established, 1937 *

26 Convention to organize Minnesota Territory held at Stillwater 1848 *

31 The Foshay Tower, then the state's tallest building, was dedicated, 1929 *

SEPTEMBER

1 A massive forest fire wiped out the Hinckley area and killed over 400, 1894 *

2 Battle of Birch Coulee, Dakotas surrounded 160 soldiers for 30 hours, killing 38, 1862*

V.P. Teddy Roosevelt tells state fair fans, "Speak softly and carry a big stick," 1901

3 The first session of the Minnesota territorial legislature began, 1849 *

The "golden spike" driven completing Northern Pacific's route to the Pacific, 1883

Minnesota's second earthquake occurred near Brainerd, 1917 *

Naval dirigible *Shenandoah* destroyed on way to St. Paul 1925 *

4 Business executive Donald Peterson born in Pipestone 1926

5 A major forest fire wiped out Chisholm and surrounding area 1908 *

6 St. Paul-born Billy Miske fought Jack Dempsey for heavyweight title 1920

Entertainer Kathi Wolfgramm of the Jets born in Minneapolis 1971 *

7 Frank and Jesse James and Younger brothers held up Northfield bank 1876 *

8 Great harness racing horse Dan Patch broke world record at 1 min. 55$^1/_4$ sec. 1906 *

Artist-illustrator Austin Eugene Briggs born in Humboldt 1908

3M lab technician Richard G. Drew developed Scotch tape, 1930 *

10 U.S. Hockey Hall of Fame coach Clifford R. Thompson born in Minneapolis 1893

Yankee outfielder and home-run champ Roger Maris born in Hibbing 1934 *

11 5-cent Drs. Mayo stamp issued at Rochester 1964

12 *Great Northwest* balloon ascension at Minneapolis 1881 *

13 Finnish descendants celebrate St. Uhro's Day*

14 Swedish-Americans tried to establish Forefathers Day on this day, but it disappeared

Feminist writer Kate Millett, author of *Sexual Politics,* born in St. Paul 1934

15 Grand Portage National Monument designated in Grand Portage, 1951 *

16 Steamship *Manistee* left Duluth and sank in Lake Superior storm, killing 23, 1883

17 René Boucher started Fort Beauharnois 1727

U.S. Supreme Court Chief Justice Warren E. Burger born in St. Paul 1907 *

New Minnesota Vikings played first game, against Chicago Bears, at Metropolitan stadium 1961

18 Western film writer C. Gardner Sullivan born in Stillwater 1886

First direct primary in United States held in Minnesota, 1900

19 Governor announced gold discovered near Vermilion Lake 1865 *

Mary Richards (Mary Tyler Moore) moved to Minneapolis and began TV situation comedy 1970 *

23 Zebulon Pike established a camp on Pike Island 1805 *

First balloon ascension in Minnesota, by William Markoe, 1857 *

Dakota Uprising ended at Wood Lake with defeat of Chief Little Crow 1862 *

24 First successful surgical removal of gall bladder in U.S., performed by Justus Ohage at St. Paul's St. Joseph Hospital 1886

F. Scott Fitzgerald, author of *The Great Gatsby,* born in St Paul 1896 *

Character actor Larry Gates born in St. Paul 1915

Baritone Cornell MacNeil, great Verdi interpreter, born in Minneapolis 1922

25 Founder of North Stars, Walter Bush Jr., born in Minneapolis 1929 *

Model and sportswear executive Cheryl Tiegs born in 1947 *

26 269 women and children, with a few men, released by Dakotas after Uprising 1862 *

U.S. Hockey Hall of Famer Frank C. Brimsek born in Eveleth 1915

29 Actress Virginia Bruce (Helen Virginia Briggs) born in Minneapolis 1910

Farmer James Lee Jenkins shot two bankers in Ruthton 1983 *

OCTOBER

1 Pierre Le Sueur and men reached mouth of Blue Earth River 1700 *

Western Minnesota was made part of Missouri Territory 1812 *

Mayo Clinic opened as St. Mary's Hospital in Rochester 1889 *

2 Indians ceded 10 million acres of Red River Valley to the U.S., 1863

3 Rock singer Eddie Cochran born in Albert Lea 1938

Baseball player Dave Winfield born in St. Paul 1951 *

Rosalie E. Wahl was appointed first woman on the state supreme court 1977 *

4 Falls of St. Anthony almost killed 1869 *

5 Political activist Philip Francis Berrigan born in Minneapolis 1923 *

6 5-cent Finland Independence stamp issued at Finland 1967

8 American Communist leader Gus Hall (Arvo Kusta Halberg) born in Iron 1910

Aeronautical engineer Robert Rowe Gilruth born in Nashwauk 1913

9 Minnesota legislature designated today Leif Erikson Day 1931

10 Congress passed Minnesota Senator Andrew J. Volstead's bill to amend the Constitution to make liquor sales illegal 1919

12 Sawmill town of Cloquet and 25 other small towns burned, killing hundreds, 1918 *

13 State constitution and application for statehood approved 1857
Target Center in Minneapolis opened 1990 *

14 Fort Snelling was officially closed as an active U.S. Army post 1946

16 U.S. Supreme Court Justice William O. Douglas born in Maine 1898 *
Novelist Kathleen Winsor, who shocked readers with *Forever Amber,* born in Olivia 1916

17 Singer Gary Puckett born in Hibbing 1942
6-cent Fort Snelling stamp issued at Fort Snelling 1970

18 Author Richard Sargeant Hodgson born in Breckenridge 1924

19 U.S. Hockey Hall of Famer Tony Conroy born in St. Paul 1895

20 Marine, oldest civilian settlement in state, organized 1858

21 Minnesota North Stars play first hockey game against California 1967 *

22 Jacob Wetterling, 11, abducted while riding bike near home in St. Joseph 1989 and not found by 1993

25 Actress Marion Ross, the mother in "Happy Days" and grandmother in "Brooklyn Bridge," born in Albert Lea 1928
Novelist Anne Tyler born in Minneapolis 1941*
Minnesota Twins won 1987 World Series over St. Louis Cardinals, at Minneapolis

27 Minnesota Twins won 1991 World Series over Atlanta, at Minneapolis

29 Actress Winona Ryder (real name: Horowitz) born in Winona 1971

30 Twins' Tom Kelly is named American League Manager of the Year 1987

31 Political leader Andrew J. Volstead born in Goodhue County 1860
Humorist and columnist Hayden Carruth born in Mount Pleasant 1862

NOVEMBER

1 First church for settlers dedicated at St. Paul 1841
Monumental snowfall in Minnesota, 24 inches in 24 hours, 1991

2 St. Paul Ice Palace and Winter Carnival Association formed 1885 *

3 Rice County town of Walcott destroyed by fire 1895
Timberwolves played their first regular season game in Seattle, losing 106-94,1989

4 Sculptor James Earle Fraser born in Winona 1876 *
Oscar-winning actor Gig Young born in St. Cloud 1913 *
Football Hall of Famer Alan Page elected first black on Minnesota Supreme Court 1992 *

5 Women were given the right to vote for school affairs 1875
Minneapolis Symphony Orchestra gave its first concert, under Emil Oberhoffer, 1903

7 Four-day giant storm began over the Great Lakes 1913 *
G. F. Kaercher of Ortonville became first woman elected clerk of Supreme Court 1922
Major snowstorm dropped 22 inches on Faribault 1943

8 Controversial Kensington Runestone discovered near Alexandria 1898 *
Astronaut Dale A. Gardner born in Fairmont 1948
Elgin Baylor of Lakers shot game record of 64 points, 1959 *
Timberwolves played their first regular home game, losing to Chicago 96-84, 1989

10 Longfellow's *Song of Hiawatha* involving Minnehaha Falls published, 1855 *
Timberwolves won for the first time, against Philadelphia, 125-118, 1989

11 Catastrophic Armistice Day blizzard on the Mississippi River 1940 *

12 *Reader's Digest* co-founder DeWitt Wallace born in St. Paul 1889 *

13 First recorded sit-down strike in U.S. at Hormel Packing Co., Austin 1933
Roger Steen, guitarist with the Tubes, born in Pipestone 1949 *

14 Diplomat Mary Pillsbury Lord born in Minneapolis in 1904
Pulitzer Prize-winning journalist Harrison Evans Salisbury born in Minneapolis 1908 *
St. Paul-born boxer Mike O'Dowd took the middleweight title from Al McCoy 1917

15 Winona founded by steamboat captain Orren Smith 1851 *
Elgin Baylor of the Lakers made record 71 points in game against Knicks, 1960 *

16 Merritt brothers found the first iron in the Mesabi Range 1890 *

19 Treaty signed, leaving Minnesota borders unclear 1794
Northern States Power nuclear reactor spilled radioactive storage water at Monticello, 1971 *

21 Actor Ralph Meeker (real name: Rathgeber) born in Minneapolis 1920

22 Artist Adolf Arthur Dehn born in Waterville 1895

Writer/illustrator/director Terry (Vance) Gilliam born in Minneapolis 1940

Slowest basketball game in history forced 24-second rule 1950 *

23 Pulitzer Prize biographer William Andrew Swanberg born in St. Paul 1907 *

26 Pro Football Hall of Famer Joe Guyon born in Mahnomen 1892

Cartoonist Charles M. Schulz, creator of "Peanuts," born in Minneapolis 1922 *

Musician-composer Stanley Richard Lebowsky born in Minneapolis 1926

28 Freighter *Mataafa* broke up off Minnesota Point in Duluth, killing 9, 1905

29 Cuyuna Range founder, Cuyler Adams, died 1932 *

Olympic gold medal hockey player Bill Baker born in Grand Rapids 1956

Hockey player Neal Lamoy Broten, first American to score 100 points in a season, born in Roseau 1959

DECEMBER

1 Frigate *Minnesota* launched at Washington Navy Yard 1855 *

Children's author Adrien Pearl Stoutenburg (a.k.a. Lace Kendall) born in Darfur 1916

U.S. Hockey Hall of Famer Roger A. Christian born in Warroad 1935

2 The state legislature met for the first time, though there was no state yet, 1857 *

Actor Warren William born in Aitkin 1895

Children's author-illustrator Marilyn Goffstein born in St. Paul 1940

Ballerina Merrill Ashley born in St. Paul 1950 *

3 Ex-Secretary of Labor James Day Hodgson born in Dawson 1915

Olympic gold medal hockey player Mike Ramsey born in Minneapolis 1960

4 UN diplomat and newspaper editor J. R. Wiggins born in Luverne 1903

5 The Volstead Act (Prohibition) was repealed 1933

7 Richard Warren Sears, founder of Sears, Roebuck & Co., born in Stewartville 1863*

Musician-composer Daniel Walter Chorzempa born in Minneapolis 1944

8 Historian and writer John Ely Burchard born in Marshall 1898

10 Sinclair Lewis was presented with his Nobel Prize for Literature 1930 *

11 College administrator Ada Louise Comstock born in Moorhead 1876 *

12 Cartoonist Cliff Sterrett born in Fergus Falls 1883

U.S. Hockey Hall of Famer Michael G. Karakas born in Aurora 1911

15 One of world's richest men, oil tycoon J. Paul Getty, born in Minneapolis 1892 *

16 William H. Fruen of Minneapolis received patent on a coin-operated, liquid-vending machine 1884

Barker-Karpis gang robbed Third Northwestern Bank of $20,000, killing 2 policemen 1932

18 Mary Lund became first female artificial heart recipient, 1985 *

19 Singer Charlie Ryan was born in Graceville 1915

Basketball player Kevin McHale born in Hibbing 1957

20 First pro football player "Pudge" Heffelfinger born in Minneapolis 1867 *

Oscar-winning director George Roy Hill born in Minneapolis 1922 *

22 Forefathers' Day, celebrating the landing of the Pilgrims, was celebrated in early Minnesota

William Watts Folwell, first president of U. of M., was inaugurated 1869 *

Writer Myron Brinig born Minneapolis in 1900

23 Poet Robert Elwood Bly born in Madison 1926 *

Pitcher Jerry Koosman born in Appleton 1943 *

24 Vietnam commander and CIA top-ranker Robert Everton Cushman, Jr., born in St. Paul 1914

25 Sculptor Paul Manship born in St. Paul 1885 *

26 Largest execution in U.S. history, of 38 Dakotas who murdered unarmed citizens, at Mankato 1862 *

Tough-guy actor Richard Widmark born in Sunrise City 1914

28 Southern Minnesota left with no government after Iowa was admitted as a state 1846

Actor Lew Ayres born in Minneapolis 1908 *

29 Emmy-winning actor Ed Flanders born in Minneapolis 1934 *

INDEX OF PEOPLE, PLACES, AND ORGANIZATIONS

PHOTO CREDITS

3M: 119
American Radio Company: 99
E.F. Burchard 913c, J.S. Geological Survey: 126
Larry Busacca/Retna: 108
Mel Chin, Revival Field 1991, mixed media installation, St. Paul, Minnesota. Revival Field is funded by the National Endowment for the Arts through a grant to the Citizen's Environmental Coalition of Houston, Texas. Its Minnesota presentation is sponsored by the Walker Art Center and the Science Museum of Minnesota, in cooperation with the Minnesota Pollution Control Agency: 30
Kris Galvin: 26
General Mills, Inc.: 89, 93
H.H. Bennett Studio Foundation: 58
Hennepin History Museum: 139
Hibbing Historical Society: 65
Indiana State Library: 62
Joe Magnuson: 69
Greater Minneapolis Convention and Visitors Association: 96
Minneapolis Sculpture Garden, Photo courtesy Walker Art Center. Claes Oldenburg & Coosje van Bruggen Spoonbridge and Cherry 1987-1988 stainless steel, painted aluminum. Gift of Frederick R. Weisman in honor of his parents, William and Mary Weisman, 1988: 90

Minnesota Department of Natural Resources: 24
Minnesota Historical Society: 44, 48 both, 78 top, 123, 153
Minnesota Office of Tourism: 9 middle, 15, 18, 19, 27, 29 bottom, 34, 37, 64, 67, 68, 74, 78 bottom, 94, 95, 124 bottom, 133, 150, 151, 154 both
Minnesota Twins: 138
Minnesota Vikings: 144
National Park Service Photo by Richard Frear: 4
Courtesy NAACP Public Relations: 83
New York Convention and Visitors Bureau: 92
North Star Publishing: 29 top
PGA World Golf Hall of Fame: 152
The Quaker Oats Company: 114 middle
Toronto Blue Jays: 136
University of Minnesota Sports Information Office: 142
University of Minnesota-Duluth Sports Information Office: 147
Melvin Simon & Associates, Inc.: 128
Supreme Court of Minnesota: 143
White Earth Indian Reservation: 43
Gary M. Wigdahl: 22
Laura Ingalls Wilder Home Association: 100
Wisconsin Center for Film and Theater Research: 98, 104, 109 bottom
Wisconsin Department of Natural Resources: 9 top